THE INTERNET AND CBT:

A CLINICAL GUIDE

THE INTERNET AND CBT:
A CLINICAL GUIDE

Gerhard Andersson, PhD
Department of Behavioural Sciences and Learning
Linköping University, Linköping, Sweden

CRC Press
Taylor & Francis Group
Boca Raton London New York

CRC Press is an imprint of the
Taylor & Francis Group, an **informa** business

CRC Press
Taylor & Francis Group
6000 Broken Sound Parkway NW, Suite 300
Boca Raton, FL 33487-2742

© 2015 by Andersson, Gerhard
CRC Press is an imprint of Taylor & Francis Group, an Informa business

No claim to original U.S. Government works

Printed on acid-free paper
Version Date: 20140618

International Standard Book Number-13: 978-1-4441-7021-4 (Paperback)

Library of Congress Cataloging-in-Publication Data

Andersson, Gerhard, author.
  The internet and CBT : a clinical guide / Gerhard Andersson.
  p. ; cm.
  Includes bibliographical references and index.
  ISBN 978-1-4441-7021-4 (paperback : alk. paper)
  I. Title.
  [DNLM: 1. Cognitive Therapy--methods. 2. Internet. 3. Remote Consultation--methods. WM 425.5.C6]

  RC489.C63
  616.89'1425--dc23   2014023502

Visit the Taylor & Francis Web site at
http://www.taylorandfrancis.com

and the CRC Press Web site at
http://www.crcpress.com

To my students

Contents

Preface

This book is the result of several years of hard work developing and evaluating the use of the Internet in cognitive behavioural therapy (CBT). It started when two students from the psychology program in Uppsala, Sweden, knocked on my door and asked me if I could supervise their final Master of Science thesis for their psychology diplomas. The idea they had sounded odd, but I hesitated for only a few minutes. We then planned one of the first trials in the world on Internet-delivered CBT (ICBT) for headache. I am of course forever grateful that they came to my room, and later one of them and several other psychology students ended up writing their theses and completing their PhDs on the topic of ICBT. One of them – now professor Per Carlbring – became a close co-worker, and without him much of the work would never have been completed. Then followed other talented students, research students and clinicians who all have contributed much to the development of the field. I would love to list them all (which would mean several extra pages), but you can get an idea of who they are by the research papers referenced in this book. Some have worked with me for a while and invested a lot of their time creating the systems and programming. Others are extremely skilled as clinicians, treatment developers, methodologists, and believe it or not there are even those who have all of these skills (and come from Iceland …).

The Swedish ICBT research phenomena would not have been possible without the help of my colleagues and co-workers in other fields. Here I am mainly thinking about my medical colleagues. Again there are many. I just mention one – professor Nils Lindefors – who you might think would not have any interest in ICBT, being from the biological psychiatry community, but in spite of that background he made an enormous effort in implementing ICBT in regular care in Stockholm, Sweden. However, before that ICBT was implemented at the audiology clinic in Uppsala for tinnitus patients. This is home ground for me, being a clinician still and working with tinnitus patients every week.

At the Academic Hospital in Uppsala we were probably one of the first in the world to implement ICBT in regular care, and I thank all people who made that possible. In fact, the clinic is still running. I also thank my universities over the years – Uppsala University, Linköping University and Karolinska Institute. All have been very supportive and not the least providing me with resources for the research. Funding bodies have also been generous in supporting the research over the years. Colleagues at other universities in Sweden and indeed many universities outside of my country have been supportive as well. ICBT needed an organisation, and back in 2004 I had the idea to just bring in a few of the then-active researchers for an informal meeting. My co-workers in Sweden helped me finalize what became the first meeting of the *International Society for Research on Internet Interventions* (ISRII). I thank my colleagues and friends in ISRII as we now approach the seventh international meeting. We finally also have a journal of our own – *Internet Interventions* – which is up and running this year 2014.

With the rapid growth of ICBT we discovered that we needed both a national and a European society – *European Society for Research on Internet Interventions* (ESRII). I have been privileged to work closely with colleagues in Europe; in particular, my collaboration with the researchers in Amsterdam has been and still is very active in projects funded by the European Commission.

What is perhaps the most amazing thing about ICBT and the work described in this book is the huge interest from people in need of help for their psychological problems. Thousands have participated in research and clinical treatment only in Sweden and indeed many more across the world. A major advantage of ICBT is that it can reach many people, but of course I am thankful for all the time invested by our research participants in the trials.

I also want to thank my editors Caroline Makepeace, Naomi Wilkinson and Julia Molloy for their trust in me getting this book written. Finally, I thank my wonderful family for their support when finalizing this book. Book writing takes time and then it is great to have a life outside of the office.

Gerhard Andersson
Linköping, February 2014

Chapter 1

Introduction

What you will learn

In this chapter you will learn about:

- A background to this book.
- Defining the Internet.
- Spread of the Internet in society.
- The role of CBT in health care and the lack of practitioners.
- How the Internet has reached the clinic.

A background to this book

This book is not only about how the Internet has changed the scene for cognitive behavioural therapy (CBT), but also how the Internet can be used for the delivery of CBT without any loss of effectiveness.

I will take on a "user's perspective" and readers will have different backgrounds in relation to the Internet and the use of guided self-help. Although the main task of this book is to introduce and explain how the Internet can be used in treatment, there are other important topics that confront the clinician doing CBT. In light of this, Chapter 2, 'Resources on the Internet' is motivated by the fact that most consumers of health care seek information on the Internet before and after consultations with medical professionals! But can we trust the information online? This and other questions are covered, including problematic Internet use (so-called Internet addiction). We know from the literature that online support groups are widely prevalent all over the world, and a client may be engaged in a support group at the same time as being in face-to-face CBT. The pros and cons of online support groups is worth reflecting on and therefore a chapter on this phenomenon (Chapter 3) is includeed. It can be useful to know which forums to recommend or avoid if you are asked. Clients find them and use them, although the effects are far from certain.

Internet use is gradually finding its way into our everyday clinical life, and some clinics are already using online medical records. Even for those who prefer to stick with face-to-face CBT (nothing bad about that – there are plenty of clients for all of us), it is likely that outcome auditing will be via online questionnaires as the paper-and-pencil versions are increasingly becoming obsolete, and are mainly reserved for persons who are not able to use computers. But can questionnaires just be transferred directly? And what about diagnostic interview procedures? These questions are covered in Chapter 4, dealing with assessments over the Internet. Online assessment will likely be the standard fairly soon, but as with all activities over the Internet privacy and security are crucial. This is a topic I return to now and again in this book. The good news is that it is possible to have safe solutions, but security is a moving target, as is the Internet and the platforms we use to access it (with some readers perhaps pausing to check their email on their smartphone right now!).

After covering these topics we move on to the main theme of the book, Internet interventions with a focus on CBT. There are numerous definitions and terms used for CBT interventions delivered via the Internet. This is reflected in this book, where it is impossible not to use different terms when referring to what has been done in research. Barak and colleagues (2009) outlined the following definition, which is useful also for the provision of CBT over the Internet:

> A web-based intervention is: a primarily self-guided intervention program that is executed by means of a prescriptive online program operated through a website and used by consumers seeking health- and mental-health-related assistance. The intervention program itself attempts to create positive change and/or improve/enhance knowledge, awareness, and understanding via the provision of sound health-related material and use of interactive web-based components. (Barak et al., 2009, page 5).

Using this definition the authors have outlined three broad web-based intervention subtypes: (1) web-based education interventions, (2) self-guided web-based therapeutic interventions, and (3) human-supported web-based therapeutic interventions. The first category is mainly covered in Chapter 2 and is separated from CBT interventions. The second and third categories are covered in depth throughout the book. Self-guided interventions are often characterized as unguided and are likely to include automated aspects. They also tend to be open for the general public without any need for a clinical consultation. Such programs are described in Chapter 5.

Chapters 6 through 9 cover human-supported web-based therapeutic interventions, also referred to as e-therapy (Abbot et al., 2008), guided Internet-delivered self-help (Andersson et al., 2008), guided Internet-delivered CBT, and several other names which can be confusing. Since this book is about CBT the term *guided Internet-based CBT* (ICBT) will be used, as it is increasingly used in the literature. The main difference between the self-guided and supported interventions is not necessarily in the actual treatment programs which may indeed be identical. The difference lies in the support. According to Marks et al. (2007), an intervention has to delegate at least some of the treatment decisions to the computer to distinguish computerized interventions from pure self-help books. However, this is a rather blurred distinction as it is perfectly possible to guide a client over the Internet when working with a self-help book. In my understanding, guided ICBT can vary from being technically sophisticated with automated reminders and online interactive programs to fairly simple downloadable and printable text files, an approach that has been called net-biblio CBT (Marks et al., 2007). The support provided in guided ICBT can vary dramatically as well, and there are programs which basically take about the same amount of therapist time as face-to-face CBT and programs where the guidance can take just a few minutes per client each week.

After covering guided ICBT in Chapters 6 to 9, an additional approach that does not involve any prepared self-help material but rather a therapy that is delivered over the Internet in real time is described. This approach goes under different names such as Internet psychotherapy, e-counselling, online therapy and email therapy (Barak et al., 2009; Rochlen et al., 2004). There is one approach that will not fit in easily here as it is not delivered in real time, and this is email therapy. That approach is covered briefly in Chapter 10. CBT-oriented clinicians, teachers, and students are increasingly using the Internet as a means to facilitate training and supervision. The literature on this topic lags behind but is an important new development and this is covered in Chapter 10.

Finally, we mention some recent developments about which we do not know much yet, concerning use of smartphones and using tablets (e.g., iPad) in face-to-face sessions. In the final chapter other aspects and a look into the future are provided. The rest of this chapter is a brief introduction to the Internet and why it is time to consider using Internet-administered CBT to expand the use of self-help.

Defining the Internet

The Internet has changed the world since its inception. The changes have been rapid and dramatic. Not only do many people all over the world use the Internet on a regular basis for information and communication, it is increasingly used for other services such as handling money, business, dating and a range of other human activities. How did this begin? Although this question is not the topic of this book, a few words can be said about it, as the Internet revolution is part of our modern history. It all begins with how we use computers, and there we already have a link with clinical psychology and CBT. CBT researchers saw the potential in delegating tasks to computers early, with professor Isaac Marks at the Institute of Psychiatry, Maudsley, UK, being one of the pioneers (Marks et al., 1998). It is not an exaggeration to state that the Internet has dramatically changed the scene for computerised interventions and assessments.

The Internet can be defined as a global system of computer networks interconnected via servers that "communicate" via shared computer language (called *Internet protocol suite*). The most common one that the reader may have heard of is TCP/IP, which stands for Transmission Control Protocol (TCP) and Internet Protocol (IP). Today IP networks are the result of a series of advancements which began with local area networks (LANs) in the 1980s (and even earlier), and eventually the World Wide Web (WWW) which took off in the early 1990s. In lay terms the Internet has four layers and each requires its own protocol. First is the link layer which contains technologies for local network communication. Second is the Internet layer which connects different local networks (which is the main idea behind the Internet). Third is the transport layer, where web hosts communicate (servers). Finally, at the highest level is the application layer, which handles more specific protocols used for communication with a range of purposes.

Spread of the Internet in society

The Internet has numerous applications in our society which has motivated the dramatic increase in the number of people who are connected. In many parts of the world, most adults have access to the Internet. In Europe, for example, access has increased 376% between 2000 and 2011, and 61.3% use the Internet on a regular basis. In North America the figure is even higher, with 78.6% having access, but in Africa the figure is much lower with only 13.5% (www.Internetworldstats.com). However, within Europe there are regional differences; in the United Kingdom 84.1% use the Internet and in Sweden 93% which basically only leaves out persons who for various reasons cannot use computers or mobile phones. Norway has a remarkable figure of 97%. In Romania, however, we see a lower figure with only 39% using the Internet. Overall, it is safe to say that most people in the Western world use and have access to the Internet, but that the third world countries and Asia have a smaller proportion connected.

The Internet is accessed in many ways. Many worksites have their staff connected, and people also have Internet access at home, which of course includes persons who are eligible for CBT. In addition, many public spaces such as restaurants and universities provide Internet access. In the early days many people used dial-up (e.g., over the phone line), but now broadband access is common, including Wi-Fi and access over the mobile network 3G/4G cell technology/cell phones. While costs vary, Internet access is often provided at low cost for the user, although there are exceptions such as hotels.

The uses of the Internet are extensive. Dating back to the mid 1990s we have witnessed an explosion in terms of web pages on various topics. One common use of the Internet is to search for health information, which includes not only information on the characteristics of health problems, but also information on treatment options and online communities for patient organisations (more on this topic is be covered in Chapters 2 and 3). Persons with health problems (and other people as well) may use the Internet to post information about themselves. Blogs are one such example. There is a large literature on these topics, but also some gaps of knowledge such as how much our patients seek information about CBT on the Internet and to what extent they post information about their experiences of CBT on the Internet.

Another use of the Internet is communication and email or equivalent communication networks. This enormous amount of information exchange is also relevant for CBT as many clinicians use email in their clinical services (this topic is covered in Chapter 6). Web conferencing is also commonly used by professionals and sometimes in clinic as well. Other uses include business and shopping. Many readers of this book may have ordered the book online, and there is also a market for other clinical materials such as instructional videos on how to conduct CBT.

Entertainment is another field, and in addition to music we have recently seen an expansion of streamed videos and online television. The amount of services provided over the Internet is expanding and includes online banking, job seeking, purchasing tickets for entertainment and travel, hotel reservations and bill paying. Increasingly these services are not available off-line and cost more if done over the telephone.

The social sphere has also been influenced by the spread of the Internet. There are dating sites and interest groups, but perhaps even more dramatic is the rapid expansion of social networking, with Facebook being one of the most common. Here we see a trend toward more closed communities, which is different from the openness that has characterised the World Wide Web since the 1990s.

Many CBT clinicians and researchers are probably using the Internet in their daily working lives, with uses such as data transfer (sending a document to a colleague as an attachment), education (either as a teacher or doing an online course yourself), perhaps giving advice and supervision, and reading the most recent research articles (most scientific journals are available online, and some for free such as *Plos One, Internet Interventions* and *BMC Psychiatry*).

CBT and need for alternatives to face-to-face CBT

As practitioners know, CBT is a broad psychotherapy orientation which covers a range of treatment techniques and modalities. In contrast to most other psychotherapy orientations CBT has been found to work not only as individual face-to-face treatment, but also as a group treatment and as guided self-help. There are adaptations and applications of CBT for mood disorders such as depression, basically all anxiety disorders (e.g., panic disorder), relationship problems, and a range of somatic health conditions such as chronic pain, cancer, cardiovascular problems and tinnitus (Butler et al., 2006).

CBT often is recommended in treatment guidelines such as the National Institutes for Health and Clinical Excellence (http://www.nice.org.uk). One reason is that CBT has been investigated in fairly rigorous controlled trials, and another is that the outcomes have been good or at least promising. In fact, if a psychological treatment has been tested in a trial for a condition it is very often CBT.

Response rates to CBT often exceed 50% and sometimes are much higher than that, such as CBT for social anxiety disorder and panic disorder, where at least 70% show major improvement. In contrast to medications, there are few side effects of CBT, although they are less well documented than in pharmacological research. In other words, CBT appears to be effective and safe. This is however not evidence of the superiority of CBT over other forms of psychotherapy or treatments. Other therapy forms such as interpersonal psychotherapy for depression (Cuijpers et al., 2011) are at least as effective as CBT, and psychodynamic treatment has been found to work in a few trials. However, for most conditions such as anxiety disorders and health problems there are very few if any other psychotherapy orientations tested, and CBT is unchallenged. Moreover, almost exclusively CBT has been transferred to other delivery formats such as guided self-help, telephone delivery, and group treatment, at least in research.

Why is it important to develop alternatives to face-to-face treatments? There are at least three reasons. One is the fact that there are not enough trained clinicians in CBT who are able to provide evidence-based treatment to all those who might benefit from it. In a world of limited resources, cost of treatment must be considered as well. A second reason has to do with distances to specialist clinics and general practices where CBT is delivered. This was pointed out by Lovell and Richards (2000), who recommended that clinicians consider other effective but less costly alternatives to face-to-face CBT, which often requires 12 to 20 one-hour sessions according to treatment manuals. Related to this are the problems some clients may face when allocating time for appointments, taking time off work or finding someone to take care of their children when travelling to the therapist's office. A third motive for developing alternatives to face-to-face treatments is client preference. There are clients who prefer online treatments over face-to-face treatments, and providing treatment from a distance can in some cases reduce the stigma of being identified as a "mental patient".

Getting back to the alternatives, there is a long history of CBT self-help both in research and in clinic. The treatment options described in this book rely on previous research on guided self-help, and self-help has been a part of the CBT scene for a long time. This means that CBT aims to reduce the importance of a therapist for the treatment and to increase client independence. Since CBT is based on change in the client's own environment and home work, utilising self-help materials is not far away from what CBT clinicians practice. Keeley et al. (2002) surveyed 265 therapists in the United Kingdom and found that self-help materials were used by 88.7% of therapists in their clinical practice as a supplement to individual therapy (see Box 1.1 for a description of self-help books). Most often the self-help used was in the form of self-help books and the high percentage differs markedly from the low uptake of computerized self-help documented by Whitfield and Williams (2004), who found that only 2.4% of 329 therapists used computerised self-help. They did not however rule out using this treatment format in the future (90%), and it is possible that the rapid expansion of evidence-based and easily accessible Internet treatment has changed this low uptake. On a more positive note there is evidence to suggest that guided self-help is as effective as face-to-face treatments (Andersson et al., in press; Cuijpers et al., 2010) and later in this book evidence suggesting that guided Internet

---

Box 1.1 What is a good CBT self-help text?

There is an abundance of self-help books on the book market and most are not based on CBT. Even the ones based on CBT and describing CBT techniques are rarely tested in research. This is a problem because some self-help books are sold under the assumption that the treatment will be as effective as the face-to-face treatment tested in a research trial. A review of some of the books available reveals a mixed picture. There are short books that may present only a small part of what would be covered in a full CBT treatment. On the other hand, some books are more on the academic side, presenting much information and research on the topic. Research on reading levels and text comprehension have been conducted, but there is a paucity of research on how much difference reading level makes for the outcome. Much of the research on guided self-help, including Internet-based treatments, includes participants who are well educated, and it is possible that groups with low education or with language barriers are less likely to accept self-help treatments.

What constitutes a good self-help book? Suggestions include the following:

- A chapter should introduce the condition for which the treatment is aimed and include help for the reader to self-diagnose. This includes a checklist and information on what the cutoffs for a probable diagnosis are when completing a self-report measure.

- Easy-to-understand advice on when to refrain from doing self-help and when to seek further assistance (e.g., medical advice) should be included. This might take the form of advice to only pursue the treatment after a medical visit to rule out serious conditions that would render the treatment unsuitable.

- The book should contain a rationale for how the treatment might work and why. Presentation of a treatment rationale is always present in CBT and hence should be part of self-help CBT as well.

- Each treatment chapter should represent what would occur in a regular CBT treatment. For example, if behavioural activation is included in a self-help book on depression, that chapter (or chapters) should include a rationale, an outline of the contents, well-described exercises and a summary. Language needs to be balanced and convey a sense of understanding and empathy (see Richardson et al., 2010). The text should consider that readers may differ in background regarding ethnicity, religious orientation and sexual orientation. If all examples are of white middle-class heterosexual couples many users of the book may be left out. Examples including cases where it has been difficult to implement the treatment can generate interest in the text and increase willingness to work with the exercises.

- A suggested schedule for working with the book should be provided. Often this means working on one chapter per week, but it can also be a pointer as to when to go back and repeat a chapter.

- Homework is a defining feature of CBT and should also be part of a self-help book. In this setting it is more of "Now try this in your life" – go out and do the exercises and register and make a note of how it went in the book. The book may provide registration sheets which can facilitate registration of exercises (for example exposure to fear of social situations in social anxiety disorder). Sometimes these are available as downloads on the publisher's site.

- Finally, a good self-help book must provide closure at the end, including advice on relapse prevention and how to implement the skills learned in the treatment in the future. Self-assessment and summary of the progress made can also be included.

treatments can be equally effective is presented. This leads us to the next topic of how the Internet has reached the clinic.

The Internet reaches the clinic

Information technology is increasingly integrated in modern health care today. One example in Sweden is computerised medical filing systems (in closed hospital networks). There is also increasing use of online booking systems, and in Stockholm county and several other places in Sweden patients can access their "health care contacts" via the Internet and book appointments directly without needing to go through a telephone contact (see Figure 1.1). In this book online questionnaires and treatment systems are described, and these have

Figure 1.1 My health care contacts first page. Way in for patients seeking health care contacts in Stockholm country region.

also been integrated in specialist clinics in Sweden, with the Karolinska Institute unit www. Internetpsykiatri.se being one of the most well known. In Australia there are several clinics like the https://thiswayup.org.au/clinic in Sydney.

There are no exact figures on how much the Internet has been integrated in different forms of health care, but it is gradually increasing. However, one thing that holds back progress is security issues. Everyone who manages his or her bank affairs via the Internet knows that security is crucial, which is shown by the need for a system that handles security issues with two-factor authentication in order to decrease the probability that the requestor is presenting false evidence of identity.

This is a moving target, in particular in health care, where the demands for security are increased, sometimes to the extent that the systems become less user-friendly. However, the reader should keep security in mind throughout this book. While there are solutions to these problems, they are sometimes costly, in particular for the private practitioner. More commercial systems include security measures, but there is always a risk, if ever so little, that systems can be hacked. Clinicians need to remember that older systems with paper files, completed questionnaires with patient names left out on the desk, etc., were not very safe either.

A new area of security thinking and problems to solve has emerged with modern mobile phones (smartphones). This topic will be revisited later in the book, and we do not want to scare the reader away since there are solutions to these security issues.

Practical implications and key points

- The Internet has been with us for almost 20 years and is here to stay. This is already having implications for the practice of CBT.

- Users of the Internet increase steadily, and there are many uses of the Internet. A client seeking help may have searched the Internet for health information and information about CBT. This is likely to influence expectations. Scientific information is more easily available now and clients can have direct access to the latest research, which also can influence their expectations in CBT.

- CBT is a well-known and recognised form of psychotherapy with plenty of empirical support for a range of conditions. However, there will never be enough clinicians calling for alternative low-intensity interventions (from the clinician's point of view but equally demanding for the clients). Self-help material is a crucial part of CBT and guided self-help has been found to be as effective as seeing a client face-to-face. However, the content of self-help books is important and therefore recommendations have been given.

- The Internet has reached many clinics and in different forms. In some countries medical files are online and patients can seek health care directly from home via the Internet. Handling sensitive information over the Internet demands secure solutions that should be as safe as handling one's bank affairs online. This is a field in development, and in clinic the need for security should be balanced against the need for user friendliness. For example, older clients may be confused if they constantly need to change passwords to log in, and not all information may be sensitive, but security never should be compromised.

References

Abbot J-AN, Klein B, Ciechomski L. (2008). Best practices in online therapy. *Journal of Technology in Human Services, 26*, 360–375.

Andersson G, Bergström J, Buhrman M, Carlbring P, Holländare F, Kaldo V, Nilsson-Ihrfelt E, Paxling B, Ström L, Waara J. (2008). Development of a new approach to guided self-help via the Internet. The Swedish experience. *Journal of Technology in Human Services, 26*, 161–181.

Andersson G, Cuijpers P, Carlbring P, Riper H, Hedman, E. (In press). Internet-based vs. face-to-face cognitive behaviour therapy for psychiatric and somatic disorders: a systematic review and meta-analysis. *World Psychiatry*.

Barak A, Klein B, Proudfoot JG. (2009). Defining Internet-supported therapeutic interventions. *Annals of Behavioral Medicine, 38*, 4–17.

Butler AC, Chapman JE, Forman EM, Beck AT. (2006). The empirical status of cognitive-behavioral therapy: a review of meta-analyses. *Clinical Psychology Review, 26*, 17–31.

Cuijpers P, Donker T, van Straten A, Andersson G. (2010). Is guided self-help as effective as face-to-face psychotherapy for depression and anxiety disorders? A meta-analysis of comparative outcome studies. *Psychological Medicine, 40*, 1943–1957.

Cuijpers P, Geraedts AS, van Oppen P, Andersson G, Markowitz JC, van Straten, A. (2011). Interpersonal psychotherapy of depression: A meta-analysis. *American Journal of Psychiatry, 168*, 581–592.

Keeley H, Williams C, Shapiro DA. (2002). A United Kingdom survey of accredited cognitive behaviour therapists' attitudes towards and use of structured self-help materials. *Behavioural and Cognitive Psychotherapy, 30*, 193–203.

Lovell K, Richards D. (2000). Multiple access points and level of entry (MAPLE): ensuring choice, accessibility and equity for CBT services. *Behavioural and Cognitive Psychotherapy, 28*, 379–391.

Marks I, Shaw S, Parkin R. (1998). Computer-assisted treatments of mental health problems. *Clinical Psychology: Science and Practice, 5*, 51–170.

Marks IM, Cavanagh K, Gega L. (2007). *Hands-on help. Maudsley monograph no. 49*. Hove: Psychology Press.

Richardson R, Richards DA, Barkham M. (2010). Self-help books for people with depression: the role of the therapeutic relationship. *Behavioural and Cognitive Psychotherapy, 38*, 67–81.

Rochlen AB, Zack JS, Speyer C. (2004). Online therapy: review of relevant definitions, debates, and current empirical support. *Journal of Clinical Psychology, 60*, 269–283.

Whitfield G, Williams C. (2004). If the evidence is so good – why doesn't anyone use them? A national survey of the use of computerized cognitive behaviour therapy. *Behavioural and Cognitive Psychotherapy, 32*, 57–65.

📖 Further reading

Norcross JC, Santrock JW, Campbell LF, Smith TP, Sommer R, Zuckerman EL. (2000). *Authoritative guide to self-help resources in mental health*. New York: Guilford Press.

Watkins PL, Clum GA. (Eds.). (2008). *Handbook of self-help therapies*. New York: Routledge.

Chapter 2

Resources on the Internet

What you will learn

In this chapter you will learn about:

- Forms of online information that can be accessed by clients and clinicians.

- What is out there for clients, significant others and clinicians?

- Ways to assess the quality of web sites.

- Problematic Internet use.

- How to handle clients who have searched the Internet for advice.

Background

As I have mentioned, clients are likely to engage in online searches. This can occur either before or after they have seen their CBT clinician.

An example might be a person, let's call her Clare, who for the last month has experienced fatigue and low mood and now seeks information. Clare books an appointment with her general practitioner (GP) but before that she does a search on the Internet and finds "Chronic fatigue syndrome" and reads a bit about that on Wikipedia. She does not think that fits in well with what she is feeling and does not read further (if she had done so she would have found more information on depression that would have fit better). Her husband Rob is worried about her and has searched the Internet as well. Since Rob has a sister who has been through a depression as an adolescent, he searched directly for that to remind himself what it is like to be depressed. Interestingly, he does not tell his wife that he has searched the Internet. Then comes the appointment with the GP. The GP gets the picture fairly rapidly, discusses the diagnostic criteria for depression with Clare, and conveys the message that depression is a medical problem that can be treated effectively with either medication or psychological treatment. As many other people, Clare is somewhat reluctant toward medication (van Schaik et al., 2004) and she asks what the doctor means by psychological treatment. The GP then explains that she can be offered cognitive behaviour therapy (CBT) and tells her that this is likely to help her and that CBT has been found to be effective in research. Due to lack of time the consultation ends, but a new appointment is booked. Clare is encouraged to consider the option of CBT but is told that she can also try medication if she wants to.

The GP did not ask Clare about what she had read online or elsewhere before the consultation and chronic fatigue syndrome was not even mentioned. On the other hand Clare was very pleased with the meeting and was encouraged by the information that help was available. She was somewhat confused that the doctor said she could decide herself instead of just telling her how to get better. Back at home she discussed the visit with her husband. Neither Clare nor her husband knew much about CBT, but Rob has a colleague at work whom he knows has been in CBT for stress problems a few years back. Together Clare and Rob sit down in front of the computer to find out more about CBT and depression.

What forms do online resources take?

The Internet has changed over the years and will continue to change in the future. Today, in 2014, there are many search engines available, but Google dominates. Google is a large company that hosts and develops a number of Internet-based services and products and generates profit primarily from advertising through its AdWords program. Google launched its web search engine in 1998 and like other web search engines Google works by storing information about many web pages. In November 2013, Google controlled 71% of the search engine market for desktops (Net Marketshare, 2014), with Yahoo (6%), Baidu (16.5%) and Bing (5.5%) all having minor shares of the market. (Google is even stronger for mobile and tablet searches.) Given that Google uses advanced algorithms for searches and also advertisements, the result of a search does not necessarily lead to the same outcome depending on which computer is used, in what country the search is done, and several other aspects. People also search in different ways, and the relevance of a search depends on the results it gives back. Many search engines use methods to rank the results to provide what is likely to be the best result first. How this is done is beyond the scope of this book, but the methods used to rank web pages have changed over time and can also be influenced by restrictions such as only presenting results in the native language. Increasingly today searches on the Internet are done from mobile phones and tablets, although the share is relatively small with 13.42% compared to 85.8% for desktop browsers (Net Marketshare, 2014).

Many searches today are likely to result in a Wikipedia.org page on top of the list. When I at this very moment search Google for *panic disorder, major depression* and *social anxiety disorder* (three common conditions for which CBT is recommended), I end up in Wikipedia hits for all three as number one on the list. This also occurs if I type in *cognitive behaviour therapy*. There might be some sponsored links on top as well, but overall Wikipedia has dramatically changed the scene for web searches.

What then is Wikipedia? It is basically an open and free encyclopaedia that is written collaboratively by volunteers who post material without reimbursement. Anyone registered can also edit material, which makes the encyclopaedia easy to update but also temporarily vulnerable. For instance, in the Swedish Wikipedia an erroneous entry of CBT was added (autumn 2011) which took some time to remove. But since Wikipedia is easily editable faulty descriptions usually do not last long.

In addition to Wikipedia numerous other forms of hits can be found via Google search. There are, for example, sponsored sites, which can present information and advertisements for products that are not necessarily evidence-based. Complementary medicine approaches can be found when searching for some conditions. Sponsored sites can also be in the form of advertisements for individual clinicians or hospitals. Many university clinics have their web sites and sometimes resources for patients and information for the general public. Pharmaceutical companies are another form of probable hit, in particular when searching for information about a specific medication. Online bookstores frequently turn up in searches, and also documents that have been published without considering copyright issues. There are also special interest organisations both for patients and professionals. In addition, there are numerous sites providing information on research, including open access papers that are free to download and read.

What does the Internet provide us and our patients?

Accessing health information is the third most common Internet activity, and searching the Internet for a significant other's health condition is also common (Fox, 2011). When people face a health decision, the Internet is their second most influential source of information after clinician advice (Couper et al., 2010). This clearly suggests that both patients and clinicians who engage in CBT are likely to use the Internet frequently but there is little research to support this, although the topic has been commented on for more than a decade (Riley & Veale, 1999).

What kind of information can you find on the Internet? Obviously this depends on how you search and also if you go directly to a web page that has been recommended. For example, the Swedish Behaviour Therapy Association provides a list on the Internet of practicing CBT therapists, and some private practitioners have their own web pages for marketing purposes and to inform clients about their services. However, many persons in distress may not know so much about CBT before they do their search, and it is therefore important to know what is out there if you search for information on topics like "panic disorder." You may end up on a page that does not even mention CBT as a treatment option.

One use of the Internet is to directly seek advice from an "Ask the doctor" service (Umefjord et al., 2003), which usually does not require a previous interaction between the doctor and the enquirer. This may occur for various reasons. Umefjord and his colleagues found that convenience (52%), anonymity (36%), doctor is too busy (21%), difficult to find time to visit a doctor (16%), difficult to get an appointment (13%), feeling uncomfortable when seeing a doctor (9%) and not being able to afford a doctor's visit (3%) were reasons to use an "ask the doctor" service. They also found that seeking a second opinion, discontent with previous doctors and a wish for a primary evaluation of a medical problem, asking embarrassing or sensitive questions, seeking information on behalf of relatives and preferring written communication were reasons indicating that there is indeed a need for this kind of service. Obviously, there are responsibilities involved when giving advice online and many clinicians prefer not to answer questions or are even not allowed to do so. However, persons seeking advice and information may also find patient organisations online, which provide information, advice and sometimes organise support groups (more on this in the next chapter).

There are also official web sites where questions regarding medical issues can be asked via filtered search engines. Examples include **www.nhs.uk** in the United Kingdom, **www.healthinsite.gov.au** in Australia, and **www.nlm.nih.gov/medlineplus** in the United States. There are also consumer-oriented sites specifically recommending online treatment such as **www.beacon.edu.anu**, but this is not a replacement for scientific studies.

For both patients and clinicians, the web can provide treatment guidelines which recommend CBT (and other treatments as well). In the United Kingdom the National Institute for Health and Care Excellence (NICE) guidelines are online (**www.nice.org**), and there are several other open web sites that are either tax funded (governmental) or run by independent organisations. Treatment guidelines by organisations like the American

Psychiatric Association (**www.psych.org**) and the American Psychological Association (**www.apa.org**) are two examples, but there are several other national examples (such as the treatment guidelines on the treatment of anxiety and depression issued by the Swedish National Board of Health and Welfare). CBT organisations such as the British Association for Behavioural and Cognitive Psychotherapies (**www.babcp.org**) are mainly for members but can also be found by patients.

Overall, we as clinicians need to be aware that our clients search the web and visit some of the sites that are meant for professionals. Therefore it is important to have a fair and respectful language on public sites, and this is also important in professional online discussion forums even though they only serve members. In addition to sites provided by organisations, there are private persons who have sites, although they are less likely to turn up in more general searches. Another category of web pages is provided by pharmaceutical companies where information about their products, help to "self-diagnose" and information about specific conditions like generalised anxiety disorder are provided.

Finally, when doing a Google search, information on research studies is likely to turn up. In addition to open access scientific papers that can be downloaded and read by everyone (for example BMC Psychiatry and Plos One), there are research papers that have been uploaded on researchers' own web pages. Researchers who have access to library facilities are privileged, and ordinary clinicians cannot easily get hold of the most recent research in the same way. This is changing as now many scientific funding bodies strongly encourage or even require that researchers make their research publicly available and this has facilitated the dissemination of research findings.

While searching with browsers like Google is one way to find research, many clients are well educated and know about public Medline (**http://www.ncbi.nlm.nih.gov/pubmed**) and search for research information themselves. In practice this means that some clients may be well read and know about the most recent research, and as a clinician you may make the mistake of not knowing that your client knows about the recent new study you have not even heard about yourself!

How can we assess the quality of web sites?

When the Internet was flooded by information about health by the end of the 1990s researchers saw the need to evaluate the quality of web sites as they varied greatly (Eysenbach & Diepgen, 1998). There are several studies on the quality of mental health information on the Internet. One example is a study by Griffiths and Christensen (2000), who evaluated the quality of web sites on depression, and since then many studies have been published on the quality of mental disorder information web sites (for review see Reavley & Jorm, 2011).

There are at least four ways to evaluate web sites. First, since the Internet is open we can leave it to the clients to make judgments on their own. While this retains the freedom of the Internet it does not necessarily lead to the best evidence-based information. Clients are also susceptible to what web browsers prioritize, and sponsored links. Second, developers of web sites can be careful and adhere to ethical guidelines in line with good clinical practice. This prevents some but not all questionable Internet activities as some sites may ignore ethics or not have the time to get the web site certified. Third, professionals (both researchers and clinicians) and patient organisations can use systematic approaches to assess and rate available web sites themselves. This can lead to a list of recommended sites and also a list of sites to avoid or warn the client not to use. A fourth option is to have the web site assessed for readability.

The HON

One example of the second way to assess sites, which is up to the organisation or person responsible for the site, is to have it assessed to get it certified. The Health On the Net (HON) Foundation provides one of the many voluntary web site certification schemes (Boyer et al., 1998). HON is a Swiss nonprofit organisation with a mission to guide clients and clinicians toward good Internet health information (**http://www.hon.ch**). HON proposed its first code of conduct for Internet health information in 1996. The current version, available in 35 languages, highlights principles they suggest web developers should follow (see Table 2.1).

Table 2.1 Principles of the Health On the Net (HON) Foundation Code of Conduct

Unhelpful thinking style	Some typical thoughts
Authoritative	Author qualifications should be indicated.
Complementarity	Information should support, not replace, the clinician-client relationship.
Privacy	Privacy and confidentiality of visitor's personal data should be respected.
Attribution	Sources of published information should be provided along with dates.
Justifiability	Claims relating to benefits and performance should be evidence based.
Transparency	Accessible presentation and accurate contact details should be provided.
Financial disclosure	Funding sources should be identified.
Advertising policy	Advertising should be clearly distinguished from editorial content.

Source: Boyer et al. 1998.

The DISCERN

The third way to evaluate web sites is to rate them yourself. Clinicians and clients can use the 16-item DISCERN quality criteria (Charnock et al., 1999) to determine the quality of health information on the Internet (**www.discern.org.uk**). The DISCERN Project was funded from 1996 to 1997 by the British Library and the NHS Executive Research and Development Program. The DISCERN has a brief questionnaire with 16 items (see Table 2.2). Each DISCERN item is rated on a scale from 1 to 5, with higher scores indicative of greater quality. The DISCERN ratings are described as:

> 1: The answer to the item is a definite no. The quality criterion has not been met at all

> 2 to 4: The answer to the item is partial. The quality criterion has been met to some extent, and

> 5: The answer to the item is a definite yes. The quality criterion has been completely met.

For each item, the DISCERN Handbook provides clear criterion definitions and examples of how rating is done. The DISCERN has good internal consistency and interrater agreement (Ademiluyi et al., 2003). There is also a briefer DISCERN with only six items (Khazaal et al., 2009).

Table 2.2 DISCERN quality criteria for consumer health information on treatment choices

1. Are the aims clear?
2. Does it achieve its aims?
3. Is it relevant?
4. Is it clear what sources of information were used to compile the publication (other than the author or producer)?
5. Is it clear when the information used or reported in the publication was reported?
6. Is it balanced and unbiased?
7. Does it provide details of additional sources of support and information?
8. Does it refer to areas of uncertainty?
9. Does it describe how each treatment works?
10. Does it describe the benefits of each treatment?
11. Does it describe the risks of each treatment?
12. Does it describe what would happen if no treatment is used?
13. Does it describe how the treatment choices affect overall quality of life?
14. Is it clear that there may be more than one possible treatment choice?
15. Does it provide support for shared decision making?
16. Based on the answers to all of the above questions, rate the overall quality of the publication as a source of information about treatment choices.

Source: Charnock et al. 1999.

Readability

Readability refers to how easy written information is to read and understand, and is obviously important as web sites mostly rely on written information. Many things can reduce readability beyond the obvious fact that it must be possible to read letters clearly to be able to read a text. Aspects rendering a text less readable are jargon (for example, in the form of polysyllabic words) and complex linguistic structures (for example, in the form of lengthy sentences). There are several tests to evaluate the readability of web sites. The Flesch Reading Ease Score, Flesch-Kincaid Grade Level Formula and Simple Measure of Gobbledygook have been used to assess readability of Internet health information (e.g., Walsh & Volsko, 2008). All three readability tests can be performed with an online tool (**www.online-utility.org/english/readability_test_and_improve.jsp**), which allows users to enter a web site address. The Flesch Reading Ease Score (Flesch, 1948) estimates grade reading level based on the average number of sentences and syllables per 100 words. Higher scores indicate higher readability. The Flesch-Kincaid Grade Level Formula translates the 0 to 100 Flesch Reading Ease Score into an American grade level, estimating the number of years of education required to understand the text. Lower scores indicate higher readability. The Simple Measure of Gobbledygook (McLaughlin, 1969) uses the number of polysyllabic words (words with at least three syllables) to calculate an estimated grade reading level. Similar to the Flesch-Kincaid Grade Level, lower scores indicate higher readability. The U.S. Department of Health and Human Services describes a text with readability above nine years of education as difficult for many people (Walsh & Volsko, 2008).

In sum, there are several ways that clinicians and patients can get an idea of the quality of web sites. In addition to these, there are scientific papers on the quality of information on the Internet that can help clinicians recommend the best available sites. However, as the Internet changes quickly, the recommended sites today may not be the same two months later.

Box 2.1 Searching the Internet

An example of social anxiety disorder

Social Anxiety Disorder (SAD) was formerly known as social phobia, and is a common condition across the world, with prevalence rates well above 10% (Furmark, 2002).

SAD is characterised by avoidance of social situations that are perceived as threatening and a persistent fear of one or more social performance situations in which embarrassment may occur. Far from all sufferers seek treatment, and there is a gap between help-seeking and the number of people who have SAD. It is likely that persons with SAD seek information on the Internet. Indeed, Erwin et al. (2004) investigated a sample of 434 individuals who responded to an Internet-based survey (posted on an anxiety disorder clinic web site). They found that 92% of the respondents met the criteria for SAD. There were some negative consequences of Internet use in this group. For example, participants reported that the Internet had made them more passive and less socially active. They also reported that they used the Internet because they experienced more comfort interacting on the Internet than face-to-face. On a more positive note respondents reported that they had acquired new information about SAD through the Internet and had learned about psychotherapy and medication treatments.

Given these findings it is interesting to know what information is out there on SAD. This was investigated by Khazaal et al. (2008) who did a systematic search and grading of quality of web-based information using two key terms: "social phobia" and "social anxiety disorder". They used the HON label and DISCERN scale as quality indicators and also investigated reading level. Out of 200 links they were able to include 58. The overall quality of the sites was poor. Only 11 (19%) had the HON label. The average Flesch-Kincaid reading grade was 7.34, which is below 8 (the recommended standard level). The mean DISCERN score was 36, which must be regarded as a low score (Reavley & Jorm, 2011). There was a difference between sites having the HON label and those without in that the HON label sites had a significantly higher DISCERN score. This study was conducted in 2006 and it is likely that the situation has changed, with better sites on SAD.

From a clinical point of view it is likely that patients with SAD have searched the Internet before they reach the clinic. It may also be the case that they use the Internet at the expense of face-to-face interactions. However, as presented later in this book, persons with SAD have been found to benefit from Internet-based treatment, and therefore the Internet may be more of a blessing than a curse for persons with SAD.

Problematic Internet use

Although this book describes how useful the Internet can be for CBT clinicians, we cannot escape the fact that Internet use can also be negative. Three different aspects of problematic Internet use are discussed here. First, the concept of Internet addiction is covered. Second, commentary on the forms problematic Internet use may take is presented, and third we cover the risk of finding negative and harmful information on the Internet or posting sensitive material about yourself as a client.

One can overdo Internet use as well as one can overeat, drink too much, gamble too much, exercise too much, and a range of other behaviours that in excess become problematic or harmful. In the late 1990s there was a discussion about problematic Internet use, and the concept "Internet addiction" was introduced (Griffiths, 1998). Now more than 10 years later problematic Internet use is still being discussed, and there has been a debate over whether Internet addiction should be introduced as a diagnostic entity in the *Diagnostic and Statistical Manual of Mental Disorders*, 5th edition (*DSM V*) (Weinstein & Lejoyeux, 2010). This did not happen, however.

Four components have been suggested as essential for a diagnosis of Internet addition:

1) Excessive Internet use which is associated with a loss of sense of time or a neglect of basic drives (such as eating and sleeping)

2) Withdrawal symptoms, including anger, tension, anxiety and/or depression when the computer (now probably the smartphone and tablet as well) is not available

3) Tolerance development, which can include the need for better computer equipment, more software, unlimited access, more hours of use, and so forth

4) Adverse consequences, including arguments, lying, poor school or work achievement, social isolation and fatigue.

This concept of Internet addiction must be regarded as tentative and there are no well-validated diagnostic instruments (but there are several self-report inventories). For a CBT clinician, the list above can serve as a reminder that some clients may overuse the Internet to the extent that it resembles an addiction or compulsion. The health problems associated with Internet addiction are mainly related to sleep deprivation and probably stress-related problems. From a clinical point of view it can work both ways. Clients with psychiatric disorders may use the Internet in problematic ways and it can also be the case that overuse of the Internet may lead to psychological problems (Ko et al., 2012). Research is still unclear regarding the temporal associations, but there have been some successful attempts to develop treatments for problematic Internet use, including pathological gambling that often occurs on the Internet (Carlbring & Smit, 2008).

Pathological gambling is one example of the form problematic Internet use may take. Other examples are sexual preoccupations (cybersex), shopping/selling, overuse of social networks, buying illegal drugs and increased loneliness. The latter problem was investigated in an early study by Kraut et al. (1998) showing that loneliness increased when participants were provided with Internet access. However, later findings have not been consistent with the notion of Internet use leading to loneliness and it is again likely that it can be either good or bad and sometimes a bit of both.

From a CBT perspective, problematic Internet use can sometimes take the form of "safety behaviour", in other words behaviour that is in the service of controlling anxiety but instead of being helpful makes the anxiety persist (e.g., Salkovskis et al., 1996). Turning to the Internet for relief and control of anxiety can very well serve the function of a safety behaviour that may need to be targeted in CBT. Nowadays, we have problematic use of mobile phones (smartphones) which can also be something that is used for ineffective anxiety management. However, smartphones can also be used to facilitate the treatment (see Chapter 10).

The third risk of Internet use relates to what can be found on the Internet. There can be harmful information; for example, instructions on how to engage in self-injury, how to lose weight for persons with anorexia and a range of other potentially dangerous information. Perhaps a bit less problematic would be finding negative information about a treatment that is not evidence-based or finding information about treatment that totally lacks research support but still claims excellent results.

A final potential negative consequence, and there are probably many more I have not covered, is the risk that clients (and this can be therapists as well) post sensitive information about themselves on blogs and on their Facebook sites. For example, I know there are clinicians who have experienced that their clients blog about the treatment session immediately after it has been completed! Again, I hesitate to dismiss all such activities as negative and harmful. There are cases when it can be a good thing to stay in touch with your friends on Facebook and get immediate feedback if you have made progress in your treatment. The lesson for us as therapists to learn is that clients may use social media without our awareness.

Clients who have searched the Internet: some do's and don'ts

Here is a proposal for a few questions you can ask and advice on what you could do and not do:

1) Ask the client if they use the Internet and/or smartphone/mobile phone on a regular basis. If so, ask how often. The rationale for asking about online behaviour should be clearly stated: "I want to ask a few questions about use of the Internet. The reason is that it can be helpful for us to know and that the Internet nowadays can form a significant part of people's lives. I know for example that some of my clients have searched the Internet for information about CBT. There are many things out there on the Internet and not all of it is true. Are you ok with me asking you about your Internet use?"

2) If they use the Internet ask if they have searched for health information, and in particular if they have read anything about CBT on the Internet. Have an open attitude and do not judge the client.

3) Ask if they are active in social networks or online groups, like support groups. Keep in mind that clients may find support on the Internet, but also that they may feel excluded from social networks like Facebook. You may also ask if they post information about themselves (e.g., blog or Facebook) and if they are happy with that. Included here can be an agreement on what should stay in the therapy room.

4) Ask if they feel stress about the Internet, like checking email, updating their Facebook page, etc. For some clients Internet use is almost like an addiction and for some a safety behaviour. It can also be a source of stress and low mood; hence, a question about negative aspects of Internet use can be important. Do not forget positive consequences as well. There may be both negative and positive consequences.

5) Probe for embarrassment. Clients may feel ashamed about their online behaviour, including not telling their significant others that they have searched for information on mental health, participated in online discussion forums, etc. There may be room here to ask about further negative aspects like gambling and cybersex.

Practical implications and key points

- There is much information available on the Internet and various ways to access it. Wikipedia is one common web site which contains a great deal of information about psychopathology and psychotherapy.
- Clients and clinicians can get information about specific conditions (like depression) and treatment options on the Internet. There are also professional resources and scientific information that may be accessed by clients and professionals.
- The quality of web sites varies, and there are ways to assess that. Since the Internet is always changing, searches need to be updated constantly. There are, however, studies in which the quality of web pages has been rated for consistency, credibility and readability and as a clinician it can be a good idea to know which web sites to recommend or not to recommend.
- Problematic Internet use can be part of the client's problem. Clients may overuse the Internet, may use it with negative consequences (like stress) and may also use the Internet as a safety behaviour. Clinicians can benefit from asking about online behaviour early in treatment as it can have an impact on the planning and practice of CBT.

References

Ademiluyi G, Rees CE, Sheard CE. (2003). Evaluating the reliability and validity of three tools to assess the quality of health information on the Internet. *Patient Education and Counselling, 50*, 151–155.

Boyer C, Selby M, Scherrer JR, Appel RD. (1998). The Health On the Net code of conduct for medical and health Websites. *Computers in Biology and Medicine, 28*, 603–610.

Carlbring P, Smit F. (2008). Randomized trial of Internet-delivered self-help with telephone support for pathological gamblers. *Journal of Consulting and Clinical Psychology, 76*, 1090–1094.

Charnock D, Shepperd S, Needham G, Gann R. (1999). DISCERN: An instrument for judging the quality of written consumer health information on treatment choices. *Journal of Epidemiology and Community Health, 53*, 105–111.

Couper MP, Singer E, Levin CA, Fowler FJ Jr, Fagerlin A, Zikmund-Erwin BA, Turk CL, Heimberg RG, Frescoa DM, Hantula DA. (2004). The Internet: Home to a severe population of individuals with social anxiety disorder? *Journal of Anxiety Disorders, 18*, 629–646.

Eysenbach G, Diepgen TL. (1998). Towards quality management of medical information on the Internet: evaluation, labelling, and filtering of information. *British Medical Journal, 317*, 1496–1502.

Flesch R. (1948). A new readability yardstick. *Journal of Applied Psychology, 32*, 221–233.

Fox S. (2011). *Health topics: 80% of Internet users look for health information online* (Pew Internet & American Life Project, February 1). Retrieved September 9, 2011, from http://www.106S 114S. pewInternet.org/~/media/Files/Reports/2011/PIP_HealthTopics.pdf

Furmark T. (2002). Social phobia: Overview of community surveys. *Acta Psychiatrica Scandinavica, 105*, 84–93.

Griffiths KM, Christensen H. (2000). Quality of web based information on treatment of depression: Cross sectional survey. *British Medical Journal, 321*, 1511–1515.

Griffiths M. (1998). Internet addiction: does it really exist? In J Gackenbach, editor. *Psychology and the Internet. Intrapersonal, interpersonal and transpersonal implications* (pp. 61–75). San Diego: Academic Press.

Khazaal Y, Chatton A, Cochand S, Coquard O, Fernandez S, Khan R. et al. (2009). Brief DISCERN, six questions for the evaluation of evidence-based content of health-related websites. *Patient Education and Counselling, 77*, 33–37.

Khazaal Y, Fernandez S, Cochand S, Reboh I, Zullino D. (2008). Quality of web-based information on social phobia: A cross-sectional study. *Depression and Anxiety, 25*, 461–465.

Ko CH, Yen JY, Yen CF, Chen CS, Chen CC. (2012). The association between Internet addiction and psychiatric disorder: A review of the literature. *European Psychiatry, 27*, 1–8.

Kraut R, Patterson M, Lundmark V Kiesler S, Mukopadhyay T, Scherlis W. (1998). Internet paradox. A social technology that reduces social involvement and psychological well-being? *American Psychologist, 53*, 1017–1031.

McLaughlin GH. (1969). SMOG grading: A new readability formula. *Journal of Reading, 12*, 639–646.

Net Marketshare. (2014). Search Engine Market Share (February 2014). Retrieved February 15, 2014, from http://marketshare.hitslink.com

Reavley NJ, Jorm AF. (2011). The quality of mental disorder information websites: A review. *Patient Education and Counselling, 85*, e16–25.

Riley S, Veale D. (1999). The Internet and its relevance to cognitive behavioural psychotherapists. *Behavioural and Cognitive Psychotherapy, 27*, 37–46.

Salkovskis PM, Clark DM. Gelder MG. (1996). Cognition-behaviour links in the persistence of panic. *Behaviour Research and Therapy, 34*, 453–458.

Umefjord G, Petersson G, Hamberg K. (2003). Reasons for consulting a doctor on the Internet: Web survey of users of an Ask the Doctor service. *Journal of Medical Internet Research, 5*, e26.

van Schaik D, Klijn A, van Hout H, van Marwijk H, Beekman A, de Haan M, van Dyck R. (2004). Patients' preferences in the treatment of depressive disorder in primary care. *General Hospital Psychiatry, 26*, 184–189.

Walsh TM, Volsko TA. (2008). Readability assessment of Internet-based consumer health information. *Respiratory Care, 53*, 1310–1315.

Weinstein A, Lejoyeux M. (2010). Internet addiction or excessive Internet use. *American Journal of Drug and Alcohol Abuse, 36*, 277–283.

📖 Further reading

Joinson AN. (2003). *Understanding the psychology of Internet behaviour. Virtual worlds, real lives*. Basingstoke: Palgrave MacMillan.

Reavley NJ, Jorm AF. (2011). The quality of mental disorder information websites: a review. *Patient Education and Counselling, 85*(2), e16–25.

Weinstein A, Lejoyeux M. (2010). Internet addiction or excessive Internet use. *American Journal of Drug and Alcohol Abuse, 36*, 277–283.

Chapter 3

Online support groups

What you will learn

In this chapter you will learn about:

- Self-help groups on the Internet.
- The effects of online support groups.
- How to handle support groups as a CBT clinician.

Background

Like many people with recurrent depression Joan often felt that people around her could not fully understand her condition. In CBT she had learned a lot of useful things and instead of being passive when depressed she now stayed active, and that often helped her get back on track. But she felt alone during those times. Her family of course knew when she was down, but since she coped so well with the mood swings they did not comment on her state, which added to her feeling of loneliness. The situation changed when she found an online support group for depression. There she could discuss her feelings and her struggles with persons who she felt understood exactly what she meant. In fact, she had been in contact with one person outside of the forum and they discussed meeting, as the new friend lived in a city not far away from where Joan lived. In the online support group there were several ongoing discussions that were of interest for Joan.

Although CBT had been discussed, more often medication was discussed, as members of the group had very different experiences of medication and the health care system. Joan noted early on that there were a few individuals who were most active, and she had herself posted only a few comments and one question. It was in association with one of these comments she had emailed directly to her new friend.

Online support groups – what are they?

One aspect of Internet use is the easily available peer-to-peer support opportunities. Online support groups (also called Internet peer support) are a form of self-help based on the assumption that people with similar problems can help each other by coming together. They are available through different Internet platforms such as email lists, chat rooms, or forums (online bulletin boards). Most common is probably the last form, as the asynchronous format has advantages over the real-time chat forums. More recently, Facebook has taken over as a form of online bulletin board in which pictorial elements are commonplace. An online support group is a form of mutual support, and with the Internet there are numerous opportunities for persons who like to discuss, ask questions and provide answers in relation to their health problems. As with all groups, online support groups can vary greatly.

A first distinction is whether the group is self-guided with facilitators or if professionals are involved monitoring the discussion. In other words online support groups can evolve without any professional involvement but can also be organized by professionals. One example of the latter is a form of Internet chat group in Germany that was organised after the completion of inpatient treatment for depression (Bauer et al., 2011). Professional involvement in online support groups can be very restrictive, mainly intervening when inappropriate activities occur such as aggression towards other group members and dangerous advice regarding self-harm. But involvement can also be more active such as participating in the discussions as a full member and posting discussion points.

A second distinction relates to the function of the group. The support can be emotional, informational or instrumental in its main form, but is often a combination of all three. To be more specific, support groups have the potential to decrease isolation, reduce the impact of stressors, increase sharing of health and self-management information and provide role modelling (Pfeiffer et al., 2011). Barak and co-workers (2008) highlighted several potential functions of online support groups. For example, they discussed personal empowerment and argued that online support groups can provide this.

A third distinction of online support groups has to do with the structural characteristics of the group and the behaviour of the members. Support groups can differ in size from just a few persons to several thousand. Indeed, given the large number of people who use the Internet it is not surprising that researchers have concluded that online support groups are at least as prevalent as face-to-face support groups (Kaplan et al., 2011). A quick search in December 2013 showed 4,110 Yahoo support groups related to depression only, indicating the huge number of groups.

Online support groups can be closed and open only by invitation or open for all interested persons with no obligations or entry criteria. Members may come and go, and many (often a majority) of the members are not active but rather passive observers of the discussions in the online forum (McKenna & Bargh, 1998).

A fourth distinction has to do with the mechanisms that may operate in online self-help groups. One such mechanism is the *online disinhibition effect* (Joinson, 1998), the observation that people may express things on the Internet that they would normally not say or do in person when confronting people. In the context of mutual support groups it is obviously necessary for at least some members to reveal information about their lives, such as experiences of health care in the case of online support groups for health problems. Both honesty and self-disclosure are important ingredients in self-help groups and according to Barak et al. (2008) the disinhibition sometimes seen on the Internet is likely to speed up the therapeutic functions of support groups. However, disinhibition and revelation of personal secrets have a potential cost (Kelly & McKillop, 1996), and as online support groups often are open (members can go in and out), it is hard to control who will get the information.

On the other hand, while regular support groups to some extent can preserve anonymity it is much easier to preserve this in online support groups where identity can be disguised. This is not always an asset, as the lack of visual information about a sender can lead to inappropriate reactions, making the risk for misunderstandings substantial in support groups based on text only. For example, a member of an online support group can change name, age, gender, ethnicity and just about everything to convey an impression that he or she is another person. Obviously this has changed with the increasing use of social networks such as Facebook where anonymity is discouraged.

In sum, online support groups have been around for close to 20 years now and are still growing in number (see Figure 3.1 for an example). With the advent of social networking, support groups can take a slightly different form, but for many health conditions there are online support groups in a range of languages. We now turn to the obvious question of whether participation in online support groups leads to better health.

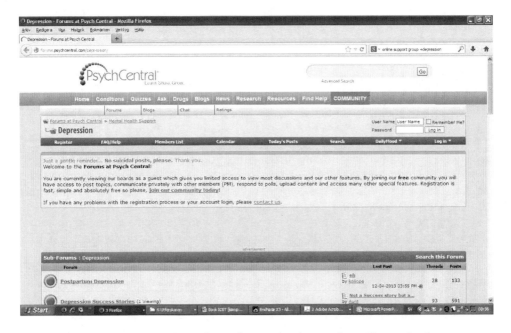

Figure 3.1 PsychCentral depression forum (**http://forums.psychcentral.com/depression/**).

Research on the effects of online communities

Online support groups have been investigated in several research trials, sometimes in the form of stand-alone interventions, but also as part of an intervention and even as a control group in CBT research, for example in some studies from my research group (e.g., Andersson et al., 2005).

Starting with the effects of online support groups for common mental health problems, Griffiths and colleagues (2009a,b) systematically reviewed studies investigating the effects of online support groups on symptoms of depression. In one early study by Houston et al. (2002), and included in the review by Griffiths, significant reductions in depressive symptoms were found following participation in online support groups. However, the literature summarized by Griffiths was not of high quality and the authors concluded that there was a paucity of high-quality research investigating the effects of online support groups on symptoms of depression. More recently, Kaplan et al. (2011) conducted a randomized controlled trial with 300 participants. They had been diagnosed with either a schizophrenia spectrum or an affective disorder. Included participants were randomized to either Internet peer support via a listserv, Internet peer support via a bulletin board or a control condition. The study could not find that participation in online support groups (which was not moderated or structured) led to enhanced well-being. On the contrary, persons who participated more actively in the peer support groups were more likely to report distress than the ones who participated less or not at all. It is worth pausing here to reflect on what we can expect from online discussion groups. Barak et al. (2008) argued that online support groups do not aim at effectiveness in terms of distress-related outcomes. Rather, they have as their goal emotional relief and elevated sense of control, which are elements of empowerment (Barak et al., 2008). While this assertion rings true it is still the case that support groups in general sometimes are presented as treatments and alternatives to traditional care, but there are studies in which the effects of online discussion forum participation have been investigated in terms of health-related outcomes.

One area in which there has been much research activity is the role of online cancer forums. Overall the literature on the benefits from participation in online cancer groups is mixed (Hoey et al., 2008). More recently, Salzer et al. (2010) investigated the benefits of Internet-based peer interaction in a group of 78 women recently diagnosed with breast cancer. Participants were randomized to either an Internet peer support group or to an Internet-based educational control condition. Follow-ups at 4 and 12 months were included. The study failed to find any benefits from peer support on measures of perceived social support, self-efficacy and hope. Moreover, the peer support group did worse than the control group on the primary outcome measure dealing with symptoms and functioning. However, the authors reported that many women actively participated in the Internet peer support group and were satisfied with the support. A second study on Internet peer support included 921 survivors of various cancers (Hoybye et al., 2010). This was a trial in which treatment as usual (a rehabilitation program) was compared with a Web-based lecture and participation in an Internet support group following the rehabilitation program. The Internet-based support was hence an add-on to the usual rehabilitation. As with the previous trial the results were not in line with the expectations, as the Internet condition did worse than the control group at six months follow-up. Taken together, these two more recent studies raise concerns regarding the benefits of online peer support for cancer.

A different use of online support groups is to add online chat forums following inpatient rehabilitation, and this has been tested in a series of trials conducted in Germany by Hans Kordy and co-workers (Golkaramnay et al., 2007). Overall, the findings are promising and represent an innovative use of online support groups that are directly linked with previous treatment (see Box 3.1).

My own experiences from using online discussion groups in research trials have been mixed. In some of our research trials participation in a moderated discussion group has served as a control condition and with few exceptions minor changes have occurred in terms of symptom relief. One exception however was a study on older adults with hearing loss in which the control group perceived a lot of benefit from their participation in a discussion forum (Thorén et al., 2011). In addition to serving as a control group we have used online discussion forums as an adjunct to Internet-delivered CBT and while there are clients who appreciate being in a group we have no clear indications that the discussion group added anything to the outcome in studies on depression and anxiety disorders. Other research groups have also included online forums as part of the treatment with no clear indications that it adds to the outcome (e.g., Titov et al., 2008).

Box 3.1 Online chat groups as aftercare following face-to-face treatment

In Germany at the Centre for Psychotherapy Research in Heidelberg, Hans Kordy and his co-workers have developed an interesting approach to aftercare following inpatient treatment. In Germany it is common to treat patients with mental disorders as inpatients, including patients with anxiety and depression who are mostly treated as outpatients in countries like the United Kingdom. The researchers in Germany developed and tested a form of online support where they set up chat forums with 8 to 10 participants who met with a therapist on the chat room once per week for a duration of 90 minutes. The groups were open and had no manual. They lasted 12 to 15 weeks and were intended to serve as a bridge after the inpatient treatment they had received. The therapists who guided the groups knew all group members, either because they had actually seen them in treatment or had interviewed them at discharge. In a trial they compared the effects of the online aftercare with a matched group who did not participate in the chat forums (Golkaramnay et al., 2007; Bauer et al., 2011). At 12 months after discharge chat participants (n = 114) had a significantly lower risk (25%) for a negative outcome compared to the control group (38.5%). Unfortunately this was not a randomized controlled trial but the findings are encouraging and represent an innovative use of online support group work that has several benefits from preventing relapse after therapy in the clinic.

What should I, as a clinician, say about online support groups?

While this book is mainly about using the Internet in CBT I felt that a separate chapter on online support groups was needed, as this is a common phenomena in clinical practice, although clinicians do not ask about participation in online groups. In certain areas such as working with adolescents it may be more obvious that clients are out on the Internet and that being a member of an online group or social network is the rule rather than the exception for most young persons. Nowadays, this is often in the form of closed social networks such as Facebook, but online discussion forums on specific topics such as eating disorders and self-harm are still widely available for anyone who would like to join.

As a CBT clinician there are two important issues to consider when the topic of online group participation is discussed. The first question is concerned with the potential benefits and harms associated with participation. Barak et al. (2008) concluded that against common belief information provided by lay people in online support groups is rarely erroneous or harmful. This is not to say that it cannot occur. Clients may see things that clearly conflict with the message presented in CBT but may also gain confidence from having stories about the benefits of CBT being presented. Since group processes occur in online groups, things may occur in online groups that are beyond the control of the therapist but that still may have an impact on the treatment.

The second question to consider with clients who participate in online groups (and again please note that your clients are out there even if you did not know about it), is whether the client shares experiences in therapy with other persons in the online forum and how this is received. For example, clients may get advice from others who have been in CBT themselves. Just imagine a response to a posting that you are in CBT for anxiety and someone in the forum comments "I tried this but it was totally useless. The therapist wanted me to do this thing he called exposure but it just did not work for me". Anyone who gets this response may feel discouraged and if online group participation is a secret in the treatment it cannot be handled in a later session. Even worse, there are therapists who are named in the forums, which can be a daunting experience. On a more positive note, some 'lay CBT' may be practiced in the forum and it can very well be that the client is gaining strength rather than bad advice from being active in a forum.

Practical implications and key points

- Online discussion forums are common and more clients than you think are members of such groups.

- The effects of participation in online forums are mixed. Some persons benefit and some do not. Many do however feel empowered and gain support from persons who have the same problems as they do.

- CBT clinicians may consider asking about online group participation as the activities in the forum may have an impact on CBT.

References

Andersson G, Bergström J, Holländare F, Carlbring P, Kaldo V, Ekselius L. (2005). Internet-based self-help for depression: A randomised controlled trial. *British Journal of Psychiatry, 187*, 456–461.

Barak A, Boniel-Nissim M, Suler J. (2008). Fostering empowerment in online support groups. *Computers in Human Behavior, 24*, 1867–1883.

Bauer S, Wolf M, Haug S, Kordy H. (2011). The effectiveness of Internet chat groups in relapse prevention after inpatient psychotherapy. *Psychotherapy Research, 21*, 219–226.

Golkaramnay V, Bauer S, Haug S, Wolf M, Kordy H. (2007). The exploration of the effectiveness of group therapy through an Internet chat as aftercare: A controlled naturalistic study. *Psychotherapy and Psychosomatics, 76*, 219–225.

Griffiths KM, Calear AL, Banfield M. (2009a). Systematic review on Internet Support Groups (ISGs) and depression (1): Do ISGs reduce depressive symptoms? *Journal of Medical Internet Research, 11*(3), e40.

Griffiths KM, Calear AL, Banfield M, Tam, A. (2009b). Systematic review on Internet Support Groups (ISGs) and depression (2): What is known about depression ISGs? *Journal of Medical Internet Research, 11*(3), e41.

Hoey LM, Ieropoli SC, White VM, Jefford M. (2008). Systematic review of peer-support programs for people with cancer. *Patient Education and Counseling, 70*, 315–337.

Houston TK, Cooper LA, Ford DE. (2002). Internet support groups for depression: A 1-year prospective cohort study. *American Journal of Psychiatry, 159*, 2062–2068.

Hoybye MT, Dalton SO, Deltour I, Bidstrup PE, Frederiksen K, Johansen C. (2010). Effect of Internet peer-support groups on psychosocial adjustment to cancer: A randomised study. *British Journal of Cancer, 102*, 1348–1354.

Joinson A. (1998). Causes and implications of disinhibited behavior on the Internet. In J Gackenbach, editor. *Psychology and the Internet. Intrapersonal, interpersonal and transpersonal implications* (pp. 43–60). San Diego: Academic Press.

Kaplan K, Salzer MS, Solomon P, Brusilovskiy E, Cousounis P. (2011). Internet peer support for individuals with psychiatric disabilities: a randomized controlled trial. *Social Science & Medicine, 72*, 54–62.

Kelly AE, McKillop KJ. (1996). Consequences of revealing personal secrets. *Psychological Bulletin, 120*, 450–465.

McKenna KYA, Bargh JA. (1998). Coming out in the age of the Internet: identity "demarginalization" through virtual group participation. *Journal of Personality and Social Psychology, 73*, 681–694.

Pfeiffer PN, Heisler M, Piette JD, Rogers MA, Valenstein M. (2011). Efficacy of peer support interventions for depression: A meta-analysis. *General Hospital Psychiatry, 33*, 29–36.

Salzer MS, Palmer SC, Kaplan K., Brusilovskiy E, Ten Have T, Hampshire M et al. (2010). A randomized, controlled study of Internet peer-to-peer interactions among women newly diagnosed with breast cancer. *Psycho-Oncology, 19*, 441–446.

Thorén E, Svensson M, Törnqvist A, Andersson G, Carlbring P, Lunner T. (2011). Rehabilitative online education vs. Internet discussion group for hearing aid users: A randomized controlled trial. *Journal of the American Academy of Audiology, 22*, 274–285.

Titov N, Andrews G, Schwencke G, Drobny J, Einstein D. (2008). Shyness 1: Distance treatment of social phobia over the Internet. *The Australian and New Zealand Journal of Psychiatry, 42*, 585–594.

📖 Further reading

Bargh JA, McKenna KYA. (2004). Internet and social life. *Annual Review of Psychology, 55*, 573–590.

Davison KP, Pennebaker JW, Dickerson SS. (2000). Who talks? The social psychology of illness support groups. *American Psychologist, 55*, 205–217.

Chapter 4

Assessments over the Internet

What you will learn

In this chapter you will learn about:

- How self-report measures can be transferred to the Internet.
- How Internet administration of diagnostic instruments works.
- Psychometric properties of online questionnaires.
- How to integrate online measurements in your daily practice.

Background

Mark had just begun face-to-face therapy and his therapist suggested that he fill out a depression questionnaire weekly so that they could get a grasp on his progress. The therapist asked Mark if he was a regular Internet user, and since Mark said he was, the therapist suggested that they would create an online profile for Mark that he could log into and fill out the measure online that could be viewed by the therapist before each upcoming session. Mark could also post messages to the therapist and check his appointments online, which was an added convenience. In addition, the web site provided an overview of Mark's progress so that he could monitor how he was doing himself. When therapy ended Mark commented that it had been useful to have the opportunity to complete measures online since he sometimes lost papers and forgot appointments when he was in distress.

Clinicians working in medical settings are obliged to document the progress of their clients, and this includes psychological treatments as well. Increasingly, clinicians working with CBT use validated self-report measures to evaluate progress and outcome. The Internet has made it possible to transfer self-report measures to online administration. Moreover, researchers have worked to develop screening instruments to obtain preliminary diagnoses, and with smartphones opportunities have emerged regarding ecologically valid real-time measures of the problem of interest (e.g., anxiety) (Boschen & Casey, 2008).

Self-report questionnaires

Self-report instruments have been administered over the Internet for almost as long as the Internet has been around (Buchanan, 2002). Completing a questionnaire on the Internet can be similar to completing it on a piece of paper, with a few differences.

First, online administration allows one questionnaire item to be displayed at a time instead of having all items presented together. Second, Internet administration can prevent items from being skipped or missed. Error can be minimized further by changing font size on the screen. Third, progress bars can be displayed so the client can get a feel for the time it will take to complete measures.

There are several other advantages as well. Online administration allows immediate scoring, and feedback can be presented instantly on the screen. Online questionnaires can also have interactive functions such as skipping further questions if a screening question indicates that the client does not have the problems measured by the questionnaire. There are also indications that online administration can increase willingness to disclose and share sensitive information (see discussion in the previous chapter on the disinhibition effect).

For the clinician and researcher online administration also saves time, as there is no need to enter data from the questionnaire to a computer. Online questionnaires of course result in less paper being used for administration, and another advantage is that items easily can be added or changed if needed. With a paper-and-pencil questionnaire a spelling error may be difficult to change if many copies of the questionnaire exist, but online questionnaires can be changed immediately, as the clinician or researcher has access to a user-friendly interface where items on measures easily can be changed without particular programming skills.

In addition, with online weekly measures it is possible to monitor suicidal ideation and deterioration, which can be flagged for the clinician who might have a heavy caseload. This is practiced at the Internet psychiatry unit at Karolinska Institutet, Stockholm, where patients treated for anxiety and depression need to log in and complete weekly measures when they access the treatment. When the patient scores high on an item measuring suicidal ideation this is flagged to the therapist who gets a message that the patient needs attention. The therapist also gets an overview on the therapist administration page (so-called back-end). An example is provided in Figure 4.1.

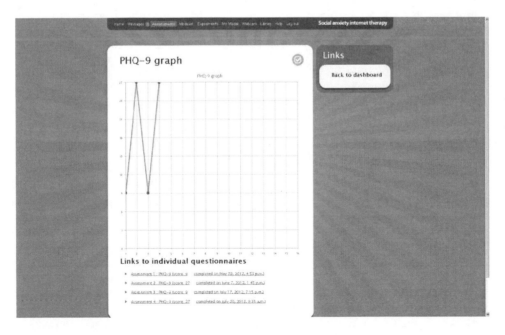

Figure 4.1 Example of a PHQ-9 graph (Patient Health Questionnaire 9).

Potential problems

There are of course some potential problems with online questionnaires. One important aspect relates to *security,* which is relevant for all clinical Internet applications (Bennett et al., 2010). There are several types of security that are important at the stage of collecting questionnaire data. Using Bennett et al.'s terminology (2010), the first is *methodological security,* which relates to the design of the application, the technology used, and how data are managed. Here we have questions regarding password protection and how a person registers to get into the system. Another issue in this category is how data are stored and managed.

The second type of security is *technical security,* which covers all the technical aspects of the application. This includes the software included in the application (which may involve external components). Validation of user input is another technical aspect. There are also computer-specific considerations such as protection from unauthorised access and firewalls.

The third type of security issue identified by Bennett et al. is *procedural security.* This has more to do with how the system is maintained and updated when new threats emerge or when deficits are identified.

A second potential problem when transferring questionnaires to the Internet is the fact that many validated measures are copyright protected and test publishers may not have routines for how to handle questions regarding online use. There are measures that are free to use and increasingly online use will become the standard. One partial solution we have used in research is to pay for online administration via an agreement with the test publisher. There may also be solutions where all of the data collection is handled by a separate body such as a company that is dedictated to this aspect. This may be sensitive since the clinician may not be in full control of the data collected.

A third problem has to do with the human factor. Clients may not be careful enough with sensitive data on their computer; they may fail to log out, so that other persons can see their responses to the questionnaire. This is not very different from paper-and-pencil questionnaires that are completed at home, except clients may not be aware of the unintended risk of showing others what they do on their computer.

Relating to the human factor is the risk that systems are too difficult for certain clients to handle and they may be put off by problems logging in or lost passwords. Clinicians can also make mistakes, and technology may fail not only from the server provider but also locally in cases when the client's Internet connection is not working.

How to transfer from paper and pencil

There are several points to consider when transferring paper-and-pencil questionnaires to the Internet. Since this book does not deal with the programming side of things (and most CBT clinicians are not programmers), the technical challenges are often best handled by information technology (IT) technicians who will know how the programming should be handled. For clinicians who work at hospitals there may be IT departments with staff who are used to handling queries regarding online questionnaires and may even have a system set up that the clinician can use with some training. University settings also have their own IT services and some private practitioners are linked with larger organisations who can assist when starting to use online measures. I recommend that this be the starting point when considering using the Internet in treatment, as many of the important questions regarding security, data management and secure communication between therapist and client are relevant already at this stage.

Further it is recommended that the online questionnaires be embedded within the treatment system. There are many commercial solutions for online questionnaires and I recommend that security and data management be given priority including where the data are stored. A challenge for current online questionnaire systems is that it should be possible to navigate through the web page using various platforms. An increasing number of persons use their smartphones and tablets as computers and the web page should be built so that the screen changes when the questionnaire is displayed on these platforms.

The online questionnaire should be easy to set up for the clinician, which is possible if there is a text editor attached to the program. Be careful to read the items several times and to test the system yourself, preferably also with the output if the questionnaire is scored by the system.

When starting to use online questionnaires it is important to know that while self-report measures have been found to work well when administered over the Internet, separate norms may be needed (Buchanan, 2002), and it is not recommended to change the format when evaluating treatment outcome. In other words if the client first completes measures online and then the post-treatment measures using paper-and-pencil format, the two formats may not be the same as it would be if both test occasions had been on either the Internet or paper and pencil.

A final word regarding implementation has to do with the prospect of obtaining daily measures in the client's own environment. Smartphone applications are being developed very rapidly, and ratings can be made with them, although it is not practical to complete long assessments on the phone unless the client wants to.

Research on online assessments

There have been several research studies conducted on the administration of questionnaires over the Internet. It is desirable that a questionnaire is transferred with maintained psychometric characteristics in relation to paper-and-pencil administration, including internal consistency, factor structure and correlation with other constructs. In addition the International Test Commission (2006) recommends presenting evidence that the two versions produce scores with comparable means and standard deviations, comparable reliabilities and a correlation at the expected level from the reliability estimates. This has been obtained for several questionnaires used in CBT. For example, we recently validated the use of the Beck Depression Inventory (BDI-II) (Beck et al., 1996). Holländare et al. (2010) recruited patients from primary care and psychiatric care and they completed the BDI-II and another depression instrument both on paper and on the Internet. The order was randomized to control for order effects (e.g., one way of filling out the measure influencing the next way the same questionnaire is filled out). Results showed that the psychometric properties of the two administration formats were mostly equivalent (both excellent). In line with some other studies we found significant interaction effects between format and order. We did not view this as a major problem as long as the administration format is unchanged when repeated measurements are made.

There are several other examples of relevance for CBT. In the field of anxiety disorders, online questionnaires have been validated for panic disorder (Carlbring et al., 2007), social anxiety disorder (Hirai et al., 2011), obsessive-compulsive disorder (OCD) (Coles et al., 2007) and generalized anxiety disorder (Zlomke, 2009), to give a few examples. Within behavioural medicine there are other examples, such as tinnitus (Andersson et al., 2003).

One crucial question has to do with what clients and clinicians prefer. This is a moving target as clients are increasingly familiar with the Internet and few are suspicious about online measures as long as they are perceived to be secure. In one study conducted with patients in regular practice it was found that patients reported high levels of satisfaction with Internet administration and that they actually preferred this method of monitoring outcome to paper administration at the office (Zimmerman & Martinez, 2012). Clinicians, though, may be unfamiliar with online questionnaires, but to the best of my knowledge this has not been investigated.

Box 4.1 Psychometric properties of online questionnaires

There are several separate publications on the psychometric properties of online questionnaires. As with questionnaires in general, items in a questionnaire should correlate with each other to the extent that a sufficient alpha coefficient is obtained. Usually, the so-called Cronbach's alpha coefficient should be at least 0.70, but preferably at least 0.90 in order for the measure to be said to tap one construct.

In research on online questionnaires it is common to report Cronbach's alpha coefficients. For example, Hedman et al. (2010) used a strategy in which they used data from two separate samples and basically compared with the psychometric properties.

One measure included was the Liebowitz Social Anxiety Scale self-assessment (Baker et al., 2002). Hedman et al. reported identical Cronbach's alpha for Internet and paper-and-pencil administration (a = 0.94). They also reported correlations between measures, but arguably the approach with two different samples does not directly answer the question if the two administration formats are exchangeable.

Hirai at al. (2011) did a similar study but with a nonclinical sample. In agreement with Hedman et al. excellent Cronbach's alpha coefficients were seen, and in addition factor structures for the two formats were similar. However they also investigated measurement invariance, which is achieved when parameters of the measurement model are equivalent across groups. Using this more sophisticated method the authors could not demonstrate measurement invariance between the two assessment modalities for any of the social anxiety measures. A more tedious way to evaluate Internet administration is to do a controlled study. Carlbring et al. (2007) conducted a randomized crossover trial with two test occasions close in time. They included 494 people who had registered for a trial on panic disorder and were randomly assigned to fill in the questionnaires either on the Internet or the paper-and-pencil versions, and then to fill in the same questionnaires again the next day using the other format. Results showed similar psychometric properties for the two administration formats. However, analyses of order effects led the researchers to conclude that the administration format should be stable across measurement points.

In many ways it could be argued that online measurements have not taken enough advantage of the computer media. For example, while it is common to use online questionnaires in research and in clinical practice it is much less common to include pictures and movies in the assessment procedures. A fairly common use however is to use online questionnaires that use screening items and then skip extra questions if a negative response has been given. This has of course been possible with paper-and-pencil questionnaires but is much more user-friendly with online questionnaires.

Diagnostic procedures

While it is clear that online administration of self-report questionnaires yields equivalent (or better) measurement characteristics as when administrated via paper and pencil, it is not as clear that complete diagnostic interview procedures can be delivered via the Internet. The main obstacle is the fact that procedures which rely on self-report do not correspond sufficiently well with the results of an interview with a trained clinician (Eaton et al., 2000). For example, in a study from my research group, we investigated the validity of the Composite International Diagnostic Interview – short form, which is a structured diagnostic instrument (Kessler et al.,1998). We administered the instrument (called CIDI short form) via the Internet to a group of persons who had sought help for panic disorder, and then interviewed all persons in a live psychiatric interview (the gold standard: Structured clinical interview for *DSM-IV* Axis I Disorders [SCID-I]) (First et al., 1997). Agreement between the two approaches was not satisfactory (Carlbring et al., 2002). After these disappointing results we decided to complement self-reported diagnostics with a live telephone interview to add reliability to the diagnostic procedures in our trials. Experiences from another research group were more positive, as Farvolden et al. (2003) found agreement between a web-administrated screening test and subsequent diagnostic interviews, with the exception of generalized anxiety disorder for which agreement was not as good.

Although it is insufficient to use only self-report (similar to questionnaires) to obtain medical diagnoses, it is possible to use web cameras given that the security issues are handled. I am not aware of much research in this area but know that clinicians sometimes use web cameras with, for example, Skype when interviewing patients from a distance (Armfield et al., 2012). Of course there are medico-legal issues involved and for some clinics it is necessary to see the patient at least once in real life. When this is not needed or required, self-reported data can as mentioned be supplemented with telephone interviews which often gives sufficient information regarding diagnostic categories. There is also research to support this (Crippa et al., 2008). When doing treatment on somatic conditions it can be useful to require that the patient has an established contact with general practice. Indeed, general practice may even be responsible for the referral. For the private practitioner considering using the Internet for assessment and treatment it is important to consider the medico-legal aspects as they may differ between countries and professions.

Experimental measures

In this chapter I focus on self-report which basically just means a transfer of paper-and-pencil tests to computer administration. There are however other categories of tests that are often used in CBT research and more recently in treatment. A large body of literature describes different forms of information processing tests that are often computer based, such as the emotional Stroop colour naming task and the dot probe task (see Harvey et al., 2004, for a description), and research has been done on how these tests can be administered over the Internet (e.g., Johansson et al., 2008). The main limitation has to do with timing and collecting exact response times from computers that are outside of the laboratory (e.g., the more technical side of measurement), but there are also some procedural problems with administering tests outside of the laboratory. A recent development is attention modification training (using a modified version of the dot probe task), which has been found to work in some studies (e.g., Amir et al., 2009). However, when we delivered the same treatment via

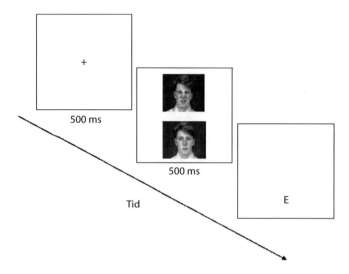

Figure 4.2 Example of bias modification training.

the Internet it did not seem to work as well (Carlbring et al., 2012). An example of a screenshot is given in Figure 4.2.

How can online assessments be integrated with clinical services?

The main theme of this book is to use the Internet in CBT, and within CBT assessment is a crucial part. Increasingly, assessment and documentation in medicine are computerized, meaning that many clinicians, even within CBT, work with computers and the Internet on a daily basis. Medical notes are increasingly computerized and there is a move towards allowing patients to have access to their own medical records from home. With this rapid development, it is very likely that online assessments will be integrated within regular services. For some this may even be a first step towards integrating modern information technology in their services. There are many advantages with using online questionnaires once security issues have been handled, and online questionnaire assessments will gradually replace paper-and-pencil assessments, although there will be persons for whom this may not be possible. There are many ways to start using online questionnaire assessments and different ways to handle issues regarding security, ownership of data, and if a system can be bought or built from scratch. In most online treatment portals assessment is integrated, but there are also cases where the assessment and treatment are managed from different places.

Practical implications and key points

- It is now known that established self-report questionnaires can be administered over the Internet with maintained measurement characteristics. However, clinicians are advised to stick with one format when evaluating treatment outcomes.

- As with all clinical activities over the Internet, security is important when collecting information over the Internet.

- While screening procedures can be implemented on the Internet it is not yet possible to diagnose medical/psychiatric conditions properly without at least talking to the patient over the phone.

- There are some experimental tests of information processing that have been possible to transfer to the Internet. However, many of the advantages of the Internet have not been fully endorsed in assessment procedures.

- A first step to integrate Internet in treatment services is to start with online assessment that can supplement or replace paper-and-pencil assessments and also be administered in the client's own environment.

References

Amir N, Beard C, Taylor CT, Klumpp H, Elias J, Burns M, Chen X. (2009). Attention training in individuals with generalized social phobia: A randomized controlled trial. *Journal of Consulting and Clinical Psychology, 77*, 961–973.

Andersson G, Kaldo-Sandström V, Ström L, Strömgren T. (2003). Internet administration of the Hospital Anxiety and Depression Scale (HADS) in a sample of tinnitus patients. *Journal of Psychosomatic Research, 55*, 259–262.

Armfield NR, Gray LC, Smith AC. (2012). Clinical use of Skype: A review of the evidence base. *Journal of Telemedicine and Telecare, 18*, 125–127.

Baker SL, Heinrichs N, Kim HJ, Hofmann SG. (2002). The Liebowitz Social Anxiety Scale as a self-report instrument: A preliminary psychometric analysis. *Behaviour Research and Therapy, 40*, 701–715.

Beck AT, Steer RA, Brown GK. (1996). *Manual for the Beck Depression Inventory-II*. San Antonio, TX: Psychological Corporation.

Bennett K, Bennett AJ, Griffiths KM. (2010). Security considerations for e-mental health interventions. *Journal of Medical Internet Research, 12*(5), e61.

Boschen MJ, Casey LM. (2008). The use of mobile telephones as adjuncts to cognitive behavioral psychotherapy. *Professional Psychology: Research and Practice, 39*, 546–552.

Buchanan T. (2002). Online assessment: desirable or dangerous? *Professional Psychology: Research and Practice, 33*, 148–154.

Carlbring P, Apelstrand M, Sehlin H, Amir N, Rousseau A, Hofmann S, Andersson G. (2012). Internet-delivered attention training in individuals with social anxiety disorder: A double blind randomized controlled trial. *BMC Psychiatry, 12*, 66.

Carlbring P, Brunt S, Bohman S, Austin D, Richards JC, Öst L-G, Andersson G. (2007). Internet vs. paper and pencil administration of questionnaires commonly used in panic/agoraphobia research. *Computers in Human Behavior, 23*, 1421–1434.

Carlbring P, Forslin P, Ljungstrand P, Willebrand M, Strandlund C, Ekselius L, Andersson G. (2002). Is the Internet administered CIDI-SF equivalent to a human SCID-interview? *Cognitive Behaviour Therapy, 31*, 183–189.

Coles ME, Cook LM, Blake TR. (2007). Assessing obsessive compulsive symptoms and cognitions on the Internet: Evidence for the comparability of paper and Internet administration. *Behaviour Research and Therapy, 45*, 2232–2240.

Crippa JA, de Lima Osorio F, Del-Ben CM, Filho AS, da Silva Freitas MC, Loureiro SR. (2008). Comparability between telephone and face-to-face structured clinical interview for DSM-IV in assessing social anxiety disorder. *Perspectives in Psychiatric Care, 44*, 241–247.

Eaton WW, Neufeld K, Chen, L-S, Cai G. (2000). A comparison of self-report and clinical diagnostic interviews for depression. Diagnostic interview schedule and schedules for clinical assessment in neuropsychiatry in the Baltimore epidemiologic catchment area follow-up. *Archives of General Psychiatry, 57*, 217–222.

Farvolden P, McBride C, Bagby RM, Ravitz P. (2003). A Web-based screening instrument for depression and anxiety disorders in primary care. *Journal of Medical Internet Research, 5*, e23.

First MB, Gibbon M, Spitzer RL, Williams JBW. (1997). *Structured clinical interview for DSM-IV Axis I Disorders (SCID-I)*. Washington, DC: American Psychiatric Press.

Harvey AG, Watkins E, Mansell W, Shafran R. (2004). *Cognitive behavioural processes across psychological disorders. A transdiagnostic approach to research and treatment.* Oxford: Oxford University Press.

Hedman E, Ljótsson B, Rück C, Furmark T, Carlbring P, Lindefors N, Andersson G. (2010). Internet administration of self-report measures commonly used in research on social anxiety disorder: A psychometric evaluation. *Computers in Human Behavior, 26*, 736–740.

Hirai M, Vernon LL, Clum GA, Skidmore ST. (2011). Psychometric properties and administration measurement invariance of social phobia symptom measures: paper-pencil vs. Internet administrations. *Journal of Psychopathology and Behavioral Assessment, 33*, 470–479.

Holländare F, Andersson G, Engström I. (2010). A comparison of psychometric properties between Internet and paper versions of two depression instruments (BDI-II and MADRS-S) administered to clinic patients. *Journal of Medical Internet Research, 12*(5), e49.

International Test Commission. (2006). International guidelines on computer-based and Internet-delivered testing. *International Journal of Testing, 6*(2), 143–171.

Johansson L, Carlbring P, Ghaderi A, Andersson G. (2008). Emotional Stroop via Internet among individuals with eating disorders. *Scandinavian Journal of Psychology, 49*, 69–76.

Kessler RC, Andrews G, Mroczek D, Ustun B, Wittchen H-U. (1998). The World Health Organization composite international diagnostic interview short-form (CIDI). *International Journal of Methods in Psychiatric Research, 7*, 171–185.

Zimmerman M, Martinez JH. (2012). Web-based assessment of depression in patients treated in clinical practice: Reliability, validity, and patient acceptance. *Journal of Clinical Psychiatry, 73*, 333–338.

Zlomke KR. (2009). Psychometric properties of Internet administration of Penn State Worry Questionnaire (PSWQ) and Depression, Anxiety, and Stress Scale (DASS). *Computers in Human Behavior, 25*, 841–843.

📖 Further reading

Birnbaum MH, editor. (2000). *Psychological experiments on the Internet*. San Diego: Academic Press.

Emmelkamp PM. (2005). Technological innovations in clinical assessment and psychotherapy. *Psychotherapy and Psychosomatics, 74*, 336–343.

Chapter 5

Open access and unguided treatment programs

What you will learn

In this chapter you will learn about:

- What characterizes open access and unguided programs.
- How open access programs are intended to work.
- The effects of unguided open access programs.
- How open access programs can be used as an adjunct to face-to-face CBT.
- Ways to improve adherence and effects of unguided open access programs.

Background

George suffered from anxiety and low mood for many years, but had made a decision that he would not go see a psychologist (or shrink). He had however been on medication provided by his GP, and the last time he saw his GP for renewal of his sleep medication he was a bit surprised when she mentioned that there are good programs on the web which provide psychological treatment for free. She had just mentioned it in passing and did not directly recommend that George should start using such a program, but it made him curious and when he went home he did a search and found MoodGYM from Australia. He thought he had nothing to lose so he registered and had a look at the program. He was glad that he did not have to talk to someone and still felt that it was a reliable source as he noted that the program was not intended for severe cases (and he did not think his problems were that great).

What is an open access treatment program?

Programs that deliver CBT over the Internet can either be closed or open, with or without registration. The closed category often involves careful assessment procedures and visits to the clinic for face-to-face assessment. These treatments also tend to be guided by a clinician and are often hosted by universities or clinics. That form is covered in the upcoming chapters. In this chapter we focus on CBT programs that are open for the public, often free of charge and always unguided. In terms of content the open access CBT programs can be similar to closed programs, but there are some differences depending on if guidance is given. In order for a program to be fully open and unguided it should not be possible to handle user information that calls for urgent management. For example, it is not feasible to collect information about suicidal ideation since that information cannot be handled in a different manner than providing automated advice on where to seek help. Therefore open access programs are often aimed at clients with less severe or urgent problems and are largely designed to prevent ill health rather than to treat clinical populations. Open access programs may be used as adjuncts to face-to-face therapies (and guided by a therapist or layperson), but that is not how they are designed. In many ways the open access CBT programs are what many people would expect from the Internet. Easily accessible, low cost and without any requirements from the user or the provider. They are however intended to work in the same manner as standard CBT. Open access programs often include the main treatment components of CBT. An example of what can be included in an unguided program is presented in Figure 5.1.

There are several advantages with unguided open access. First, they can lead to many more people getting access to CBT and if found to be effective they have the potential to save costs for society. They can also be less stigmatizing as there is no need for contact between the user and a clinician. Getting in touch with an open access program may be the first step in a stepped care process, and for some it can lead to seeking more evidence-based help (Christensen et al., 2006b). Moreover, open access Internet treatment programs have the advantage of being possible to present anonymously (Christensen, 2010), which is not possible in closed programs delivered in health care settings. Many functions in open access programs are automated and the user may find the program engaging. For some individuals an open access CBT program can be very effective and there may be no need for further treatment after completing the program.

There are however also some well-known disadvantages with the open access programs. The most well known is the large dropout rate from unguided open access programs (Eysenbach, 2005). Many people who register as users do not complete the treatment or do not even start. A second potential disadvantage relates to the lower effects seen in research

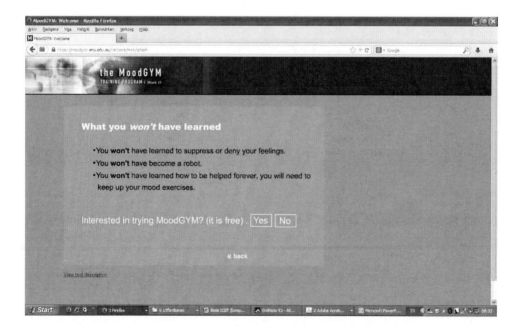

Figure 5.1 Screenshot from the MoodGym program (**http://moodgym.anu.edu.au/welcome/new/splash**).

on unguided programs versus guided programs, although there are a few exceptions. A third disadvantage has to do with client safety and the need to advise persons with severe problems not to use the program. In addition, not collecting information about potentially problematic conditions such as severe mental health problems can occur. Finally, a user may decide not to pay attention to the disclaimers and hence persons with severe problems may access the treatment in spite of the disclaimers discouraging this. In terms of content there is an understandable tendency for unguided open access programs to focus on lighter mental health problems, and hence they rarely contain full treatment packages from face-to-face treatment protocols.

In sum there are both pros and cons with open access CBT programs not monitored by clinicians. They cost much less and can reach a very large audience. They may however also be discouraging for some users who leave the program with a negative experience. Researchers within the field of Internet treatments are not in agreement with regard to the value of open access programs. The evidence against open access programs is not strong; for example that they could make clients less motivated for face-to-face CBT. It could also be argued that although dropout rates from open access programs are huge and adherence often poor, there are some clients who benefit. As the extra cost for providing one extra person with an open access program is minimal nothing is lost, and in terms of reaching underserved regions there may not be much of an alternative. The situation is not very different from the self-help book market, where it is probably the case that many buyers of self-help books never end up reading them, or only read a portion.

There is a jungle of open access programs based on CBT, and one way to get a good idea of the available programs in English is to visit the Beacon web site (**http://www.beacon .anu.edu.au/**) (Figure 5.2), which aims to list and rate quality health web sites, collect user characteristics and publish user feedback (Christensen et al., 2010). Beacon does not cover all Internet treatments and mainly lists sites that have been tested in research

Figure 5.2 The Beacon website (**http://www.beacon.anu.edu.au/**).

(mostly English), but it is a useful resource for clinicians and researchers who are interested in online CBT.

Research on the effects of open access treatment programs

Systematic reviews

Several systematic reviews and meta-analyses on Internet-delivered treatments exist, but none which focus only on open access and self-guided programs across different conditions. Cuijpers et al. (2011) conducted meta-analyses of self-guided treatments for depression where there had been no contact with a clinician. I was also involved in that study. We were only able to include seven controlled trials in the review with a total of 1,362 respondents. The majority (6/7) of the studies were on Internet-delivered treatment. The overall mean effect size showed a significant but small (effect size $d = 0.28$ which is a small effect size) difference between self-guided psychological treatment and control groups at post-test. Other reviewers have found similar small effects of unguided programs for depression when compared to guided treatments (Andersson & Cuijpers, 2009; Richards & Richardson, 2012). Overall, effects are substantially smaller when Internet treatments for depression are unguided, and this has been known for a while (Spek et al., 2007). Less is known regarding unguided open access programs for anxiety.

Anxiety programs

There are several programs described on the Beacon web site for anxiety disorders that are open and free to use with or without registration, most of which have not yet been tested in research. An example is the e-couch web site (**http://www.ecouch.anu.edu.au/**) from the group behind MoodGYM.

Farvolden and co-workers (2005) developed and tested an open access program for panic disorder and found that a very high proportion dropped out with only 12 (1.03%) out of 1,161 of registered users completing the 12-week program. However, gains were seen for participants who used the program to some extent. For example, for 152 users who completed at least three sessions there was a reduction in the number of panic attacks, but in spite of the potential benefit from the psychoeducation the very low adherence remains a crucial problem.

More recently, Klein and co-workers (2011) published a large trial in which they investigated the effects of five fully automated self-help programs for five anxiety disorders (generalized anxiety disorder [GAD], panic disorder, obsessive-compulsive disorder [OCD] and posttraumatic stress disorder [PTSD]). As with many open access Internet treatments the adherence to the programs dropped dramatically from 7,245 completing the pre-treatment assessment to 2,235 completing 12 weeks of treatment (with an additional 350 still being in progress). However of these 2,235 only 225 completed the post-treatment assessment (1,913 completed treatment but not the assessment). The authors focused their report on the 225 who completed the study and for these completers the results were promising with fairly large within-group effects. This study suggests that while automated open access programs lead to substantial loss of interest for many people, the ones who actually stay and complete the treatment are likely to benefit from it.

Although there are a few studies on the treatment of anxiety with unguided Internet treatments, far more work has been done on the guided CBT interventions presented in the next chapter, many of which have been found to work as well as regular face-to-face CBT.

Depression and low mood

MoodGYM

Returning to research on open access programs for symptoms of depression, the most widely disseminated open access program in the world is probably MoodGYM, which has been tested in many studies including trials with some form of clinician contact and support (Christensen et al., 2004). A screenshot is shown in Figure 5.3. A remarkable number of persons have registered and used MoodGym from all across the world (Christensen, 2010), with more than 400,000 registered users (in 2012). Again as expected a large majority do not complete the program when it is unguided but for the ones who do, it appears to be effective even though no guidance is given.

Batterham et al. (2008) reported data from around 82,000 users who had accessed MoodGYM in 2006. Only 27% completed one module and 10% completed two or more modules. The interesting thing with that study was that they investigated what factors predicted adherence and found that better adherence was predicted by higher depression severity, higher anxiety severity, a greater level of dysfunctional thinking, younger age, higher education, being female and being referred to the site by a mental health professional. In other words it appears as if persons with more problems who are educated (and more likely women) seem to be more suitable for unguided depression treatment.

Detailed process research by Christensen and co-workers (2006a) found that a single treatment module was not enough, but when more modules were added depression scores decrease, although dropout rate can increase in unguided programs. In their research trial they compared six different versions of MoodGYM in a fully automated randomized controlled trial. In addition to the finding that one module was not enough, they found large dropout rates with only 20% completing the assigned intervention.

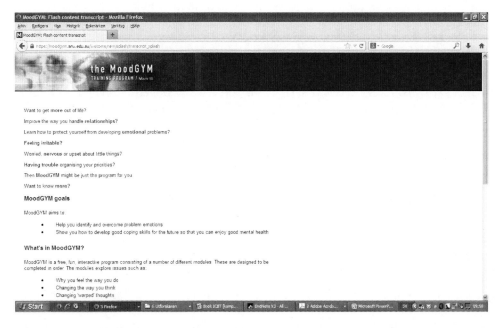

Figure 5.3 MoodGYM ingredients (**http://www.moodgym.anu.edu.au/welcome/new/splash/transcript_ splash**).

ODIN

A program from the United States called ODIN (Overcoming Depression on the Internet) is another early depression program that has been tested in research. To date, three randomized controlled trials have been published using ODIN (Clarke et al., 2002, 2005, 2009).

The ODIN program (**http://www.feelbetter.org**) consists of seven modules that are mainly cognitive in orientation, and hence this depression treatment does not include behavioural activation. Overall, effect sizes in the studies have been small when compared to treatment as usual (even lack of effects in their first trial), but in the second study reminders were used either via mail or phone and then treatment effects were found (albeit small).

The third trial included a total of 160 young adults aged 18 to 24 years. In this controlled study, in which the treatment was compared to "treatment as usual", the researchers again used reminder postcards that were mailed periodically to encourage use of the intervention. However there was no additional therapist contact. A small but still statistically significant between group effect was found in favour of the treatment. Effects were however stronger for women.

Deprexis

Deprexis is a depression treatment that has been developed in Germany and is available in English and Swedish translations (**http://www.deprexis.com/**). I have been involved in some of the studies on Deprexis. While most of the modules are typical of CBT for depression, there are also modules that reflect other approaches to CBT such as mindfulness.

The program has 10 modules that can be completed in around 10 to 60 minutes, depending on the user. The modules are presented as simulated dialogues during which concepts and techniques are explained and illustrated. The user is to be engaged in the exercises, and responses are solicited regularly during the program.

Deprexis is adaptive and includes tailoring of content according to responses made. All modules are accompanied by illustrations such as drawings, photographs and flash animations. The modules included are (1) Behavioural Activation, (2) Cognitive Modification, (3) Mindfulness and Acceptance, (4) Interpersonal Skills, (5) Relaxation, Physical Exercise and Lifestyle Modification, (6) Problem Solving, (7) Childhood Experiences and Early Schemas, (8) Positive Psychology Interventions, (9) Dreamwork and Emotion-Focused Interventions and (10) Psychoeducation. In addition to the content modules, there is one introductory and one summary module. The inclusion of a module on dreamwork and emotion-focused therapy is not straightforward CBT but fits in well with the rest of the program and is attractive for some users (Moritz et al., 2012).

To date three controlled trials have been published on this program, all on the German version. The first was a study with 396 individuals with symptoms of depression (Meyer et al., 2009). This fairly large trial showed a larger than usual effect (for being an unguided program), but there was a large dropout rate.

A second trial investigated whether guided versus unguided use of Deprexis would differ when compared with a waiting list control group (Berger et al., 2011). In this trial with 66 individuals diagnosed with depression there were minor differences in favour of the guided version (not statistically significant) and both treatments were better than the waiting-list group. However, when a treatment was unguided there were diagnostic telephone interviews with all participants and hence the Deprexis program was not fully unguided without any human contact. The dropout rate was small with 88% completing post-treatment assessment in the unguided group, suggesting that doing an interview may prevent some dropout. Although it can be argued that this was not a fully unguided treatment it may still be representative for how a clinician or general practitioner may prescribe Internet treatment following a clinical interview.

The most recent trial on Deprexis included 110 participants who were not diagnosed during the trial but could have been so previously (Moritz et al., 2012), in which case they were asked to provide the name of their previous psychiatric contact (therapist). However, this was not a requirement for participating in the trial. There were two groups in the trial to which participants were randomly allocated (immediate treatment versus waiting list). When the treatment period had ended 82% had completed the treatment, which is a very high figure for an unguided program. There was however some nontherapeutic contact in the middle of the treatment period via email. Results showed that the Deprexis group had improved more than the waiting list control group. However, the between-group differences were rather small and one reason could be that the control group improved as well. This is not an uncommon finding in depression trials. For a screenshot of Deprexis see Figure 5.4.

Figure 5.4 Example of the Deprexis program (Meyer et al., 2009).

Living Life to the Full

In the United Kingdom the Living Life to the Full program has been developed by Chris Williams (**http://www.llttf.com/**) and is available at no cost. This is a very attractive program, based on the five areas approach (Williams & Chellingsworth, 2010), which targets milder psychological problems (anxiety and depression). It is presented in user-friendly language, but not much is known about the effects as an Internet-delivered treatment, although a large-scale trial is now in progress.

Health-related problems

Unguided Internet treatments for health conditions are also available (see **http://www. beacon.anu.edu.au/** for a list). One example is the open access program for smoking cessation developed by Ricardo Muñoz and co-workers (Leykin et al., 2012). Since smoking is such a huge public health problem Muñoz and his group argue that the program can help a large number of people stop smoking even though the dropout rates are huge, stating "Internet-based smoking cessation interventions can help large numbers of smokers quit. Large-scale international outcome studies can be successfully implemented using automated Internet sites" (Leykin et al., 2012, p. 1).

This program is available in Spanish as well as in English. The number of people that can access the site is amazing. In a descriptive study of usage the authors report that in the first year of recruitment, 94,158 individuals from 152 countries visited the site (Muñoz et al., 2012). An interesting aspect of that study was that users could personalize the site by choosing from among nine site elements (a Prequit Checklist, Stop Smoking Guide, Nicotine Replacement Therapy Guide, Taking Control of Your Life, individually timed email messages, Mood Management Intervention, Virtual Group, a Journal, and a Cigarette Counter).

While most people who access the site never return to it or provide informed consent, quit rates for the ones who completed the intervention were good. For example at 12-months follow-up 449 out of 1,096 (45.4%) reported that they had stopped smoking, and given that this is an unguided, open access program this should be regarded as a major achievement. (For a screenshot see Figure 5.5.)

Figure 5.5 The San Francisco Stop Smoking Site (**https://www.stopsmoking.ucsf.edu/es/intro/munoz. aspx**).

Another program focuses on problem drinking (there are several programs available but most are not based on CBT). The program, Minderdrinken (**http://www.minderdrinken.nl**), is available in the Netherlands, and has been tested in research (Riper et al., 2008) and found to be effective (although there was a substantial dropout rate of around 40%).

There is also a program for insomnia called *Sleep Healthy Using the Internet* (SHUT-i; **http://www.shuti.net**), that has been tested in a small trial with very promising results (Ritterband et al., 2009). This program provides text, pictorial, animation and audio formats. The feedback is automated and tailored. Given the high prevalence of insomnia, programs like SHUT-i could be an important adjunct to management of sleep problems in society. Other programs for insomnia are available (see Chapter 9), but this one is the unguided program with the most support.

A full list of all open access programs based on CBT is not possible to provide, but a majority have not been tested in research. Increasingly, however, more knowledge is gained regarding their effects and availability is increasing as programs are being translated into different languages. For example, MoodGYM has been translated into Chinese. More research is needed to confirm that treatments are effective in different countries. It is also important to document many different aspects when evaluating new programs. One example is given in Box 5.1.

Box 5.1 Example of research on one open access program

An example of a carefully evaluated unguided open access program for depressive symptoms is the study done by Esther de Graaf, Syliva Gerhards and their co-workers in the Netherlands. They used a depression-specific program called *Colour Your Life* (**http://www.kleurjeleven.nl**)* that was developed by the Trimbos Institute in the Netherlands.

The program consists of eight weekly 30-minute online sessions and an additional booster session. Homework is recommended after each session and the whole program is based on CBT principles, specifically a Dutch version of the coping with depression treatment developed by Lewinsohn and co-workers (Lewinsohn et al., 1986).

Colour Your Life is interactive and multimedia based. In common with many current psychosocial intervention studies, the researchers first published their research protocol where they outlined what they planned to do (de Graaf et al., 2008). In the later controlled trial the investigators randomly allocated 303 persons with depression to either the *Colour Your Life* program, treatment as usual, or a combination of treatment as usual and *Colour Your Life*. Surprisingly there were no differences between the three groups after the treatment or at six months follow-up (de Graaf et al., 2009a). Few adhered to the treatment, with 36% completers in the treatment group and 13% in the combined group. Even for those who did complete the treatment there were no group differences. On the other hand there were reductions in depressive symptoms in all three groups which was confirmed in a later one-year follow-up (de Graaf et al., 2011), but again no between-group differences. However, interestingly, cost-effectiveness analyses of the same trial showed that costs were lower in the *Colour Your Life* group (Gerhards et al., 2010) compared to the other two groups.

The researchers published additional reports of the study outcomes, for example a prediction study which showed that something called "extreme positive responding" on a measure of dysfunctional attitudes was associated with better outcomes in the *Colour*

*Please note that a site called **http://www.come-alive.co.uk/colour-your-life-course.htm**) is available in English but has nothing to do with the depression treatment from the Netherlands.

Your Life group (de Graaf et al., 2010). This measure can be viewed as measuring optimism. In another report they found that homework completion and treatment expectancy were associated with better outcomes (de Graaf et al., 2009b), but perhaps even more interesting is a qualitative study of a subsample of 18 patients who had completed the Internet treatment (or the combined treatment) (Gerhards et al., 2011). In this study it was clear that the lack of support could be perceived as negative. For example, one of the quotes in the paper read "That thing doesn't talk back, (...) I haven't got any contact with it. Whereas when I talk to you, then you react, and then you straightaway reach a much deeper level than with the computer" (Gerhards et al., 2011, p. 122).

Following these rather negative results (with the exception of the health economic benefits) the researchers behind the trial concluded that: "Adding therapist support to online self-help interventions might improve adherence." (de Graaf et al., 2009b, p. 230). In spite of the lack of additional benefits of the *Colour Your Life* program in this study conducted in primary care settings in the Netherlands, it may be that the treatment as usual is responsible for the lack of differences. The within-group effects were substantial and depressive symptoms have a tendency to drop over time for many patients. However, poor adherence remains a problem in common with many unguided Internet treatments.

How and when should I recommend open access treatments?

In this chapter I have briefly provided examples of unguided open access programs. Given the evidence to date I would be hesitant to recommend unguided treatments to patients with more than mild symptoms if no other treatment or assessment is provided. The risk of not completing the treatment is too great and the wrong treatment may be given to the patient. However, if some form of diagnostic information is incorporated and if adherence to the treatment can be fostered, for some patients an unguided open access program might be the first step in becoming familiar with the concepts of CBT. I doubt that non-completion can be very harmful and a similar argument can be raised against self-help CBT books that are probably often left unread on bookshelves after perhaps reading the first chapter. It is also clear that there are subgroups of patients who benefit much from unguided programs (Titov et al., 2008), and it is possible that new ways to mimic the support function of a live therapist can be developed. As a clinician I can also see another important role for the unguided open access treatments if they are provided with some form of guidance or presented in parallel to other interventions. In this light, I recommend the following:

1) Find out whether your patient is familiar with the Internet.

2) Assess suitability in relation to severity/characteristics of the problems and also in relation to patient characteristics. For example a quit smoking web site might be useful to recommend to anyone, whereas for a much distressed depressed person it may not be suitable to recommend self-guided treatment.

3) Only recommend programs on the Internet that are evidence based or at the very least based on treatment protocols that have been tested in research.

4) If you recommend an open access program be sure to check with the patient in a follow-up session (or telephone call) to see how the program was perceived.

5) Consider supporting the patient more directly by incorporating the psychoeducation and the exercises from the program in your own treatment with the patient.

6) Do not hesitate to use empirically supported Internet treatments as adjuncts to your own treatment (e.g., a program for insomnia when your main treatment is focused on anxiety), but you need to be familiar with the open access treatment and make an effort not to confuse the patient with conflicting messages from you and the Internet treatment program.

Practical implications and key points

- CBT programs have been developed for online use without any professional guidance. Some programs are free of charge and most are offered without any guidance. Programs may include automated elements to increase adherence.

- Internet open access programs are intended to work as regular CBT treatments but are often presented as complements to face-to-face care.

- Effects of unguided CBT Internet treatments tend to be smaller than if some kind of support is given and dropout rates are usually substantial. However, open access programs can reach less well-served regions.

- Clinicians should consider using unguided Internet treatments as a complement to their own services and also to guide the treatments themselves to prevent dropouts.

References

Andersson G, Cuijpers P. (2009). Internet-based and other computerized psychological treatments for adult depression: A meta-analysis. *Cognitive Behaviour Therapy, 38*, 196–205.

Batterham PJ, Neil AL, Bennett K, Griffiths KM, Christensen H. (2008). Predictors of adherence among community users of a cognitive behavior therapy website. *Patient Preference and Adherence, 2*, 97–105.

Berger T, Hämmerli K, Gubser N, Andersson G, Caspar F. (2011). Internet-based treatment of depression: A randomized controlled trial comparing guided with unguided self-help. *Cognitive Behaviour Therapy, 40*, 251–266.

Christensen H. (2010). Increasing access and effectiveness: Using the Internet to deliver low intensity CBT. In J Bennett-Levy, H Christensen, P Farrand, K Griffiths, D Kavanagh, B Klein, M Lau, J Proudfoot, D Richards, J White, C Williams, editors. *Oxford guide to low intensity CBT interventions* (pp. 53–67). Oxford: Oxford University Press.

Christensen H, Griffiths KM, Jorm A. (2004). Delivering interventions for depression by using the Internet: Randomised controlled trial. *British Medical Journal, 328*, 265–268.

Christensen H, Griffiths KM, Mackinnon AJ, Brittliffe K. (2006a). Online randomized trial of brief and full cognitive behaviour therapy for depression. *Psychological Medicine, 36*, 1737–1746.

Christensen H, Leach LS, Barney L., Mackinnon AJ, Griffiths KM. (2006b). The effect of web based depression interventions on self-reported help seeking: Randomised controlled trial. *BMC Psychiatry, 6*, 13.

Christensen H, Murray K, Calear AL, Bennett K, Bennett A, Griffiths KM. (2010). Beacon: A web portal to high-quality mental health websites for use by health professionals and the public. *Medical Journal of Australia, 192*(11 Suppl), S40–S44.

Clarke G, Eubanks D, Reid E, Kelleher C, O'Connor E, DeBar LL, Lynch F, Nunley S, Gullion C. (2005). Overcoming depression on the Internet (ODIN) (2): A randomized trial of a self-help depression skills invervention program with reminders. *Journal of Medical Internet Research, 7*, e16.

Clarke G, Kelleher C, Hornbrook M, DeBar L, Dickerson J, Gullion C. (2009). Randomized effectiveness trial of an Internet, pure self-help, cognitive behavioral intervention for depressive symptoms in young adults. *Cognitive Behaviour Therapy, 38*, 222–234.

Clarke G, Reid E, Eubanks D, O'Connor E, DeBar LL, Kelleher C, Lynch F, Nunley S. (2002). Overcoming depression on the Internet (ODIN): A randomized controlled trial of an Internet depression skills invervention program. *Journal of Medical Internet Research, 4*, e14.

Cuijpers P, Donker T, Johansson R, Mohr DC, van Straten A, Andersson G. (2011). Self-guided psychological treatment for depressive symptoms: A meta-analysis. *PLoS ONE, 6*(6), e21274.

de Graaf LE, Gerhards SA, Arntz A, Riper H, Metsemakers JF, Evers SM, Severens JL, Widdershoven G, Huibers MJ. (2009a). Clinical effectiveness of online computerised cognitive-behavioural therapy without support for depression in primary care: Randomised trial. *British Journal of Psychiatry, 195*, 73–80.

de Graaf LE, Gerhards SA, Arntz A, Riper H, Metsemakers JF, Evers SM, Severens JL, Widdershoven G, Huibers MJ. (2011). One-year follow-up results of unsupported online computerized cognitive behavioural therapy for depression in primary care: A randomized trial. *Journal of Behavior Therapy and Experimental Psychiatry, 42*, 89–95.

de Graaf LE, Gerhards SA, Evers SM, Arntz A, Riper H, Severens JL, Widdershoven G, Metsemakers JF, Huibers MJ. (2008). Clinical and cost-effectiveness of computerised cognitive behavioural therapy for depression in primary care: Design of a randomised trial. *BMC Public Health, 8*, 224.

de Graaf LE, Hollon SD, Huibers MJ. (2010). Predicting outcome in computerized cognitive behavioral therapy for depression in primary care: A randomized trial. *Journal of Consulting and Clinical Psychology, 78*, 184–189.

de Graaf LE, Huibers MJ, Riper H, Gerhards SA, Arntz A. (2009b). Use and acceptability of unsupported online computerized cognitive behavioral therapy for depression and associations with clinical outcome. *Journal of Affective Disorders, 116*, 227–231.

Eysenbach G. (2005). The law of attrition. *Journal of Medical Internet Research, 7*(1), e11.

Farvolden P, Denisoff E, Selby P, Bagby RM, Rud, L. (2005). Usage and longitudinal effectiveness of a Web-based self-help cognitive behavioral therapy program for panic disorder. *Journal of Medical Internet Research, 7*(1), e7.

Gerhards SA, de Graaf LE, Jacobs LE, Severens JL, Huibers, MJ, Arntz A, Riper H, Widdershoven G, Metsemakers JF, Evers SM. (2010). Economic evaluation of online computerised cognitive-behavioural therapy without support for depression in primary care: Randomised trial. *British Journal of Psychiatry, 196*, 310–318.

Gerhards SA, Abma TA, Arntz A, de Graaf LE, Evers SM, Huibers MJ, Widdershoven GA. (2011). Improving adherence and effectiveness of computerised cognitive behavioural therapy without support for depression: A qualitative study on patient experiences. *Journal of Affective Disorders, 129*, 117–125.

Klein B, Meyer D, Austin DW, Kyrios M. (2011). Anxiety online: A virtual clinic: preliminary outcomes following completion of five fully automated treatment programs for anxiety disorders and symptoms. *Journal of Medical Internet Research, 13*, e89.

Lewinsohn PM, Munoz RF, Youngren MA, Zeiss MA. (1986). *Control your depression*. New York: Prentice Hall.

Leykin Y, Aguilera A, Torres LD, Perez-Stable EJ, Munoz RF. (2012). Interpreting the outcomes of automated Internet-based randomized trials: Example of an international smoking cessation study. *Journal of Medical Internet Research, 14*(1), e5.

Meyer B, Berger T, Caspar F, Beevers CG, Andersson G, Weiss M. (2009). Effectiveness of a novel integrative online treatment for depression (Deprexis): Randomized controlled trial. *Journal of Medical Internet Research, 11*(2), e15.

Moritz S, Schilling L, Hauschildt M, Schroder J, Treszl A. (2012). A randomized controlled trial of Internet-based therapy in depression. *Behaviour Research and Therapy, 50*, 513–521.

Muñoz RF, Aguilera A., Schueller SM, Leykin Y, Perez-Stable EJ. (2012). From online randomized controlled trials to participant preference studies: Morphing the San Francisco stop smoking site into a worldwide smoking cessation resource. *Journal of Medical Internet Research, 14*, e64.

Richards D, Richardson T. (2012). Computer-based psychological treatments for depression: A systematic review and meta-analysis. *Clinical Psychology Review, 32*(4), 329–342.

Riper H, Kramer J, Smit F, Conijn B, Schippers G, Cuijpers P. (2008). Web-based self-help for problem drinkers: A pragmatic randomized trial. *Addiction, 103*, 218–227.

Ritterband LM, Thorndike FP, Gonder-Frederick LA, Magee JC, Bailey ET, Saylor DK, Morin CM. (2009). Efficacy of an Internet-based behavioral intervention for adults with insomnia. *Archives of General Psychiatry, 66*, 692–698.

Spek V, Cuijpers P, Nyklicek I, Riper H, Keyzer J, Pop V. (2007). Internet-based cognitive behaviour therapy for symptoms of depression and anxiety: A meta-analysis. *Psychological Medicine, 37*, 319–328.

Titov N, Andrews G, Choi I, Schwencke G, Mahoney A. (2008). Shyness 3: Randomized controlled trial of guided versus unguided Internet-based CBT for social phobia. *The Australian and New Zealand Journal of Psychiatry, 42*, 1030–1040.

Williams C, Chellingsworth M. (2010). *CBT. A clinician's guide to using the five areas approach*. London: Hodder Arnold.

📖 Further reading

Bennett GG, Glasgow RE. (2009). The delivery of public health interventions via the Internet: Actualizing their potential. *Annual Review of Public Health, 30*, 273–292.

Bennett-Levy J, Christensen H, Farrand P, Griffiths K, Kavanagh D, Klein B, et al. editors. (2010). *Oxford Guide to Low Intensity CBT Interventions*. Oxford: Oxford University Press.

Chapter 6

Guided Internet-based CBT (ICBT) programs: Introduction

What you will learn

In this chapter you will learn about:

- How guided self-help can be transferred to the Internet.
- The role of the therapist in guided Internet-based CBT (ICBT).
- The overall effects of ICBT in systematic reviews.
- Health economical benefits of guided ICBT.
- How ICBT is perceived.
- Ethical considerations.

Introduction

Lucy had considered seeking psychological treatments for her stress problems for years, but the only time she had visited a psychologist he had not taken much interest in what troubled her the most – the stress she experienced in her life. She had been offered antidepressants from her GP but declined the offer, as she also did when it was suggested she go to a physiotherapist to learn relaxation. She felt she did not have the time for face-to-face therapy as it would not fit in well in her daily busy life with work, a dog and two children at school needing her assistance every day. She read an article in the newspaper about a stress management course on the Internet that had been found to be effective, and the researchers now were looking for research participants for a new study. She thought about it for a day and then registered on the web site. In the description of the study it said that she would have a personal guide throughout the program and that the stress management course was based on CBT. Following a set of questionnaires and a telephone interview, she was accepted for the trial and began working with the first treatment module, after instruction. Following the eight-week stress management course she felt much improved and in particular appreciated the weekly feedback from her online therapist. One thing she would have liked was to be in contact with other persons in the same situation on the web, which had not been part of the study.

Guided ICBT versus face-to-face CBT?

In contrast to most unguided treatments, guided ICBT was originally and often still is derived from studies on bibliotherapy where some form of guidance is provided by a professional (Watkins, 2008). Most research and clinical implementations of guided ICBT have involved texts similar to self-help books in addition to interactive online features and multimedia components such as films (Barak et al., 2009). Any program (including the automated open access programs reviewed in the previous chapter) can be used as guided treatments, although the therapist should be able to communicate with the client based on progress in the treatment program.

A few years ago we defined one approach to guided ICBT:

> [A] therapy that is based on self-help books, guided by an identified therapist who gives feedback and answers to questions, with a scheduling that mirrors face to face treatment, and which also can include interactive online features such as queries to obtain passwords in order to get access to treatment modules. (Andersson et al., 2008, p. 164.)

A clear difference between this definition and automated programs like MoodGYM is that that the level of technical complexity of the programs can be minimal, and in fact when we started with our first research trial on headache, we only had a static web page and emailed text documents to our research participants (Ström et al., 2000). Today, with broadband access widely available, more interactive web sites can be used but the demand for high security has increased.

In this chapter we describe the approach that has been most studied in research and also the approach that is closest to guided self-help, and how CBT therapists work with their clients (e.g., homework assignments and personal feedback on homework completion). In Chapter 1 some recommendations regarding what makes self-help texts work were given. This is of course dependent on the condition being treated, and hence we give more specialized information on the content of the programs in the following three chapters dealing with mood disorders, anxiety disorders and finally somatic conditions like chronic pain and tinnitus.

An important question for the reader with background and training in CBT is how ICBT relates to regular CBT. It could be argued is that guided ICBT is more or less identical to face-to-face CBT and that it is only a question of format, where face-to-face CBT uses verbal communication in the session (albeit often with the addition of text or figures written on a whiteboard) and guided ICBT presents the information mainly via text as well as feedback and therapeutic advice that would be presented in session by a live therapist.

In addition to this, there are more differences than just the way the information is presented. For example, in group-based CBT group processes are inherently involved (Burlingame et al., 2002) that may either boost or hinder the therapeutic progress. (I have been running CBT groups for many years and am often struck by how different groups are.) In guided ICBT it is most common that communication with the client is *asynchronous* and not direct. (See Chapter 10 for real-time ICBT.) In other words guidance and therapeutic support are given after some reflection, although most of the communication tends to be in the form of encouragement (see next heading on the role of the therapist). Most forms of ICBT do not allow *case formulation* to play any major role once a diagnosis has been established. Many CBT clinicians regard case formulation (Tarrier, 2006) as a major part of CBT and it is often part of the training of CBT therapists. Guided ICBT can however be tailored based on an individual needs analysis (more on that in later chapters), but the treatment material is often based on manuals for specific disorders and the treatment manuals therefore need to incorporate specifics so that each client who reads (or listens to or watches) the treatment feels that the treatment fits with his or her problems.

Another difference between face-to-face CBT and guided ICBT is that the latter often includes much *more information* than is possible to convey in a time-limited face-to-face CBT treatment. In face-to-face CBT the therapist and client often prioritize and adapt the pace of the treatment according to the patient's capabilities. In the worst case, this can lead to what psychologist Glenn Waller has called "therapist drift" (Waller, 2009), which means that some therapists drift away from doing evidence-based CBT to doing "talking therapy" instead. This does not occur in ICBT, at least not within the program, but potentially from the guiding therapist.

Clients often fail to complete the full treatment program, and poor adherence is a problem in many studies on ICBT, although less of a problem in guided ICBT than in unguided (see Chapter 5). Somewhat unexpectedly, this does not always mean that non-completers gain less, but rather that the treatment dose needed is less than a full 10-week 180-pages of text long treatment. In addition, for some clients the major effects of treatment are realized fairly early, after four to six weeks, leaving less room for further improvement. In spite of this, I recommend that clients complete the full treatment programs, as the overlearning (e.g., further exposure to feared situations) and plans for preventing relapse are likely to be of benefit for the client.

Another advantage of guided ICBT over face-to-face therapy is that the client can repeat (re-read) the program contents, the advice from the guiding therapist, and the whole treatment history with previous questions to the therapist and corresponding feedback. While this is possible to some extent in face-to-face therapy if the session is recorded, it is probably rather rare and somewhat problematic in terms of confidentiality if the videotape (or audio-recording) is lost. Since the correspondence between the therapist and the client in guided ICBT is contained within a secure interface (similar to Internet banking) it is less risky than handling session notes, recordings, etc., in face-to-face therapies.

There are of course several limitations with guided ICBT when compared to face-to-face CBT. First, the ability to lead the patient through in vivo exposures is limited (web camera being a possibility). In addition, the feedback provided in face-to-face sessions is more direct even though the same time-lag may occur when feedback is given on homework completion.

Second, the more active parts in face-to-face CBT when the therapist gently encourages the client to move forward in exposure or activation are less likely to be as efficient in guided ICBT where it is fairly easy to escape the situation if it becomes too difficult. In other words, guided ICBT may be less aversive because the therapist has less possibilities to push the client forward, but it is also a possible disadvantage because clients in guided ICBT can easily censor treatment components they do not like.

A third disadvantage – which we discovered by doing a qualitative study on participants from a study on depression (Bendelin et al., 2011) – is that some clients in guided ICBT only read and do not change anything in their lives or complete any of the homework assignments (or at least not to the extent that change is achieved). This can of course occur in face-to-face CBT as well and I believe some readers will recognize this from their clinics, when a client returns for a weekly session with little or no change in his or her life and no completed homework (and even with little recollection of the matters discussed in the last session). An experienced CBT therapist will react to this in session and hence avoid therapist drift and doing "talking therapy", whereas for us it was somewhat surprising that a proportion of our interviewed research participants actually had read the treatment material but had not implemented any of the advice given.

A fourth disadvantage with guided ICBT with a fixed program content is the obvious risk of providing either too much or too little treatment. This is related to the issue of case conceptualization in that a therapist in face-to-face therapy adjusts the treatment plan according to patient characteristics. I strongly recommend proper assessment before recommending guided ICBT, as most of the programs I have worked with are long, and are rarely experienced as being too brief. On the other hand, some ICBT programs are indeed short, and optimally length should be adapted according to what the client is likely to be able to master.

In the next chapter tailored ICBT, where number of treatment modules is adapted according to findings in the assessment phase, is discussed. Table 6.1 provides some suggestions on how to conduct guided ICBT based on the experiences from our clinic (Bergström et al., 2009) and research (Andersson et al., 2009).

The role of the therapist in guided ICBT

In this chapter guided ICBT, in which the guidance provided by a therapist is a crucial part of the treatment, is introduced. Guiding ICBT can take many different forms and may vary in terms of the amount of time devoted to the individual client (Palmqvist et al., 2007).

The time it takes to respond to queries from clients, reading and providing feedback on homework assignments, and sorting out other difficulties can vary, but in our experience it does not take more than 10 minutes per week on average per client. In total that would lead to around 100 minutes for a 10-session program, and adding to that time for a diagnostic interview over the phone (usually about 40 minutes, with a total time of 140 minutes for all procedures). However, this number may vary from just providing brief encouragement to writing longer and more therapeutic responses to clients. It can also vary between different therapists and in response to different clients.

In the approach I have mostly used the therapist is identified with a name (and a picture on the study home page) and always responds with the first name as signature. The correspondence between the therapist and the client is best characterized as minimal guidance, or low intensity, and takes place within a secure online contact handling system that requires two-factor authentication (see Chapter 1), resembling Internet banking (with proper handling of encryption, authentication and message authentication codes). Hence both the therapist and the client can log in and read all correspondence that has occurred during the treatment.

There are also other contact possibilities such as regular telephone contact and SMS reminders, and there are occasions when these are needed (Andersson & Carlbring, 2010). For example, when dealing with more severe patients who are in a crisis, telephone support can be called for.

Regular reminders that it is time to check the treatment page can be sent via SMS with no sign revealing that it has anything to do with "treatment". For example, this could read,

Table 6.1 Some advice on how to provide guided ICBT

1. Conduct careful assessment of candidates, preferably with a structured telephone interview being the minimum and in-session interview being the optimum. If needed consult specialists (e.g., physicians when treating chronic pain).
2. Adapt the treatment for Internet administration and consider using pictures, film and audio files. However, make it possible for the patient to print out the material (as PDF), and do not rely too much on web solutions that require broadband access.
3. Consider the advice on self-help books in Chapter 1; for example use language that is not too difficult to understand and not biased.
4. Convey empathy both in the online material and in the correspondence.
5. Make clear that there is a time limit for treatment completion (a deadline) when the outcome will be monitored regardless of how much the client has completed in terms of treatment modules.
6. Recommend exercises in real life (i.e. prescribe homework), that are possible and realistic to perform and report in at a set date (e.g., report in on Sunday). Give instructions that increase the likelihood of completion, for example by giving examples on what a completed worksheet may look like.
7. Always provide feedback on completed assignments as soon as possible, preferably within 24 hours (see below on therapist factors).
8. Allow some but not too much flexibility. For example reinforce reading but also encourage trying to complete the homework assignment if feasible.
9. Have a plan for what to do if the client signals deterioration. With more severe clients it can be useful to have the client's phone number to call if the client has signaled deterioration in the internet communication.
10. Some clients will have problems with working on the computer, and some computer support may be needed. If the system breaks down it is important to answer questions directly and solve the problem as soon as possible (e.g., if the patient cannot log in to the system, an email from the system administrator quickly stating: "We have noted the problem and are working on a solution" can prevent the patient from leaving the treatment).
11. Adapt and update the program on a regular basis. Co-workers and therapists working with the treatment can provide important feedback which can be incorporated in the next version of the treatment in an iterative process.

"You have a message on your page. Please log in to read. Gerhard for the Sofie project". This kind of reminder is often automated in ICBT systems.

The approach I have worked with involves fairly limited therapist contact, but enough to establish a therapeutic alliance (more on this soon). Other approaches, such as the *Interapy* treatment (Ruwaard et al., 2011), developed by professor Freddy Lange and his team, involve much more therapist time, as the treatment includes structured writing assignments, and this form of therapy is closer to email therapy where there is much contact between the therapist and the patient (Murphy & Mitchell, 1998; see Chapter 1 for definitions).

Therapist behaviours

What is the therapist doing when guiding the client? We have categorized the responses from therapists in a trial on generalized anxiety disorder by using content analyses of how three therapists responded (in total 490 emails sent to clients in the trial). The categories found are described in Table 6.2 (derived from Paxling et al., 2013).

Table 6.2 Therapist activities in guided ICBT

Behaviour	Specification of behaviour	Examples
Deadline flexibility	Behaviours that pertain to lenience from the therapist concerning deadlines for homework submissions and allowance of extra time to work with a given treatment module	You'll get another couple of days to finish the task. You can wait with this week's task and continue with the one you're working on.
Task reinforcement	Behaviours aimed at reinforcing assignments already completed by the participant	Well done! You've described your worry thoughts in a clarifying way.
Alliance bolstering	Non-treatment specific writings that pertain to interest in the participant's life situation and care for his or her situation (This category is not related to the treatment)	How nice that you've had a good week. That must have been tough on you.
Task prompting	Behaviours prompting the participant to work with a given homework assignment, and explicit interest in future results of the participant's progress	I'm looking forward to hearing from you during the work with the coming modules. Good luck with the next task.
Psychoeducation	Information about psychological processes, goals of the treatment and explanation of purpose and meaning of the work involved in the treatment	Worrying is part of generalized anxiety disorder.
Self-disclosure	Therapist behaviours that describe circumstances in the therapist's own life situation that are similar or relevant to the patient's situation	I've also had trouble sleeping.
Self-efficacy shaping	Behaviours that prompt and reinforce the participant to spontaneously engage in the health-promoting behaviours they have learnt through the treatment	The more you practice this, the more often you'll be able to notice the thoughts.
Empathetic utterance	Writings that attempt to convey understanding and empathy for the participant's suffering, frustration or general life situation related to the treatment	I understand that you …. I can see why you ….

Source: Based on Paxling et al. (2013).

Interestingly, when we correlated the frequency of these therapist behaviours we found that task reinforcement, task prompting, self-efficacy shaping and empathetic utterances correlated with module completion. In other words these responses were associated with research participants completing more treatment modules. Deadline flexibility was negatively associated with outcome and task reinforcement positively correlated with changes on the Penn State Worry Questionnaire (Meyer et al., 1990), which was the measure of worry we used. In another study by Sanchez-Ortiz and colleagues (2011) a similar approach was taken by categorizing emails sent from a therapist guiding a program for eating disorders. They analysed the content of 712 emails and found that 14.7% of the emails therapists sent contained at least one CBT comment, while 95.4% had at least one supportive comment and 13.6% had at least one technical comment. Thus they concluded that the bulk of emails sent were of supportive character.

Overall, however, we know very little about the characteristics of effective Internet therapists and indeed in the somewhat brief contact in guided ICBT there is little room for large therapist effects. In the research I have been involved in we have found very little evidence that it makes much difference who the therapist is (Almlöv et al., 2009, 2011), but this does not mean that the therapist can write just anything. Most therapists are able to provide balanced and appropriate responses to clients and they often manage to resolve ruptures in the therapeutic contact as well, although these are rare (i.e. few patients bother to express their anger toward their Internet therapist and instead probably just drop out). An example of a fictive question from a patient is presented in Figure 6.1 (from the Swedish system at Internet psychiatry, Stockholm).

In principle, guidance can take any form (e.g., web-camera, telephone, live consultations), but by far the most common way to support ICBT has been via email. Again, this is not the same thing as receiving emails from your therapist in your inbox; the correspondence should be contained within a secure encrypted contact handling system. Titov (2010) has written about the specifics of email guidance. He refers to asynchronous electronic mail and does not cover real-time messaging (instant messaging or chat). He also acknowledged the role of writing and reading skills: "Practitioners and clients must have minimal levels of typing

Figure 6.1 Contact handling system at Karolinska (Internet psychiatry unit).

Table 6.3 Example of correspondence between client and therapist (altered to maintain privacy)

> **Client**
> Hi,
> I have now completed the second module, more or less. It was tedious to get going and doing the exercises for real. I do not know if I did it correctly and if I had done that I would probably never have finished….
> Mary
> **Therapist**
> Dear Mary,
> It is good that you do this, even when it is hard. In the next module you will move on to working with activity scheduling and weekly planning. This way of working can indeed be hard and make you tired in the short run, but it is a known effective way to influence your mood in the right direction! So, keep doing what you can since it will pay off in the end.
> Chris Jones, Psychologist

and technical skills to read, save, and send emails. In interventions where email is used to communicate complex ideas about treatment or to guide clients through an intervention, practitioners require advanced skills in communication via text format" (Titov, 2010, p. 289).

It is crucial that the therapist is well acquainted with the program he or she is guiding. Clients may ask for clarifications, but there may also be questions regarding the problem at hand, about other treatments (such as medication), and technical issues. To the best of my knowledge there are few systematic investigations on what clients ask for and the contents of their emails to their therapists. Interestingly, in one of our clinical studies on the treatment of tinnitus (see Chapter 9 for more on somatic conditions) we found that emails from clients dealing with negative aspects of treatment (e.g., delays in treatment, not completing homework, technical problems) were associated with worse outcome ($r = -0.39$), suggesting that it is not necessarily a good thing to be in contact with the therapist (Kaldo-Sandström et al., 2004).

Frequency of contact is an issue. Many systems allow clients to send in their reports anytime and are given answers more or less immediately, and some set up deadlines for sending in homework (we do that) and provide feedback after that date. If you have the responsibility for a client it should be possible for the client to contact you in case there is an urgent matter; frequent contact does not necessarily improve outcome. In one of the few studies that have systematically investigated this matter Klein and co-workers (2009) found no differences in outcome when their *Panic Online* program was administered with either frequent (three emails per week) or infrequent (one email per week) support from a psychologist.

Correspondence does not need to be long to be helpful. Table 6.3 gives an example of correspondence between the therapist and the client. Note that the therapist did not pay much notice to the client's comment that she did not know if she had done it correctly. Instead the therapist focused on task reinforcement and "self-efficacy shaping". Perhaps you would have done it differently?

The therapeutic alliance

In most forms of psychotherapy, the *therapeutic alliance* (the bond between the patient and the therapist) is regarded as an important factor, although it is emphasized more often in other therapeutic orientations than in CBT. However, the existing evidence on the role of the therapeutic alliance clearly suggests that an alliance is formed in CBT and the clients rate the alliance as being high (Horvath et al., 2011). This means that clients agree with their therapist in terms of the *tasks* and *goals* of the therapy, and that they feel they have a *bond* with the therapist.

The importance of therapeutic alliance in guided ICBT is not obvious, and the literature on the topic is mixed with regard to how important it is for outcome. Some studies show an association and some do not. In ICBT there is much less therapist contact than in face-to-face treatments (approximately 1/10 of the time), and the client may not even see the therapist in person. Thus much of the information on which the alliance is based does not exist in ICBT. However, there is a therapeutic interaction, and therapists guiding ICBT use both specific and common factors to encourage the client to work with the ICBT (see Table 6.2).

Since we know that alliance ratings tend to be just as high as in face-to-face treatments (e.g., Knaevelsrud & Maercker, 2007) the development of a therapeutic alliance does not necessarily require direct face-to-face contact with a therapist. In fact, even in static text material there is room for conveying empathy that can foster alliance. A client may perceive an understanding clinician who is behind the text material (Richardson et al., 2010). The total information available for clients when rating the alliance in ICBT can consist of interactions with a therapist online, interactions with a treatment system and text material that can possibly boost the alliance.

Returning to the research question on whether the therapeutic alliance is important in guided ICBT (with minimal therapist contact), we published a study on the topic with alliance ratings from three separate groups (Andersson et al., 2012a). We included participants with depression ($N = 49$), generalized anxiety disorder ($N = 35$) and social anxiety disorder ($N = 90$). They all completed a measure of alliance (the Working Alliance Inventory; Busseri & Tyler, 2003), which was modified for guided ICBT. The ratings were made early in the treatment (weeks 3 to 4). Results showed that alliance ratings were high in all three samples but correlations between the alliance measure and improvement were not statistically significant. Thus in the largest study on the topic to date, alliance in ICBT was again fairly highly rated by clients but did not make a difference for the outcome. On the other hand, in a more recent small study on mixed anxiety disorders we did find an association between alliance and outcome (Bergman Norgreen et al., 2013), indicating that there may be differences between different client groups in how important the alliance is.

Does it need to be a professional?

In my understanding of ICBT, guidance helps to prevent dropout and increase the effects, and this is clearly supported by the empirical literature with a few exceptions (but those studies often include some contact with the researchers, although the actual treatment is unguided) (see Johansson & Andersson, 2012). The next question is whether it matters how skilled and trained the therapist is. The importance of competence (which should be achieved via training and practice) is debated within CBT, with the literature showing mixed findings (Webb et al., 2010), but few within the CBT community would argue that training does not matter and that therapist skills are unimportant.

At the heart of the debate is whether specific techniques really are needed or if more general "common" factors such as warmth, empathy and trust, are enough for generating improvement (Wampold, 2001). Clearly, there must be more technique and less of the common factors in ICBT, but common factors are (as mentioned above) not absent. Given the offline character of guidance in most forms of guided ICBT it is possible that clinicians performing the guidance develop therapist skills gradually. For example, the speed of responding and giving appropriate guidance could be influenced by experience. We found this when we did a study comparing experienced versus inexperienced psychologists (in terms of guiding ICBT), who guided clients with social anxiety disorder through a program (Andersson et al., 2012b). While both groups were equally effective, the inexperienced therapists tended to log in more often, indicating that they spent more time with each client.

Research has been done to investigate whether the main content of guidance given makes a difference. Titov and co-workers conducted a series of controlled studies in which they investigated whether guidance can be given from a "technical" point of view, without any specific therapeutic advice. In their studies guidance from a "technician" has been found to be just as effective as when providing guidance from a "therapist" (Robinson et al., 2010; Titov et al., 2009, 2010a). On the other hand, the "technicians" in those studies were part of the research team and it is interesting to note that a controlled trial investigating the added value of telephone tracking by lay telephone counsellors failed to confer any additional benefits over self-guided treatment when the program MoodGYM was used (Farrer et al., 2011). However, MoodGYM is primarily an unguided treatment (see Chapter 5), but since there was contact with all of the research participants over the phone and the study was conducted in a national helpline service setting, this study adds to our knowledge of how ICBT can be delivered.

In most of the studies I have been part of and also in the clinical implementations the therapists have often been either students in their last year of a five-year clinical psychologist program or previous students who continued to do guided ICBT as part of their clinical activities. There are other clinicians with no background in ICBT who guide ICBT, but since we have not conducted any large-scale trial on how to train experienced CBT therapists in guiding ICBT it is fair to say that in most cases the clinician performing the guidance has had relatively little clinical experience and hence things can probably only get better with a skilled experienced clinician. It could be that experienced clinicians "overdo" it, and drift away from the manual, but factors such as writing skills are important. Further, it is important not to overload clinicians with too many cases (which at worst can lead to clinicians to mixing up clients.

Supervision is another topic that we have included in many of our trials. Supervision can be useful when the therapist is uncertain about how to respond to the client, but it can also be important to encourage the therapist, and in group supervision to listen to how other therapists handle their cases.

Therapist skills are needed when guiding a client through ICBT and when developing a treatment program. They can be useful when handling treatment failures, misunderstandings, and other problems in treatment. Overall, as attested by the fairly high ratings of therapeutic alliance in ICBT, clients tend to trust and appreciate their online therapist.

There is literature on this topic that deals with online counselling, or e-therapy (Murphy & Mitchell, 1998), which involves much more interaction and hence is closer to face-to-face CBT. This form of Internet treatment is covered in Chapter 10. But since we know from the work of Titov and co-workers that guidance does not necessarily need to be therapeutic, it is important to investigate whether professionals other than CBT clinicians can do the guidance, perhaps under the supervision of psychologists. In the era of low-intensity CBT and the Increasing Access to Psychological Treatment (IAPT) model in the United Kingdom (Clark, 2011), there is a need to investigate different models of service delivery.

The overall effects of guided ICBT in systematic reviews

The overall effects of guided ICBT are discussed here, and the next three chapters focus on depression, anxiety and somatic conditions. The answer to the question "How effective is guided ICBT?" is: "Just about as effective as face-to-face CBT", but there are exceptions. With the growing amount of studies the answer might even be: "In some cases just as good, in others less good, and in a few cases even better than face-to-face CBT". Perhaps it is not meaningful to ask such a vague question, like asking "does medication work?" (see Marks & Cavanagh, 2009 for a thoughtful discussion on this topic). We focus on specific conditions in later chapters, but here suffice it to say that guided ICBT has been tested for a wide range of problems over the last 15 years (Hedman et al., 2012).

In Table 6.4 a list of most of the conditions tested in randomised controlled trials is presented, but new studies appear almost every week so the list is not comprehensive. It would also be longer if unguided treatments were included. It does however reflect how rapidly this field has progressed, because for some of the conditions listed there are close to 20 randomised controlled trials (e.g., social anxiety disorder), and there are no studies on guided ICBT earlier than the mid-1990s.

Not listed in Table 6.4 is the range of people for whom ICBT has been developed and tested. Most of the studies have been on adults who volunteered for research trials, but there is an expanding number of studies on other target groups such as regular clinic patients, young adults and adolescents, older persons and persons with different languages and cultural backgrounds. For example, there is a study on the treatment of depression in Chinese Australians with Mandarin/Cantonese-speaking support personnel (Choi et al., 2012), and in my group we have recently conducted a study on depression in Kurdish language. More on specific applications follows in the upcoming chapters.

Table 6.4 Examples of conditions for which guided ICBT has been tested in research (randomised controlled trials)

Psychiatric conditions	Somatic conditions	Other
Depression	Headache	Couples therapy
Bipolar disorder	Tinnitus	Parent training
Panic disorder	Diabetes	Stress problems
Social phobia	Insomnia	Perfectionism
Specific phobia	Childhood encopresis	Burnout
Mixed anxiety/depression	Chronic pain	Procrastination
Health anxiety	Cancer	
Obsessive-compulsive disorder	Irritable bowel syndrome	
Generalized anxiety disorder	Erectile dysfunction	
Posttraumatic stress disorder	Hearing loss	
Pathological gambling	Chronic fatigue	
Bulimia and eating disorders	Multiple sclerosis	
	Obesity	
	Smoking	

Just as the number of research trials is growing there is a constant flow of new review articles on Internet-delivered treatments in general and also on guided ICBT. One potential problem with some of the reviews is that they tend to combine studies on different forms of Internet-delivered treatment with other forms of computerized interventions and even guided self-help with no Internet component (e.g., Cuijpers et al., 2009). These reviews are valuable but for a reader it can be confusing when guided and unguided treatments are summarized under the same heading as well as computerized treatments delivered via CD-ROM and bibliotherapy studies. Although this can be regarded as a minor problem (see Chapter 1 for more on definitions), a term like *computerized cognitive behaviour therapy* (CCBT) can encompass many different forms of treatment.

One fairly early meta-analytic review cited frequently was conducted by a Dutch research group (Spek et al., 2007). They focused on ICBT for anxiety and depression and found greater effects for anxiety disorders and somewhat smaller effects for depressive disorders. However, when taking degree of support into account they found that guided interventions had greater effects. The following year Barak and colleagues (2008) published a comprehensive meta-analysis with a range of conditions and interventions. They found a mean effect size (standardized mean difference) of 0.53, which can be regarded as a medium effect size. However, this metric does not have much meaning as they included as many as 92 studies that were very different in character. Interestingly, studies involving CBT appeared to have larger effects, but again given the speed of research not even a majority of the non-CBT conducted studies to date were included in that review. It is however one of the few review papers that has covered a wide range of studies which is very informative.

Being more focused on anxiety and depression and also on guided computerized interventions (practically all being Internet based), Andrews and co-workers (2010) included 22 controlled studies, and found a mean Cohen's *d* effect size of 0.88, which is very much in line with what can be achieved in face-to-face CBT. They also found evidence for long-term effects at a median of 26 weeks follow-up. Adding to these findings, Cuijpers and his co-workers (2010) published a meta-analysis on direct comparisons between face-to-face and guided self-help (again with most studies being done on Internet-delivered CBT). I was one of the authors of that review and we included 21 studies with 810 participants. Results clearly showed no difference between guided self-help and face-to-face treatment. If anything there was a small tendency in the opposite direction with an effect size of *d* = −0.02, in favour of guided self-help. I have worked on a few controlled trials in which we have compared face-to-face and guided ICBT and have come to the conclusion that both treatment formats are effective, but that there are clients who are more or less suitable for either format. It is also worth noting that the studies in which guided ICBT has been compared with face-to-face CBT (either individual or group CBT) often include a lot of direct contact with research participants in the assessment phase. One possibility could be that the face-to-face CBT provided has been inferior to regular CBT, but that is clearly not what we have found. In fact, we usually find large treatment effects for the clients treated with either format. (I am mainly referring to our trials on anxiety and depression here, e.g., Carlbring et al., 2005.)

In addition to the many systematic reviews on the topic there are more general reviews and "state-of-the-art" position papers (e.g., Andersson, 2009; Griffiths et al., 2007; Ritterband et al., 2003), and in these it is often apparent that different research groups have somewhat different views on the way ICBT should best be provided, which generates a healthy debate on the pros and cons of guided versus unguided treatments.

In conclusion, there are now so many studies that it is becoming less meaningful to conduct reviews on a range of conditions together as the number of trials for each separate condition is growing (e.g., on ICBT for chronic pain). Other questions remain which are in many respects the same questions asked by CBT researchers and clinicians; for example, the role of treatment *adherence*, how we can predict who is likely to benefit from ICBT, and also the role of therapeutic alliance mentioned earlier.

Comments on predictors and moderators (for who does the treatment work) are given in the upcoming chapters, as it is unlikely that the same factors should be important across conditions. Even the role of guidance may differ between conditions. It is possible that guidance is more important when treating a depressed person with ICBT than when treating an otherwise healthy person who has insomnia. The take-home message is that we need to specialize our interventions as has been done in CBT in general, even though there are commonalities and co-morbidities across problem areas. We are now in a position where guided ICBT can be regarded as evidence based and ready for dissemination. To quote Andrews et al. (2010), "We now, it seems, are beginning to know enough about the efficacy, applicability and potential cost savings from the Internet programs for people with anxiety and depressive disorders to begin to integrate these Internet services with existing mental health services." (p. 5).

Does guided ICBT save costs?

As alluded to in the above quote from Andrews et al. (2010) it can be assumed that Internet-delivered treatments, and guided ICBT as well, save costs. If just accounting for the therapist time, guiding a person in ICBT is less time consuming than seeing the client live, and provided that the effects of treatment are not compromised ICBT is then cost-effective.

There is emerging evidence that this is the case. Measuring costs is complicated and not only concerns costs of the treatment or therapist time (Drummond et al., 2005). Many current studies on cost-effectiveness adopt a *societal perspective*, including the costs of all types of health services as well as costs associated with production losses. Hence we measure things like the number of GP visits, sessions with psychiatrists, hospital days, medication usage and all other health care consumption. In addition, we collect information on the number of work loss days (absenteeism from work) and the number of work cutback days (less efficiency at work when feeling ill).

It is useful to distinguish between *intervention costs* associated with therapist support, screening interviews, computers, servers and Internet access and the *direct medical costs* that concern both formal and informal health service providers. It takes quite an effort to break down the costs for different components. (I am not personally involved in doing these analyses and work together with excellent co-workers such as Filip Smit in the Netherlands and Björn Paxling, Erik Andersson and Erik Hedman in Sweden.)

There are also other costs involved such as direct non-medical costs that arise when patients travel to health service providers and pay for parking or transportation. In addition to the costs and cost savings that are more or less the same for each new client, there are costs for developing ICBT programs and training therapists. These costs are less stable and can vary from very little to a great deal when a new ICBT system is replacing an old one.

There are an increasing number of cost-effectiveness studies on ICBT and also on guided ICBT. One important type of study directly compares costs for live therapy versus ICBT, and we did this in association with a trial on social anxiety disorder (Hedman et al., 2011). In that study we also looked at cost-utility, which is a calculation that takes quality-adjusted life years (QALIs) into account. Results showed that the gross total costs were significantly reduced at six-month follow-up, compared to pre-treatment in both face-to-face and ICBT conditions. As both treatments were equivalent in reducing social anxiety and gross total costs, ICBT was more cost-effective due to lower intervention costs ($464 per capita in the ICBT group versus $2,687 in the face-to-face group treatment).

We have also investigated cost-effectiveness for other conditions like health anxiety, irritable bowel syndrome and generalized anxiety disorder. Warmerdam and co-workers (2010) found that guided ICBT for depression was cost-effective and equally found Internet-delivered problem-solving therapy to be so.

This area of research is important not only for ICBT but also for CBT in general, as resources are not endless and it is crucial to show that society actually saves costs by providing evidence-based treatments.

How is it perceived and who wants it?

Because guided ICBT has been around for some time one may wonder how this way of delivering CBT is perceived by clinicians, clients and the public. Whitfield and Williams (2004) did a survey on the use of computerized CBT in the United Kingdom and found that a strikingly small number of CBT therapists used that treatment format (2.4%), and only 1% were using it as an alternative to patient-therapist contact. This should be viewed in relation to a previous study showing that 88% of CBT practitioners used self-help approaches on a regular basis (Keeley et al., 2002). However, the Internet is probably much more accessible than previous CD-ROM-based programs and hence it cannot be taken for granted that the same applies to ICBT now 10 years later.

A study in the United States was published with a national sample of 2,098 social workers, psychologists and other professionals. The authors found poor acceptance and uptake of online mental health treatment, with only 2% reporting that they used the Internet to provide therapy (Wells et al., 2007). Perhaps this should be seen in relation to the relatively low Internet access in the United States by that time (the data were collected in 2003), and the problems with interstate regulations (see below on ethics), but it may also be the case that attitudes among clinicians differ between countries.

A study from Norway by Wangberg et al. (2007) showed a remarkably different outcome. They found that out of a sample of 1,040 members of the Norwegian psychologist association as many as 45% had used the Internet in interactions with clients. Only 3% of the psychologists felt that use of the Internet between client and therapist was unacceptable. Interestingly, having a psychodynamic theoretical stance was related to negative attitudes toward Internet treatment. This finding was replicated in a study from the United States more recently, where Mora et al. (2008) found that CBT practitioners more strongly endorsed the use of Internet-based interventions than psychoanalytically oriented practitioners. However, in line with Wells et al. participants overall did not express strong levels of endorsement of online therapies as either adjuncts or alternatives to face-to-face treatment.

It appears that many clinicians are more hesitant toward Internet treatment for more severe conditions, as was found in an Australian study (Gun et al., 2011). The authors had both health professionals and laypeople complete a questionnaire regarding attitudes toward Internet-based treatment programs. For both groups, mild to moderate anxiety and depression respondents reported high levels of acceptance, which again indicates that differences between countries may play a role.

Much of this research has concerned anxiety and depression, and it would be useful to know how Internet treatment for other conditions is perceived by clinicians. For example, we found that patients with breast cancer and oncologists were positive toward using Internet-delivered treatment (Andersson et al., 2006). There are also interesting qualifiers that should be tested such as what clinicians think about open versus closed Internet treatments. In a study on clinicians' attitudes toward computer treatment with children and adolescents (Stallard et al., 2010), the authors found that few of their respondents thought that computerized CBT should be delivered freely online without any professional support. This was identified as a major problem, and the potential to access the treatment at home was seen as the greatest advantage.

It is far from clear that CBT clinicians know what ICBT is, how effective it is and for whom it is suitable. The difference in outcome and adherence between guided versus unguided ICBT makes things even more confusing.

Perhaps even more interesting than what clinicians think is what the clients or the would-be clients think about ICBT. There is some previous literature on this topic relating to computerized CBT (e.g., Kaltenthaler et al., 2008), but most of the information has been derived from treatment completers, which is not the same as prospective clients.

Mohr and colleagues (2010) published a unique study in which they asked more than 600 primary care patients in the United States about their interest in different forms of psychological treatment including face to face, by telephone and via the Internet. This study found clear differences in favour of face-to-face treatment as 91.9% were interested or would consider face-to-face care compared to 62.4% for telephone and 48.0% for Internet treatment. Still, being conducted in a primary care setting and in the United States this indicates that at least half would be interested in Internet delivery of psychological treatment. Mohr et al. also found some associations, for example that severity of the symptoms did not matter for preference and that perceived time constraints predicted interest in telephone and Internet treatments compared to face-to-face treatment.

It may not be easy to answer questions regarding Internet treatment unless you know what it is and how it works. In a small study Sorbi and van der Vaart (2010) asked patients with migraine to rate the program, which is a consumer-oriented way to evaluate how Internet treatment is perceived and at the same time get feedback. We have routinely asked our research participants for feedback, and this has been helpful.

Titov and his co-workers have published studies on how persons with posttraumatic stress disorder (PTSD) (Spence et al., 2011) and obsessive-compulsive disorder (OCD) (Woolton et al., 2011) view Internet therapy and if this format is preferable to face-to-face treatment. In both of these studies Internet treatment was perceived as highly acceptable, and relatively few preferred face-to-face treatment over Internet treatment (with 32% in the PTSD study, and 10% in the OCD study). It is very likely that persons who suffer from anxiety disorders in Australia (where the study was conducted) may have a particular interest in getting ICBT as face-to-face CBT may not be available in close proximity. The authors argued that ICBT may reduce barriers to accessing treatment.

Interest in receiving ICBT seems to be influenced by what is written about it in the press, what clinicians in health care believe (and say to you) and whether you know someone personally who has gone through ICBT. Most of our research trials over the years have recruited participants via advertisement (see Jones et al., 2012, for a recent study on how adverts can increase uptake of ICBT), and also via referral and self-referral when the service is provided as routine care. We return to this topic later, but it is inevitable that anything said may change, since the attitude toward Internet services (like shopping) has changed and is still changing as I write these words.

Another way to answer the question "who wants guided ICBT" is to look at persons who have actually completed ICBT. In our early studies we had a majority of participants who were well educated, perhaps reflecting a bias in favour of participating in research and doing psychological treatment among persons with higher education. There are few systematic studies on this topic, but it appears that ICBT is becoming more acceptable in the general population, and work by the Titov and Andrews groups clearly suggests that persons receiving ICBT have as severe problems as clinic patients but are more similar to persons having the disorders in the general population with regard to other characteristics (Titov et al., 2010b). The question of whether clients treated with ICBT in general care benefit as much as the research participants who are recruited via advertisement in the upcoming chapters on depression, anxiety disorders and somatic conditions is discussed later in the book. Overall, however, the evidence to date suggests that guided ICBT could be offered to regular patients even though there will be exceptions as there are for regular individual or group-based CBT.

Ethical considerations

This chapter concludes with a brief overview of the ethical considerations to be reflected upon when doing guided ICBT. Ethical issues surround all the aspects of Internet use described in this book, but when there is direct contact between client and care provider, it is similar to regular clinical practice (compared to an open access unguided program with no direct contact with the user). One useful way to approach these matters is by highlighting the particulars of Internet treatment in relation to established ethical guidelines. This was done in a review paper by Dever Fitzgerald et al. (2010), who structured their review according to the guidelines provided by the international *Universal Declaration of Ethical Principles for Psychologists* (International Union of Psychological Science, 2008). The principles are displayed in Table 6.5 in the left column. My comments in the right column are based on the review by Dever Fitzgerald et al.

Several other ethical aspects are relevant, depending on where and how ICBT is practiced. In the United Kingdom and Sweden there are regulations regarding publicly funded health care (e.g., NHS), but fewer restrictions regarding where to practice than in the United States, where it is not allowed to have clients in jurisdictions in which a psychologist does not hold a license. The practice of Internet-delivered psychological services, and in particular email-based therapy, has been discussed in the United States (Midkiff & Wyatt, 2008; Zack, 2008).

Anonymity is another sensitive matter. Since psychologists and other professionals working in health care, at least in my country, are required to keep files on the clients they treat, anonymity becomes problematic in health care. A solution is to separate the medical files from the ICBT treatment since then all personal details (like the personal ID number all citizens have in Sweden) are absent from the treatment platform and identification is contained within the medical filing system. There are different rules and regulations in different countries regarding this. In Norway, for example, it is not allowed to have any email contact with a patient, leaving telephone support as the only option when guiding ICBT (Nordgreen et al., 2010).

Another area that can be used in ICBT programs is discussion or chat forums. This is different from one-to-one contact, as clients in discussion forums may discuss sensitive topics with each other (Humphreys et al., 2000). In my research we have these groups

Table 6.5 Universal Declaration of Ethical Principles for Psychologists and my own comments in relation to guided ICBT

Principle	Comment
I. *Respect for the dignity of persons and peoples*	As with all practice of CBT *consent* is important which requires clear information about procedures. For example, clients should be informed about how much work is needed in order to gain from the treatment. What is crucial in ICBT is the importance of *privacy* and *confidentiality*, which are closely linked to Internet information security. A particular matter of relevance in ICBT is the respectful handling of *non-completers* of treatment. One ethical aspect is also *access*, and paying attention to clients who may not own a computer or have limited processing capacities requiring low tech solutions such as sending paper versions of modules to clients.
II. *Competent caring for the well-being of persons and peoples*	CBT clinicians should *do no harm* regardless of communication channel. They should also offset or correct errors that may occur. In ICBT potential errors may include sending the wrong feedback or not detecting that a client signals that he or she has deteriorated, has become suicidal, etc. In research there has been a neglect of reporting negative outcomes in trials (Barlow, 2010, Rozenthal et al., 2014), and failure to report negative outcomes is not ethical conduct. With regard to competent caring, supervision of clinicians providing the support, constant update of treatment materials (may be a simple thing like a spelling error detected by a client) are important. Proper training and ongoing discussions regarding diagnostic procedures are also recommended.
III. *Integrity*	Integrity has to do with *truthful, open and accurate communication*. In relation to ICBT this has implications regarding full disclosure of who we are and what we know about the treatment format. For example, the professional identity of the person providing the support should be known (if for example a student is providing the support). Access to personal information is another important aspect with medical records opening for patients to easily access. While expectations for improvement should be fostered there should be no exaggeration regarding cure. Clients in ICBT should not be exploited for personal, professional or financial gain.
IV. *Professional and scientific responsibilities to society*	We are dealing with the constant need to update our knowledge and do new research with the goal of making things better. It also relates to how society will handle new information. For example, guided ICBT should be presented as a complement to regular CBT and not as a cost-saving replacement. Guided ICBT costs more than unguided but is more effective. Open access treatments reach more people worldwide but have large dropout rates. While little is known regarding therapist skills in ICBT proper training and supervision should be included in all practice. The possibility of training other professional groups to guide ICBT under supervision should be explored.

Source: Based on Dever Fitzgerald et al. (2010).

monitored, which means we do take ethical responsibility if sensitive topics are posted, with the clients knowing in advance that the groups are monitored and that we may take action.

We are only in the beginning of a new field of practice and there is not even any particular license or accreditation to practice ICBT (at least not in the United Kingdom and the Scandinavian countries).

Practical implications and key points

- Guided ICBT has successfully transferred CBT self-help techniques to Internet administration. Guided ICBT is different from face-to-face CBT but shares some characteristics such as homework assignments.

- Providing therapist support is crucial to secure good outcomes, but it is not clear what form of guidance is enough. Email is the most common way to support ICBT.

- A therapeutic alliance is formed in guided ICBT, but it is unclear if it is predictive of outcome. There are overall minor differences among therapists in the success of client outcomes, but writing skills and supportive encouragement are important.

- Guided ICBT has now been tested for the main conditions for which CBT has been found to be useful, although there are few applications for more severe conditions. Systematic reviews clearly show that guided ICBT can generate as good an outcome as face-to-face CBT for anxiety disorders and low to moderate depression.

- Health economic benefits of guided ICBT are obvious and are mainly related to lower costs of intervention compared to face-to-face CBT.

- ICBT is yet not perceived favourably by clinicians, although attitudes are changing and there are differences between countries. Clients are more positive, but many probably do not know how ICBT works and that it is not a quick fix that is easier than regular CBT.

- There are obvious ethical considerations when providing guided ICBT, which also depends on where the service is delivered. The same ethical guidelines as in face-to-face CBT should apply, but special care should be taken regarding information security.

References

Almlöv J, Carlbring P, Berger T, Cuijpers P, Andersson G. (2009). Therapist factors in Internet-delivered CBT for major depressive disorder. *Cognitive Behaviour Therapy, 38*, 247–254.

Almlöv J, Carlbring P, Källqvist K, Paxling B, Cuijpers P, Andersson G. (2011). Therapist effects in guided Internet-delivered CBT for anxiety disorders. *Behavioural and Cognitive Psychotherapy, 39*, 311–322.

Andersson G. (2009). Using the Internet to provide cognitive behaviour therapy. *Behaviour Research and Therapy, 47*, 175–180.

Andersson G, Bergström J, Buhrman M, Carlbring P, Holländare F, Kaldo V, Nilsson-Ihrfelt E, Paxling B, Ström L, Waara J. (2008). Development of a new approach to guided self-help via the Internet. The Swedish experience. *Journal of Technology in Human Services, 26*, 161–181.

Andersson G, Carlbring P. (2010). Using communication channels to support Internet interventions. In J Bennett-Levy, H Christensen, P Farrand, K Griffiths, D Kavanagh, B Klein, M Lau, J Proudfoot, D Richards, J White, C Williams et al., editors. *Oxford guide to low intensity CBT interventions* (pp. 269–274). Oxford: Oxford University Press.

Andersson G, Carlbring P, Berger T, Almlöv J, Cuijpers P. (2009). What makes Internet therapy work? *Cognitive Behaviour Therapy, 38*(S1), 55–60.

Andersson G, Carlbring P, Furmark T, and on behalf of the SOFIE Research Group. (2012b). Therapist experience and knowledge acquisition in Internet-delivered CBT for social anxiety disorder: A randomized controlled trial. *PloS ONE, 7*(5), e37411.

Andersson G, Nilsson-Ihrfelt E, Strand Ekberg AK, Svensson L, Fjällskog M-L. (2006). *Breast cancer patients and oncologist attitudes towards Internet delivered self help.* Paper presented at the Second International Meeting for the International Society for Research on Internet Interventions, April 28–29, Karolinska Institute, Stockholm.

Andersson G, Paxling B, Wiwe M, Vernmark K, Bertholds Felix C, Lundborg L, Furmark T, Cuijpers P, Carlbring P. (2012a). Therapeutic alliance in guided Internet-delivered cognitive behavioral treatment of depression, generalized anxiety disorder and social anxiety disorder. *Behaviour Research and Therapy, 50*, 544–550.

Andrews G, Cuijpers P, Craske MG, McEvoy P, Titov N. (2010). Computer therapy for the anxiety and depressive disorders is effective, acceptable and practical health care: A meta-analysis. *PloS ONE, 5*, e13196.

Barak A, Hen L, Boniel-Nissim M, Shapira N. (2008). A comprehensive review and a meta-analysis of the effectiveness of Internet-based psychotherapeutic interventions. *Journal of Technology in Human Services, 26*, 109–160.

Barak A, Klein B, Proudfoot JG. (2009). Defining Internet-supported therapeutic interventions. *Annals of Behavioral Medicine, 38*, 4–17.

Barlow DH. (2010). Negative effects from psychological treatments. A perspective. *American Psychologist, 65*, 13–20.

Bendelin N, Hesser H, Dahl J, Carlbring P, Zetterqvist Nelson K, Andersson G. (2011). Experiences of guided Internet-based cognitive-behavioural treatment for depression: A qualitative study *BMC Psychiatry, 11*, 107.

Bergman Nordgren L, Carlbring P, Linna E, Andersson G. (2013). Role of the working alliance on treatment outcome in tailored Internet-based cognitive behavioural therapy for anxiety disorders: Randomized controlled pilot trial. *JMIR Research Protocols, 2*, e4.

Bergström J, Andersson G, Karlsson A, Andreewitch S, Rück C, Carlbring P, Lindefors N. (2009). An open study of the effectiveness of Internet treatment for panic disorder delivered in a psychiatric setting. *Nordic Journal of Psychiatry, 63*, 44–50.

Burlingame GM, Fuhriman A, Johnson J. (2002). Cohesion in group psychotherapy. In JC Norcross, editor. *Psychotherapy relationships that work* (pp. 71–87). Oxford: Oxford University Press.

Busseri MA, Tyler JD. (2003). Interchangeability of the Working Alliance Inventory and Working Alliance Inventory, Short Form. *Psychological Assessment, 15*, 193–197.

Carlbring P, Nilsson-Ihrfelt E, Waara J, Kollenstam C, Buhrman M, Kaldo V, Söderberg M, Ekselius, L, Andersson G. (2005). Treatment of panic disorder: Live therapy vs. self-help via Internet. *Behaviour Research and Therapy, 43*, 1321–1333.

Choi I, Zou J, Titov N, Dear BF, Li S, Johnston L, Andrews G, Hunt C. (2012). Culturally attuned Internet treatment for depression amongst Chinese Australians: A randomised controlled trial. *Journal of Affective Disorders, 136*, 459–468.

Clark DM. (2011). Implementing NICE guidelines for the psychological treatment of depression and anxiety disorders: The IAPT experience. *International Review of Psychiatry, 23*, 318–327.

Cuijpers P, Donker T, van Straten A, Andersson G. (2010). Is guided self-help as effective as face-to-face psychotherapy for depression and anxiety disorders? A meta-analysis of comparative outcome studies. *Psychological Medicine, 40*, 1943–1957.

Cuijpers P, Marks I, van Straten A-M, Cavanagh K, Gega L, Andersson G. (2009). Computer-aided psychotherapy for anxiety disorders: A meta-analytic review. *Cognitive Behaviour Therapy, 38*, 66–82.

Dever Fitzgerald T, Hunter PV, Hadjistavropoulos T, Koocher GP. (2010). Ethical and legal considerations for Internet-based psychotherapy. *Cognitive Behaviour Therapy, 39*, 173–187.

Drummond MF, Sculpher MJ, Torrance GW, O'Brien BJ, Stoddart GL. (2005). *Methods for the economic evaluation of health care programmes* (3rd ed.). Oxford: Oxford University Press.

Farrer L, Christensen H, Griffiths KM, Mackinnon A. (2011). Internet-based CBT for depression with and without telephone tracking in a national helpline: Randomised controlled trial. *PLoS ONE, 6*(11), e28099.

Griffiths K, Farrer L, Christensen H. (2007). Clickety-click: e-mental health train on track. *Australasian Psychiatry, 15*, 100–108.

Gun SY, Titov N, Andrews G. (2011). Acceptability of Internet treatment of anxiety and depression. *Australasian Psychiatry, 19*, 259–264.

Hedman E, Andersson E, Ljótsson B, Andersson G, Rück C, Lindefors N. (2011). Cost-effectiveness of Internet-based cognitive behavior therapy vs. cognitive behavioral group therapy for social anxiety disorder: Results from a randomized controlled trial. *Behaviour Research and Therapy, 49*, 729–736.

Hedman E, Ljotsson B, Lindefors N. (2012). Cognitive behavior therapy via the Internet: A systematic review of applications, clinical efficacy and cost-effectiveness. *Expert Review of Pharmacoeconomics and Outcomes Research, 12*(6), 745–764.

Horvath AO, Del Re AC, Fluckiger C, Symonds D. (2011). Alliance in individual psychotherapy. *Psychotherapy, 48*, 9–16.

Humphreys K, Winzelberg A, Klaw E. (2000). Psychologists' ethical responsibilities in Internet-based groups: Issues, strategies, and a call for dialogue. *Professional Psychology: Research and Practice, 31*, 493–496.

International Union of Psychological Science. (2008). Universal declaration of ethical principles for psychologists. Retrieved August 2012 from http://www.am.org/iupsys/resources/ethics/univdecl2008.html

Johansson R, Andersson G. (2012). Internet-based psychological treatments for depression. *Expert Review of Neurotherapeutics, 12*, 861–870.

Jones RB, Goldsmith L, Hewson P, Kamel Boulos MN, Williams CJ. (2012). Do adverts increase the probability of finding online cognitive behavioural therapy for depression? Cross-sectional study. *BMJ Open, 2*, e000800.

Kaldo-Sandström V, Larsen HC, Andersson G. (2004). Internet-based cognitive-behavioral self-help treatment of tinnitus: Clinical effectiveness and predictors of outcome. *American Journal of Audiology, 13*, 185–192.

Kaltenthaler E, Sutcliffe P, Parr G, Beverley C, Rees A, Ferriter M. (2008). The acceptability to patients of computerized cognitive behaviour therapy for depression: A systematic review. *Psychological Medicine, 38*, 1521–1530.

Keeley H, Williams C, Shapiro, DA. (2002). A United Kingdom survey of accredited cognitive behaviour therapists' attitudes towards and use of structured self-help materials. *Behavioural and Cognitive Psychotherapy, 30*, 193–203.

Klein B, Austin D, Pier C, Kiropoulos L, Shandley K, Mitchell J, Gilson K, Ciechomski L. (2009). Internet-based treatment for panic disorder: does frequency of therapist contact make a difference? *Cognitive Behaviour Therapy, 38*, 121–131.

Knaevelsrud C, Maercker A. (2007). Internet-based treatment for PTSD reduces distress and facilitates the development of a strong therapeutic alliance: A randomized controlled clinical trial. *BMC Psychiatry, 7*, 13.

Marks I, Cavanagh K. (2009). Computer-aided psychological treatments: Evolving issues. *Annual Review of Clinical Psychology, 5*, 121–141.

Meyer TJ, Miller ML, Metzger RL, Borkovec TD. (1990). Development and validation of the Penn State Worry Questionnaire. *Behaviour Research and Therapy, 28*, 487–495.

Midkiff DM, Wyatt WJ. (2008). Ethical issues in the provision of online mental health services (Etherapy). *Journal of Technology in Human Services, 26*, 310–332.

Mohr DC, Siddique J, Ho J, Duffecy J, Jin L, Fokuo JK. (2010). Interest in behavioral and psychological treatments delivered face-to-face, by telephone, and by Internet. *Annals of Behavioral Medicine, 40*, 89–98.

Mora L, Nevid J, Chaplin W. (2008). Psychologist treatment recommendations for Internet-based therapeutic interventions. *Computers in Human Behavior, 24*, 3052–3062.

Murphy LJ, Mitchell DL. (1998). When writing helps to heal: email as therapy. *British Journal of Guidance and Counselling, 26*, 21–32.

Nordgreen T, Standal B, Mannes H, Haug T, Sivertsen B, Carlbring P, Andersson G, Havik OD. (2010). Guided self-help via Internet for panic disorder: Dissemination across countries. *Computers in Human Behavior, 26*, 592–596.

Palmqvist B, Carlbring P, Andersson G. (2007). Internet-delivered treatments with or without therapist input: Does the therapist factor have implications for efficacy and cost? *Expert Review of Pharmacoeconomics & Outcomes Research, 7*, 291–297.

Paxling B, Lundgren S, Norman A, Almlöv J, Carlbring P, Cuijpers P, Andersson G. (2013). Therapist behaviours in Internet-delivered cognitive behaviour therapy: Analyses of email correspondence in the treatment of generalized anxiety disorder. *Behavioural and Cognitive Psychotherapy, 41*, 280–289.

Richardson R, Richards DA, Barkham M. (2010). Self-help books for people with depression: The role of the therapeutic relationship. *Behavioural and Cognitive Psychotherapy, 38*, 67–81.

Ritterband LM, Gonder-Frederick LA, Cox DJ, Clifton AD, West R. W, Borowitz SM. (2003). Internet interventions: In review, in use, and into the future. *Professional Psychology: Research and Practice, 34*, 527–534.

Robinson E, Titov N, Andrews G, McIntyre K, Schwencke G, Solley K. (2010). Internet treatment for generalized anxiety disorder: A randomized controlled trial comparing clinician vs. technician assistance. *PloS ONE, 5*, e10942.

Rozental A, Andersson G, Boettcher J, Ebert D, Cuijpers P, Knaevelsrud C, Ljótsson B, Kaldo V, Titov N, Carlbring P. (2014). Consensus statement on defining and measuring negative effects of Internet interventions. *Internet Interventions, 1*, 12–19.

Ruwaard J, Lange A, Schrieken B, Emmelkamp P. (2011). Efficacy and effectiveness of online cognitive behavioral treatment: A decade of interapy research. *Studies in Health Technology and Informatics, 167*, 9–14.

Sanchez-Ortiz VC, Munro C, Startup H, Treasure J, Schmidt U. (2011). The role of email guidance in Internet-based cognitive-behavioural self-care treatment for bulimia nervosa. *European Eating Disorders Review, 19*, 342–348.

Sorbi MJ, van der Vaart R. (2010). User acceptance of an Internet training aid for migraine self-management. *Journal of Telemedicine and Telecare, 16*, 20–24.

Spek V, Cuijpers P, Nyklicek I, Riper H, Keyzer J, Pop V. (2007). Internet-based cognitive behaviour therapy for symptoms of depression and anxiety: A meta-analysis. *Psychological Medicine, 37*, 319–328.

Spence J, Titov N, Solley K, Dear BF, Johnston L, Wootton B, Kemp A, Andrews G, Zou J, Lorian C, Choi I. (2011). Characteristics and treatment preferences of people with symptoms of posttraumatic stress disorder: An Internet survey. *PloS ONE, 6*(7), e21864.

Stallard P, Richardson T, Velleman S. (2010). Clinicians' attitudes towards the use of computerized cognitive behaviour therapy (cCBT) with children and adolescents. *Behavioural and Cognitive Psychotherapy, 38*, 545–560.

Ström L, Pettersson R, Andersson G. (2000). A controlled trial of self-help treatment of recurrent headache conducted via the Internet. *Journal of Consulting and Clinical Psychology, 68*, 722–727.

Tarrier N, editor. (2006). *Case formulation in cognitive behaviour therapy*. London: Routledge.

Titov N. (2010). Email in low intensity CBT interventions. In J Bennett-Levy, H Christensen, P Farrand, K Griffiths, D Kavanagh, B Klein, M Lau, J Proudfoot, D Richards, J White, C Williams, editors. *Oxford guide to low intensity CBT interventions* (pp. 287–293). Oxford: Oxford University Press.

Titov N, Andrews G, Davies M, McIntyre K, Robinson E, Solley K. (2010a). Internet treatment for depression: A randomized controlled trial comparing clinician vs. technician assistance. *PloS ONE, 5*, e10939.

Titov N, Andrews G, Kemp A, Robinson E. (2010b). Characteristics of adults with anxiety or depression treated at an Internet clinic: Comparison with a national survey and an outpatient clinic. *PLoS ONE, 5*, e10885.

Titov N, Andrews G, Schwencke G, Solley K, Johnston L, Robinson E. (2009). An RCT comparing the effects of two types of support on severity of symptoms for people completing Internet-based cognitive behaviour therapy for social phobia. *Australian and New Zealand Journal of Psychiatry, 43*, 920–926.

Waller G. (2009). Evidence-based treatment and therapist drift. *Behaviour Research and Therapy, 47*, 119–127.

Wampold BE. (2001). *The great psychotherapy debate. Models, methods, and findings*. Mahwah, NJ: Lawrence Erlbaum.

Wangberg SC, Gammon D, Spitznogle K. (2007). In the eyes of the beholder: Exploring psychologists' attitudes towards and use of e-therapy in Norway. *Cyberpsychology & Behavior, 10*, 418–423.

Warmerdam L, Smit F, van Straten A, Riper H, Cuijpers P. (2010). Cost-utility and cost-effectiveness of Internet-based treatment for adults with depressive symptoms: Randomized trial. *Journal of Medical Internet Research, 12*(5), e53.

Watkins PL. (2008). Self-help therapies: Past and present. In PL Watkins, GA Clum, editors. *Handbook of self-help therapies* (pp. 1–24). New York: Routledge.

Webb CA, DeRubeis RJ, Barber JP. (2010). Therapist adherence/competence and treatment outcome: A meta-analytic review. *Journal of Consulting and Clinical Psychology, 78*, 200–211.

Wells M, Mitchell KJ, Finkelhor D, Becker-Blease KA. (2007). Online mental health treatment: concerns and considerations. *CyberPsychology & Behavior, 10*, 453–459.

Whitfield G, Williams C. (2004). If the evidence is so good – why doesn't anyone use them? A national survey of the use of computerized cognitive behaviour therapy. *Behavioural and Cognitive Psychotherapy, 32*, 57–65.

Wootton BM, Titov N, Dear BF, Spence J, Kemp A. (2011). The acceptability of Internet-based treatment and characteristics of an adult sample with obsessive compulsive disorder: An Internet survey. *PLoS ONE, 6*, e20548.

Zack JS. (2008). How sturdy is the digital couch? Legal considerations for mental health professionals who deliver clinical services via the Internet. *Journal of Technology in Human Services, 26*, 333–359.

📖 Further reading

Andersson G. (2010). The promise and pitfalls of the Internet for cognitive behavioural therapy. *BMC Medicine, 8,* 82.

Abbot J-AN, Klein B, Ciechomski L. (2008). Best practices in online therapy. *Journal of Technology in Human Services, 26,* 360–375.

Andersson G, Carlbring P, Berger T, Almlöv J, Cuijpers P. (2009). What makes Internet therapy work? *Cognitive Behaviour Therapy, 38*(S1), 55–60.

Dever Fitzgerald T, Hunter PV, Hadjistavropoulos T, Koocher, GP. (2010). Ethical and legal considerations for Internet-based psychotherapy. *Cognitive Behaviour Therapy, 39,* 173–187.

Chapter 7

Guided ICBT: Depression

What you will learn

In this chapter you will learn about:

- How depression can be treated using guided ICBT.
- The typical contents of the programs for depression and depressive symptoms.
- Use of tailoring treatment components.
- Effects of guided ICBT for depression in research.
- Effectiveness in clinical settings.
- Other approaches than CBT.

Introduction

Linda was depressed as a teenager when she had to change schools and move to another city together with her parents. She only vaguely remembered that period, which lasted a few months. Now she was in her late 30s and was happily married with two children and a stable economic situation. However, three months prior there had been a major reorganization at work and she now had developed depression. In fact, she had been off work and had taken vacation time but just stayed at home. She heard about the Internet psychiatry unit from a friend who had been treated for panic disorder and decided to contact the unit. As she lived in the Stockholm county region she was accepted immediately, and just four days later she was called in for an interview with a psychiatrist in training. He recommended Internet treatment as she did not feel like having medication, or rather said to herself, "I do not feel that bad". The next step occurred the week after the interview when she came back to the unit to see a psychologist. This psychologist interviewed her again and informed her about the depression program. She was also showed the system on the computer and the psychologist told her that she (the psychologist) would likely be the one who would guide her through the program. Although she had heard about Internet treatment previously, she did not know that it required a lot of work and that it basically was the same treatment as seeing a psychologist, except she would do it from a distance. She felt a bit anxious about the treatment as she felt very tired, but she was also encouraged to get going and get back to life again. She then worked with the program for 10 weeks, and in particular appreciated the behavioural activation parts. Working with her beliefs and thoughts felt a bit strange at first, but she discovered that she did indeed need to do that, in particular in relation to her work. It was arranged at the start of treatment for her to come back to the unit for a follow-up visit, and when she arrived more than two months later she felt much better. She felt that she had done most of the work herself, but the support from her therapist had been helpful, in particular at one point when she almost gave up when the activity scheduling had failed totally.

How can depression be treated using guided ICBT?

In this chapter we go into more detail regarding how guided ICBT programs for depression have been structured. Most readers are familiar with the diagnostic criteria for major depressive disorder as defined by the *DSM-IV* (APA, 2000). A reminder might however be in place. A person who suffers from major depressive disorder must have *significant* symptoms of depression. These include either a depressed mood or a loss of interest or pleasure in daily activities consistently (for at least a two-week period). The altered mood must represent a change from the person's normal functioning and cover many areas of life. Other symptoms such as weight loss when not dieting or weight gain; insomnia or hypersomnia; psychomotor agitation or retardation; fatigue or loss of energy; feelings of worthlessness or excessive or inappropriate guilt; diminished ability to think or concentrate, or indecisiveness; and recurrent thoughts of death or recurrent suicidal ideation without a specific plan, or a suicide attempt, or a specific plan for committing suicide can also be part of the depression. In addition, there should be no alternative better explanation (such as a medical condition), and the symptoms should be experienced nearly every day. Major depression is a debilitating and severe health problem.

The recommendations presented in Table 6.1 are also relevant when depression is the target. Thus, homework assignments, feedback on the homework and a deadline for completion are among the important aspects to include. In Table 7.1 an overview of a selection of programs that have all been tested in randomized controlled trials is presented. There are several other programs and versions of programs not covered in the table, but the focus here is on the ones below.

Deprexis was described in Chapter 5 as an unguided program, but it has been tested as a guided program as well with good results (Berger et al., 2011). MoodGYM has also been tested as a guided program (Farrer et al., 2011), but its main use is as an unguided program; the content was also described in Chapter 5. Here the focus is on the programs that are mainly delivered as guided ICBT. The Colour Your Life program from the Netherlands is also included here, as it has been used as a guided program in earlier research. In spite of a large number of trials being conducted on Internet-delivered treatments for depression (Richards & Richardson, 2012; Johansson & Andersson, 2012), there are relatively few programs that are meant to be mainly guided ICBT. Following are some comments on each of the programs listed in Table 7.1.

The first program we developed in Sweden (the *David program*) was based on both behavioural activation and cognitive restructuring, with an emphasis on behavioural activation. This is a purely text-based treatment and the text was later published as a self-help book (Andersson et al., 2007). The decision to include both behavioural activation and cognitive components was inspired by Lewinsohn's manual *Control Your Depression* (Lewinsohn et al., 1986), but we also incorporated cognitive restructuring (five-columns method), although we decided not to include work on core beliefs (Beck, 1995). The decision to include a module on insomnia was based on our understanding that this is a common co-morbid problem. In later updated versions of the treatment we included more information on goal planning and values, but the main ingredients have remained the same.

Table 7.1 Contents of different guided ICBT programs for depression

Program and country of origin	Duration and number of modules/lessons	Main contents	Mode of presentation	Reference example supporting use
Out of depression (DAVID) Sweden	Eight weeks Five separate modules (chapters) Later adapted to seven modules by Vernmark et al. (2010)	Psychoeducation Behavioural activation Cognitive techniques Insomnia and relapse prevention	Downloadable pdf files Guidance via email Homework assignments	Andersson et al., 2005
Relapse prevention program (ISIDOR) Sweden	10 weeks Nine basic modules and seven optional advanced modules with more specific information	Psychoeducation Adding positively reinforced activities Handling negatively reinforced activities Cognitive restructuring Improving sleep Mindfulness Reducing anxiety Physical activity Long-term goals	Downloadable pdf files and text on screen. Secure contact handling system for homework and guidance via that system	Holländare et al., 2011
Tailored Internet intervention for depression (Taylor) Sweden	Up to 10 weeks but flexible. 25 modules that are prescribed according to symptom profile Four modules are fixed: psychoeducation, cognitive restructuring and relapse prevention	Modules on depression, panic, social anxiety, worry, trauma, stress management, concentration problems, problem solving mindfulness and relaxation	As above	Johansson et al. (2012a)
Depressionshjälpen Sweden	Eight weeks Seven modules	Psychoeducation Link between activity and well-being Understanding different activities and the role of reinforcement	Modules with text, videos and narrated animations Interactive web page	Carlbring et al. (2013)

→

		Make a difference in your life Thoughts and emotions Repetition and continued practice Relapse prevention	CD with mindfulness and acceptance instructions Email support with the same contact handling system as above for handling homework	
Sadness program Australia	Eight weeks Six online lessons	Behavioural activation Cognitive restructuring Problem solving Assertiveness skills	Lessons online with illustrated case stories, printable summary, additional resource documents (text files on sleep, panic and other co-morbid problems) Therapist support via email, automated reminders	Perini et al., 2009
Wellbeing program Australia	10 weeks Eight online lessons	Transdiagnostic with a focus on depression Psychoeducation Cognitive therapy Control of physical symptoms Behavioural activation Graded exposure More on cognitive therapy (e.g., core beliefs) Problem solving Relapse prevention	Same as above, but with the addition of "Stories from the Frontline" (patient stories) and FAQ Online discussion forum for each lesson	Titov et al., 2011
Interapy depression Netherlands	11 weeks Eight treatment phases	Divided into phases with written instructions 1. Inducing awareness:	A personal interactive workbook is used by participants and	Ruwaard et al., 2009

→

		writing 2. Inducing awareness: monitoring 3. Structuring activities 4. Challenging negative thoughts 5. Behavioural experiments 6. Positive self-verbalization 7. Social skills 8. Relapse prevention	a manual with templates for therapists Communication via email (within the system) Homework assignments are included	
Colour Your Life Netherlands	Eight weeks Eight lessons and one follow-up lesson	Psychoeducation, cognitive restructuring, behaviour change, relaxation, social skills relapse prevention	Text, exercises, videos and illustrations Feedback from therapist possible	Warmerdam et al., 2008

It is important to update the manuals after each new study and also when the treatment is provided in clinic (in this case the Internet psychiatry unit in Stockholm). There may be unclear text segments, a need for better illustrations, a need for expanding or diminishing the length, and other components that may need updating. Although it may conflict with the importance of treatment manuals that remain stable, it is important to let the clinicians who work with the treatment give their input. This is the way we are working with the tailored intervention, for which there is a constant need for updated and new treatment modules.

The second program from Sweden presented in Table 7.1 is the ISIDOR program that was developed with the specific aim of preventing recurrence of depression in persons with at least one previous episode of depression. Since we knew that mindfulness-based cognitive therapy (Segal et al., 2002) had been found to be a promising treatment for preventing recurrence of depression (albeit with mixed findings), we decided to include mindfulness as a component in this treatment. The program was found to reduce the risk of relapse in a group of partially remitted patients (Holländare et al., 2011).

Given the co-morbidity between depression and other problems such as anxiety disorders and health-related concerns, we have developed an approach that involves tailoring the treatment material according to the clients' current concerns and problems, including preferences and motivation. As shown in Table 7.1, a range of treatment modules are included in this program. To date, the system involves computerized assessment and a clinical telephone interview that inform the tailoring. There are three fixed modules that should be included which deal with psychoeducation, cognitive restructuring and safety behaviours. A final module on relapse prevention is included for most clients. However, in between those modules the content can be tailored, including tailoring the number of modules, as clients vary in how much they can manage to complete within a given time frame.

The fourth program from Sweden, called *Depressionshjälpen*, was developed by the company Psykologpartners and is different from the previous Swedish depression programs as it involves less text and more interactive features. In particular it has a focus on behavioural activation, which is regarded as an evidence-based treatment for depression (Cuijpers et al., 2007a). This program has been tested in one controlled trial with good outcome (Carlbring et al., 2013).

The Sadness program from Australia differs from the more text-based Swedish programs. An example of how the program might appear is presented in Figure 7.1. In common with the other depression programs this one covers both behavioural and cognitive interventions as well as problem solving.

Topics covered in this summary

Here is a list of the topics we will cover in this summary.

Tick these off as you go, and please complete each part of this summary:

1. Depression explained
2. The Vicious cycle of depression
3. How is depression treated?
4. Medication
5. What are your symptoms of depression?
6. Summary

Figure 7.1 Example from the Australian Sadness program (**https://thiswayup.org.au/self-help/learn-about-self-help/depression/#Depression**).

Of more recent origin is the transdiagnostic Wellbeing program (Titov et al., 2011), which represents another way to handle co-morbidity between anxiety and mood disorders (Figure 7.2). This program has not been directly compared against a more depression-specific program, but holds promise in terms of effects and acceptability.

Interapy is a distinctly different program. As described in Table 7.1 this program is longer and involves many assignments including substantial therapist contact. Hence the treatment takes between 22 to 44 hours of client time and about 7 to 14 hours of therapist time. Given this, it is also not surprising that Interapy includes more treatment components.

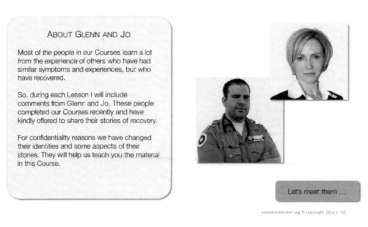

Figure 7.2 From the Wellbeing course.

Overall, however, the approach is similar to most guided ICBT interventions as the therapeutic contact is asynchronous and the program is intended to work via mainly text.

There are many more depression programs and the number increases steadily. However, the ones covered here are probably the most researched ones. As evident from the review they differ in content but share common CBT components. We now turn to the overall evidence for ICBT for depression.

The effects of guided ICBT for depression

Systematic reviews and meta-analyses

Just as the number of studies is growing rapidly, there is a parallel activity going on in which the evidence is summarized. Several systematic reviews and meta-analyses have been published, but most often ICBT has not been the sole focus of the reviews that tend to cover other computerized interventions. One such example was a meta-analytic review published by me and my colleague in Amsterdam, professor Pim Cuijpers (Andersson & Cuijpers, 2009). Following a literature search and coding, we included 12 studies with a total of 2,446 participants. Ten of the 12 studies were delivered via the Internet. The mean effect size of the 15 comparisons between Internet-based and other computerized psychological treatments versus control groups at post-test was $d = 0.41$. However, this may not be a representative figure as the effect was moderated by a significant difference between supported ($d = 0.61$) and unsupported ($d = 0.25$) treatments.

In a more recent meta-analytic review Richards and Richardson (2012) found a similar effect size of $d = 0.56$ (based on 19 studies). In line with the Andersson and Cuijpers (2009) paper, supported interventions yielded better outcomes along with greater retention. Johansson and Andersson (2012) also conducted a systematic review but focused only on ICBT interventions. While we did not conduct a formal meta-analysis in that review we calculated effect sizes. A clear linear relation was seen between degree of support and outcome (Spearman correlation of $p = 0.64$). Studies with no therapist contact either before or during treatment had an effect of $d = 0.21$, contact with the client only before the treatment an effect of $d = 0.44$, contact during treatment only an effect of $d = 0.58$ and contact both before and during treatment an effect of $d = 0.76$ (Johansson & Andersson, 2012).

ICBT versus face-to-face therapy for depression

One crucial question when presenting ICBT as a treatment option is how well the effects compare with those of face-to-face treatment. Fairly few studies exist, but the ones available most often indicate that effects are about the same, as found in the overall review by Cuijpers et al. (2010). Spek et al. (2007) studied a total of 201 persons with subthreshold depression which they randomized to ICBT, group cognitive behaviour therapy, or a waiting-list control condition. This is by far the largest comparative trial on face-to-face versus ICBT for depressive symptoms. Results showed that both active treatments were effective (actually the effect size for ICBT was $d = 1.0$ and group CBT $d = 0.65$), and there were no significant differences between the two. Both active treatments were better than the control group. It is important to note that this study focused on subthreshold depression and not diagnosed major depression. In a smaller comparative trial from our group we randomly allocated participants with mild to moderate depression to either guided ICBT ($n = 33$) or to live group treatment ($n = 36$) (Andersson et al., 2013b). Follow-ups were conducted at one year and three years after the treatment ended, making this ICBT versus live treatment study the one with the longest follow-up period in which randomization has been maintained. Within-group effect sizes for the ICBT condition at post-treatment showed a Cohen's $d = 1.46$, with a similar large effect at three-year follow-up, $d = 1.78$. For the group CBT the corresponding within-group effects were $d = 0.99$ and $d = 1.34$, respectively. Overall, there was no indication suggesting that guided ICBT should be inferior to group CBT.

More on individual studies

One interesting aspect of ICBT is that research trials have been conducted in many countries and the research is not dominated by the United States. One of the earliest controlled trials on guided ICBT for depression was the trial conducted by our group in Sweden (Andersson et al., 2005). Swedish researchers have since then completed additional trials which all point in the same direction, with large between-group effects against waiting-list control groups.

One of the more recent additions to the literature was the trial testing tailored treatment according to the symptoms reported by the participant (Johansson et al., 2012). In that trial, with a total of 121 participants, we compared tailored treatment to non-tailored "standard" ICBT, and also included a control group in the form of a monitored online discussion group. In addition to having diagnosed major depressive disorder, participants also presented with a range of co-morbid symptoms. This is a common finding among persons with depression, who very often have co-morbid problems such as insomnia and anxiety. As with many ICBT studies the duration of the treatments was short, lasting for only 10 weeks. As presented in Table 7.1 there were 25 different treatment modules to choose from in the tailored treatment, but three were fixed and given to all participants in the tailored condition. As expected, both active treatment groups improved and results were maintained at a six-month follow-up. We then went further and tested differences between subgroups in the trial. These analyses showed that the tailored treatment was more effective than the standardized treatment for the participants with higher levels of depression at baseline (who also had more co-morbid problems), both in terms of reduction of depressive symptoms and on recovery rates. This study suggests that tailored treatment can be better for more complicated depression cases with additional symptoms.

Another way to handle co-morbidity is to have less diagnosis-specific treatments. In Table 7.1 the contents of the transdiagnostic Wellbeing program are briefly presented. One advantage of transdiagnostic programs is that they present the core treatment components that are likely to be useful for persons both with or without co-morbidity. Several studies have been done on this program (e.g., Johnston et al., 2011), although this specific version was adapted for the treatment of depression (Titov et al., 2011). There are additional innovative aspects of the Wellbeing program. As it is described in the research paper it includes eight online lessons, a summary/homework assignment for each lesson, and an online discussion forum for each lesson. Regular automatic reminders and notification emails are also included.

What is highly interesting from a tailored versus transdiagnostic perspective is that the researchers provided access to additional written resources about such things as assertiveness skills, health anxiety and strategies for improving sleep. In order to add credibility and also resolve issues they provided answers to frequently asked questions about the application of skills described in the lessons, and also access to the "Stories from the Frontline", which is a collection of forum posts written by participants in previous ICBT programs covering topics relevant to the treatment. To my knowledge this approach has not been used previously, and does raise some ethical issues which require that the postings be altered to secure anonymity.

The Australian research group with Titov and Andrews as the senior researchers has done several innovative studies, and one additional example is a trial in which they investigated the efficacy and acceptability of ICBT for Chinese Australians with depression. They translated their Sadness program and culturally adapted it for the Chinese population (Choi et al., 2012). Participants were randomized to either treatment or waiting list. In addition to the translated Sadness program, they provided additional text modules and weekly telephone clinical support in Mandarin or Cantonese. They found large treatment effects with a between-group effect size of $d = 0.93$, for the depression measure.

There are other examples of translated ICBT programs for other conditions (Wagner et al., 2012), and in Sweden we have conducted a trial with Kurdish immigrants for which we translated our depression program into Kurdish. The trial had a between-group effect of $d = 1.29$ for the depression outcome measure (Brohede & Koshnaw, 2012).

Another important concern regarding guided ICBT for depression is how well the treatment works for different age groups. In addition to the trial by Spek et al. (2007) on older adults with subclinical depression, there is an open trial on a brief ICBT program called *"Managing Your Mood Programme"*, which was tested for 20 older adults in Australia and found to be effective (Dear et al., 2013).

With regard to adolescents and children much less has been done on guided ICBT for depression, but there are exceptions such as a trial by van der Zanden et al. (2012). This Dutch group tested the effectiveness of a guided Web-based group course Master Your Mood with a large group of 244 young people with depressive symptoms (aged 16 to 25 years). This trial was not restricted to diagnosed depression. Results showed that the treated participants improved more than a control group, with a large between-group effect size of $d = 0.94$.

Depression is a condition in which relapse is common. Hence there is a need to develop cost-effective treatments that can prevent the recurrence of depression. The ISIDOR program described in Table 7.1 is an example of such a program. Holländare et al. (2011) conducted a study with 84 individuals who had residual symptoms of depression and who had been treated for a depressive episode previously. The treatment lasted for 10 weeks and participants were randomly assigned to either ICBT or a control group. Results showed that significantly fewer participants in the CBT group experienced relapse in depression compared with those in the control group. Effects were also found at a six-month follow-up, and there is also a two-year follow-up (Holländare et al., 2013). This study is unique in that it is the first to show that guided ICBT can prevent relapse in depression.

Another Swedish program was recently tested by Carlbring et al. (2013). As seen in Table 7.1 this treatment is based on behavioural activation and includes components of mindfulness and acceptance-based CBT. In the trial 80 individuals were randomized to treatment or to waiting-list control. The treatment lasted for eight weeks, and a three-month follow-up was also reported. While the treatment was more interactive and less text based than previous treatments from our group, the between-group effect size was $d = 0.98$ for the main depression measure outcome (Beck Depression Inventory, BDI). This suggests that guided ICBT can include less text and still be effective.

There is at least one controlled study on the Interapy treatment for depression, developed in the Netherlands. The program is described in Table 7.1 and in the text. Fifty-four persons with depression were included in the trial and the researchers reported an 18-month follow-up. They randomized participants into immediate treatment for 13 weeks or to a wait-list control condition. Results at post treatment showed effects in line with other reports with a between-group effect size $d = 0.70$ on the BDI.

Colour Your Life is the Dutch program that has also been tested as an unguided treatment (see previous chapter). Warmerdam et al. (2008) did a controlled study on participants with depressive symptoms and compared CWD with problem-solving therapy and a third waiting list control group (total N = 263). The authors found moderate effect sizes at 12-week follow-up between the two active treatments and the control conditions (Cohen's d = 0.69 for the CBT condition and d = 0.65 for the problem-solving therapy group). An adapted version of the Colour Your Life program was tested in a controlled trial on depression in patients with diabetes (N = 255). Results showed a small between-group effect size when the treatment was compared against a waiting list control condition (d = 0.29) (van Bastelaar et al., 2011).

Although many programs have generated about the same effects (e.g., moderate to large effects when compared to waiting lists), this conclusion is not definitive as there are very few direct comparisons between programs. In the few studies available it has rather been the case that distinctly different treatments have been compared. One example is a trial by Vernmark et al. (2010), in which email-based (individualized) treatment was compared against the less time-consuming guided self-help. Studies in which guided ICBT has been compared against face-to-face treatment have been mentioned previously, but it is still not known if different ICBT programs differ in effects.

Long-term effects

Many studies on guided ICBT have included fairly short follow-up periods such as six months. There are however a few studies in which longer-term outcomes have been reported. A follow-up 3.5 years after treatment completion was however done with the participants in the trial by Vernmark et al. (2010). A total of 58% (51/88) completed the follow-up, and results showed continued lowered scores on the Beck Depression Inventory (BDI), and a majority (56.9%) had a BDI score lower than 10 (Andersson et al., 2013a). I have already mentioned our more recently completed comparative trial on guided ICBT versus group CBT, in which we included a three-year follow-up (Andersson et al., 2013b). The Interapy study included an 18-month follow-up and the authors found that the effects were sustained (Ruwaard et al., 2009). The study by Spek and co-workers (2007) was followed by a one-year follow-up (Spek et al., 2008), and they found a large pre-treatment to follow-up effect (d = 1.22). Overall, there are few follow-up studies on guided ICBT for depression.

Effectiveness

Research on CBT has been criticized for not being representative for patients seen in regular clinical settings. The distinction between efficacy studies and effectiveness studies basically is that the latter involves regular patients seen in regular settings by regular therapists. Efficacy studies more often consist of participants recruited via advertisements, seen in university or lab settings, and treated by either experts or students. An overwhelming majority of research studies on ICBT has been in the form of efficacy studies, and there are fewer studies that are based on data from regular clinical settings where ICBT is delivered as part of routine care. This topic is explored later in this book, but for now the conclusion is that there are little data available on ICBT for depression in regular care.

One exception to this is the Interapy treatment for which Ruwaard and colleagues (2012) reported effectiveness data. A total of 405 patients treated for depression were included in the report. One-year follow-up data was also reported. Within-group effects were as large as in efficacy trials, with an effect size of d = 1.9 for the BDI at post-test and 1.8 between pre-treatment to one-year follow-up. More studies on the effectiveness of ICBT for depression will likely appear in the near future.

Another recent example is a trial on the Sadness programme from Australia. Williams and Andrews (2013) reported data on 359 patients who had been prescribed with the Sadness programme in a primary care context (e.g., routine practice). Large within-group effects were seen on the PHQ-9 ($d = 0.97$), and in a subgroup analysis even larger effects were seen for more patients with more severe depression ($d = 1.49$). In line with many ICBT studies there was a significant proportion who did not complete the full program (54% completed all six lessons). However, a proportion of clients who did not complete the full program also tended to benefit if they had at least completed four lessons. Fewer of those who only completed two or three lessons benefited from the program. Thus there was a dose-response relationship.

The most recent effectiveness study is from Sweden (Hedman et al., 2014). We investigated the outcomes of all patients ($N = 1203$) who had received guided ICBT for depression between 2007 and 2013 at the Internet Psychiatry Unit in Stockholm, Sweden. The Montgomery Åsberg Depression Rating Scale-Self rated showed large improvements from pretreatment assessments to post treatment ($d = 1.27$). This is probably the largest study to date on ICBT for depression in regular care.

For whom is it suitable and what is special about depression?

Most studies on ICBT for depression have involved research participants who have been recruited via advertisements. Studies generally have strict inclusion criteria which can lead to less variation in patient characteristics, which could influence outcome. For example, almost all studies on guided ICBT for depression have excluded participants who show signs of suicidal ideation. This is of course for ethical reasons, as ICBT may not be a suitable alternative for these persons. However, it may also be that too many are excluded who could have benefitted from ICBT with no risk of their suicidal ideation becoming worse. It is known that psychological treatment can reduce hopelessness, which is a risk factor for suicide (Cuijpers et al., 2013).

There are ongoing studies on ICBT for persons with suicidal ideation, and clinical studies suggesting that suicidal ideation decreases following ICBT (Watts et al., 2012), but more research is needed. A vast majority of clients who have suicidal ideas and even plans never commit suicide. The Internet can be used for monitoring symptoms such as suicidal thoughts, reducing the risk of missing detecting when a client feels worse. Such monitoring is a standard feature of the Internet Psychiatry Unit at Karolinska University Hospital in Stockholm.

Few studies have been published on predictors of treatment outcome in ICBT for depression, although some data are presented in the trials. There are few reports of significant associations with outcome. Vernmark et al. (2010) found that there were no effects of pre-treatment medication status, gender or presence of co-morbidity. In addition, there was no correlation between change on the BDI and age, computer knowledge, previous treatment or any other of the pre-treatment variables in that trial and there was no correlation between outcome and number of modules completed in the guided self-help treatment.

In a secondary report of the first Swedish depression trial (e.g., Andersson et al., 2005), we analyzed data from 71 participants who completed a six-month follow-up (Andersson et al., 2004). A small but statistically significant negative correlation between the number of previous depression episodes and outcome was found (rho = −0.24), indicating that participants who had few previous episodes benefitted more from ICBT. Spek et al. (2008) also investigated predictors of treatment outcome in their trial and found that higher baseline BDI scores, female gender and lower neuroticism scores predicted better outcome after ICBT. The latter finding is interesting as it suggests that ICBT for depression is less suitable for persons with high scores on the personality dimension neuroticism. However, in a more recent paper reporting effects of ICBT on personality dimensions as measured by the Temperament and Character Inventory (TCI) (Cloninger et al., 1993), it was found that the dimensions of *Harm avoidance* and *Self-directedness* changed following ICBT (Johansson et al., 2013a), but the effects were related to improvement in depression rather than a direct effect of ICBT.

One clinical impression is that depressed persons may be in greater need of guidance than is the case for some other conditions. Depression may be associated with "giving up" and if there are no obvious direct consequences (which is the case when there is no therapist contact) there is a great risk of dropping out from treatment. However, it is interesting to note that the therapeutic alliance is not associated with treatment outcome in depression (see Chapter 6).

Another important aspect of managing depression in regular clinical settings is the role of concurrent antidepressant medication. Pim Cuijpers and colleagues have showed in a series of meta-analyses that combined psychotherapy and antidepressant medication is better than the monotherapies (Cuijpers et al., 2011). In many trials on ICBT concurrent medication has been allowed if it has been stabilized, but the actual effects of combined ICBT plus antidepressant medication have not been tested in controlled trials.

What about other approaches?

While the focus of this book is on ICBT, there are some Internet trials on depression treatment that originate from different theoretical perspectives. One example is a trial from my research group in which we used a psychodynamic self-help book, *Make the Leap* (Silverberg, 2005). In that study 92 individuals with depression were randomised to treatment or an active control. The treatment consisted of nine treatment modules based on psychodynamic principles (e.g., the *Make the Leap* book adapted for use with depressed clients) with online therapist contact. The active control condition was a structured support intervention and contained psychoeducation and scheduled weekly contacts online. Both interventions lasted for 10 weeks. Results showed large and superior improvements in the treatment group compared to the active control group (between-group Cohen's $d = 1.11$). Treatment effects were maintained at a 10-month follow-up.

It is interesting to note that it has been possible to transfer a treatment format originating from the CBT tradition (ICBT) to other theoretical orientations. Because many elements (diagnostic procedures, mainly text-based delivery, etc.) are similar, direct comparative trials are needed to determine if different approaches (e.g., psychodynamic versus CBT) yield similar outcomes.

Another way to study this is to let the client decide. In a small pilot study we investigated this question. For the waiting-list group participants in the psychodynamic trial we let the participants choose treatment. More than half preferred ICBT ($n = 30$) over the psychodynamic Internet treatment ($n = 14$). While differences in outcomes were small, there was a clear tendency for the ICBT group to perform better at follow-up. Exploratory analyses indicated that strength of preference was correlated with adherence to treatment and completion of the whole program and long-term outcome for the ICBT group (Johansson et al., 2013b).

There are other approaches that have also been tested for treating depression using the Internet as a treatment format. As mentioned in this chapter, Warmerdam et al. (2008)

compared ICBT against problem-solving therapy and found that it was as effective as ICBT. This is not a surprising finding as meta-analyses have confirmed that problem-solving therapy can work for depression (Cuijpers et al., 2007b), but it is possible that this treatment format could be regarded as a form of CBT as it is sometimes included in CBT as practiced in regular clinical settings.

Practical implications and key points

- Guided ICBT has been found to work for mild to moderate depression and several different programs have been tested.

- Effects are often in line with what can be found in face-to-face therapy for depression, but there is yet little data and few robust predictors of outcome that would inform treatment recommendations.

- Several new ideas have been tested in research on guided ICBT such as tailored treatment, psychodynamic treatment and letting the client decide based on preferences.

- While there is emerging evidence that guided ICBT works in regular clinical settings it is thus far less well established how well ICBT works for more severe conditions and for other mood disorders such as bipolar disorder.

- It is not yet known if ICBT would work together with antidepressant medication and if this combined treatment, in line with what has been found for face-to-face CBT, is better than monotherapies.

References

American Psychiatric Association (APA). (2000). *Diagnostic and statistical manual of mental disorders* (4th ed., text revision ed.). Washington, DC: American Psychiatric Press.

Andersson G, Bergström J, Holländare F, Carlbring P, Kaldo V, Ekselius L. (2005). Internet-based self-help for depression: A randomised controlled trial. *British Journal of Psychiatry, 187*, 456–461.

Andersson G, Bergström J, Holländare F, Ekselius L, Carlbring P. (2004). Delivering CBT for mild to moderate depression via the Internet. Predicting outcome at 6-months follow-up. *Verhaltenstherapie, 14*, 185–189.

Andersson G, Bergström J, Holländare F, Lenndin J, Vernmark K. (2007). *Ut ur depression och nedstämdhet med kognitiv beteendeterapi [Out of depression and low mood]*. Stockholm: Viva.

Andersson G, Cuijpers P. (2009). Internet-based and other computerized psychological treatments for adult depression: A meta-analysis. *Cognitive Behaviour Therapy, 38*, 196–205.

Andersson G, Hesser H, Hummerdal D, Bergman-Nordgren L, Carlbring P. (2013a). A 3.5-year follow-up of Internet-delivered cognitive behaviour therapy for major depression. *Journal of Mental Health, 22,* 155–164.

Andersson G, Hesser H, Veilord A, Svedling L, Andersson F, Sleman O, Mauritzson L, Sarkohi A, Claesson E, Zetterqvist V, Lamminen M, Eriksson T, Carlbring P. (2013b). Randomized controlled non-inferiority trial with 3-year follow-up of Internet-delivered versus face-to-face group cognitive behavioural therapy for depression. *Journal of Affective Disorders, 151*, 986–994.

Beck JS. (1995). *Cognitive therapy: Basics and beyond*. New York: Guilford Press.

Berger T, Hämmerli K, Gubser N, Andersson G, Caspar F. (2011). Internet-based treatment of depression: A randomized controlled trial comparing guided with unguided self-help. *Cognitive Behaviour Therapy, 40*, 251–266.

Brohede D, Koshnaw K. (2012). SAFIN. En randomiserad kontrollerad studie av en KBT-baserad depressionsbehandling på kurdiska via Internet. (Examensuppsats på psykologprogrammet). Institutionen för Beteendevetenskap och Lärande, Linköpings universitet [SAFIN. A randomized controlled trial of ICBT in the Kurdish language Sorani].

Carlbring P, Hägglund M, Luthström A, Dahlin M, Kadowaki Å, Vernmark K, Andersson G. (2013). Internet-based behavioral activation and acceptance-based treatment for depression: A randomized controlled trial. *Journal of Affective Disorders, 148*, 331–337.

Choi I, Zou J, Titov N, Dear BF, Li S, Johnston L, Andrews G, Hunt C. (2012). Culturally attuned Internet treatment for depression amongst Chinese Australians: A randomised controlled trial. *Journal of Affective Disorders, 136*, 459–468.

Cloninger CR, Svrakic DM, Przybeck TR. (1993). A psychobiological model of temperament and character. *Archives of General Psychiatry, 50*, 975–990.

Cuijpers P, Andersson G, Donker T, van Straten A. (2011). Psychological treatments of depression: Results of a series of meta-analyses. *Nordic Journal of Psychiatry, 65*, 354–364.

Cuijpers P, de Beurs DP, van Spijker BAJ, Berking M, Andersson G, Kerkhof AJFM. (2013). The effects of psychotherapy for adult depression on suicidality and hopelessness: A systematic review and meta-analysis. *Journal of Affective Disorders, 144*, 183–190.

Cuijpers P, Donker T, van Straten A, Andersson G. (2010). Is guided self-help as effective as face-to-face psychotherapy for depression and anxiety disorders? A meta-analysis of comparative outcome studies. *Psychological Medicine, 40*, 1943–1957.

Cuijpers P, van Straten A, Warmerdam L. (2007a). Behavioral activation treatments of depression: A meta-analysis. *Clinical Psychology Review, 27*, 318–326.

Cuijpers P, van Straten A, Warmerdam L. (2007b). Problem solving therapies for depression: A meta-analysis. *European Psychiatry, 22*, 9–15.

Dear BF, Zou J, Titov N, Lorian C, Johnston L, Spence, et al. (2013). Internet-delivered cognitive behavioural therapy for depression: A feasibility open trial for older adults. *Australian and New Zealand Journal of Psychiatry, 47*, 169–176.

Farrer L, Christensen H, Griffiths KM, Mackinnon A. (2011). Internet-based CBT for depression with and without telephone tracking in a national helpline: randomised controlled trial. *PLoS ONE, 6*, e28099.

Hedman E, Ljótsson B, Kaldo V, Hesser H, El Alaoui S, Kraepelin M, Andersson E, Rück C, Svanborg C, Andersson G, Lindefors N. (2014). Effectiveness of Internet-based cognitive behaviour therapy for depression in routine psychiatric care. *Journal of Affective Disorders, 155*, 49–58.

Holländare F, Johnsson S, Randestad M, Tillfors M, Carlbring P, Andersson G, Engström I. (2011). Randomized trial of Internet-based relapse prevention for partially remitted depression. *Acta Psychiatrica Scandinavica, 124*, 285–294.

Holländare F, Johnsson S, Randestad M, Tillfors M, Carlbring P, Andersson G, Engström I. (2013). Two-year outcome for Internet-based relapse prevention for partially remitted depression. *Behaviour Research and Therapy, 51*, 719–722.

Johansson R, Andersson G. (2012). Internet-based psychological treatments for depression. *Expert Review of Neurotherapeutics, 12*, 861–870.

Johansson R, Lyssarides C, Andersson G, Rousseau A. (2013a). Personality change after Internet-delivered cognitive behavior therapy for depression. *PeerJ, 1*, e39.

Johansson R, Nyblom A, Carlbring P, Cuijpers P, Andersson G. (2013b). Choosing between Internet-based psychodynamic versus cognitive behavioral therapy for depression: A pilot preference study. *Submitted*.

Johansson R, Sjöberg E, Sjögren M, Johnsson E, Carlbring P, Andersson T, Rousseau A, Andersson G. (2012). Tailored vs. standardized Internet-based cognitive behavior therapy for depression and comorbid symptoms: A randomized controlled trial. *PLoS ONE, 7*, e36905.

Johnston L, Titov N, Andrews G, Spence J, Dear BF. (2011). A RCT of a transdiagnostic Internet-delivered treatment for three anxiety disorders: Examination of support roles and disorder-specific outcomes. *PLoS ONE, 6*, e28079.

Lewinsohn PM, Munoz RF, Youngren MA, Zeiss MA. (1986). *Control your depression*. New York: Prentice Hall.

Perini S, Titov N, Andrews G. (2009). Clinician-assisted Internet-based treatment is effective for depression: Randomized controlled trial. *The Australian and New Zealand Journal of Psychiatry, 43*, 571–578.

Richards D, Richardson T. (2012). Computer-based psychological treatments for depression: A systematic review and meta-analysis. *Clinical Psychology Review, 32*, 329–342.

Ruwaard J, Lange A, Schrieken B, Dolan CV, Emmelkamp P. (2012). The effectiveness of online cognitive behavioral treatment in routine clinical practice. *PLoS ONE, 7*(7), e40089.

Ruwaard J, Schrieken B, Schrijver M, Broeksteeg J, Dekker J, Vermeulen H, Alfred Lange A. (2009). Standardized web-based CBT of mild to moderate depression: A randomized controlled trial with a long-term follow-up. *Cognitive Behaviour Therapy, 38*, 206–221.

Segal ZV, Williams JMG, Teasdale JD. (2002). *Mindfulness-based cognitive therapy for depression*. New York: Routledge.

Silverberg F. (2005). *Make the leap. A practical guide to breaking the patterns that hold you back*. New York: Marlowe & Company.

Spek V, Cuijpers P, Nyklicek I, Smits N, Riper H, Keyzer J, Pop V. (2008). One-year follow-up results of a randomized controlled clinical trial on Internet-based cognitive behavioural therapy for subthreshold depression in people over 50 years. *Psychological Medicine, 38*, 635–639.

Spek V, Nyklicek I, Cuijpers P, Pop V. (2008). Predictors of outcome of group and Internet-based cognitive behavior therapy. *Journal of Affective Disorders, 105*, 137–145.

Spek V, Nyklicek I, Smits N, Cuijpers P, Riper H, Keyzer J, Pop, V. (2007). Internet-based cognitive behavioural therapy for subthreshold depression in people over 50 years old: A randomized controlled clinical trial. *Psychological Medicine, 37*, 1797–1806.

Titov N, Dear BF, Schwencke G, Andrews G, Johnston L, Craske MG, McEvoy P. (2011). Transdiagnostic Internet treatment for anxiety and depression: a randomised controlled trial. *Behaviour Research and Therapy, 49*, 441–452.

van Bastelaar KM, Pouwer F, Cuijpers P, Riper H, Snoek FJ. (2011). Web-based depression treatment for type 1 and type 2 diabetic patients: A randomized, controlled trial. *Diabetes Care, 34*, 320–325.

van der Zanden R, Kramer J, Gerrits R, Cuijpers P. (2012). Effectiveness of an online group course for depression in adolescents and young adults: A randomized trial. *Journal of Medical Internet Research, 14*, e86.

Vernmark K, Lenndin J, Bjärehed J, Carlsson M, Karlsson J, Öberg J, Carlbring P, Eriksson T, Andersson G. (2010). Internet administered guided self-help versus individualized e-mail therapy: A randomized trial of two versions of CBT for major depression. *Behaviour Research and Therapy, 48*, 368–376.

Wagner B, Schulz W, Knaevelsrud C. (2012). Efficacy of an Internet-based intervention for posttraumatic stress disorder in Iraq: A pilot study. *Psychiatry Research, 195*, 85–88.

Warmerdam L, van Straten A, Twisk J, Riper H, Cuijpers P. (2008). Internet-based treatment for adults with depressive symptoms: Randomized controlled trial. *Journal of Medical Internet Research, 10*, e44.

Watts S, Newby JM, Mewton L, Andrews G. (2012). A clinical audit of changes in suicide ideas with Internet treatment for depression. *BMJ Open, 2*, e001558.

Williams AD, Andrews G. (2013). The effectiveness of Internet cognitive behavioural therapy (iCBT) for depression in primary care: a quality assurance study. *PLoS ONE, 8*, e57447.

📖 Further reading

Marks IM, Cavanagh K, Gega L. (2007). *Hands-on help. Maudsley monograph no. 49*. Hove: Psychology Press.

Martell CR, Dimidjian S, Herman-Dunn R. (2010). *Behavioral activation for depression. A clinician's guide*. New York: Guilford Press.

Persons JB, Davidson J, Tompkins MA. (2001). *Essential components of cognitive-behavior therapy for depression*. Washington, DC: American Psychological Association.

Williams C, Whitfield G. (2001). Written and computer-based self-help treatments for depression. *British Medical Bulletin, 57*, 133–144.

Chapter 8

Guided ICBT: Anxiety disorders

What you will learn

In this chapter you will learn about:

- How anxiety disorders can be effectively treated with guided ICBT.
- Contents of a range of programs for anxiety disorders.
- The potential role of tailored ICBT and treatment based on unified protocol.
- Effects in research and in clinical settings.
- Other approaches and future challenges.

Introduction

Pierre has suffered from social anxiety for as long as he can remember. The anxiety has influenced his life to such an extent that he has declined job offers and strongly feels that he is below his level of competence at work, since he avoids giving presentations and engaging in social activities with his colleagues. To his surprise he has found a girlfriend he trusts (and stayed together with for almost a year), and they are about to get married. Pierre tried psychotherapy and medication earlier in his life (he is now in his 40s) but neither helped him, with the possible exception of medication, since he was depressed at the time he received antidepressant and became better. The psychotherapy was insight oriented, which is not surprising since he lives in Switzerland, where CBT was not easily available. While he had found the therapy somewhat useful it had not helped him with his social fears. He now saw an advertisement for a trial on online CBT for social phobia and decided to apply. While he knew a bit about CBT for social phobia, he had never tried it. The Internet format suited him well as he worked in the information technology (IT) business. Progress with the program came slowly but steadily. Pierre was strongly encouraged by his girlfriend who he kept informed about the treatment. When the study period ended he had completed most of the assignments and exposure exercises and what surprised him the most was the fact that things had worked out so well at work. In a sense he had been a bit lucky as there had been some reorganization at work, and he had new colleagues which made it a bit easier to act in different ways than previously at work. In particular, he found the social skills advice useful but also the information on safety behaviours. He still experienced some anxiety when talking to colleagues but much less so and more importantly this anxiety did not provoke avoidance of social situations.

Guided ICBT for anxiety disorders

This chapter provides an overview of programs that have been developed and tested for a range of anxiety disorders. As in the previous chapter on depression treatments there are many programs available, but only a minority have been tested rigorously in research. These latter programs are the focus of this chapter. A comprehensive list of all ICBT programs for anxiety (included the ones with no evidence base) would be difficult to compile. However, there are a number of ICBT programs for anxiety disorders that have been tested for most common anxiety disorders.

As described in Chapter 6, the treatment format of guided ICBT involves therapist contact on a regular basis. The contact is often asynchronous and in general the way the ICBT programs are set up reflects the way CBT is done with patients with anxiety disorders. ICBT treatments for anxiety have been derived from treatment manuals in the field of CBT for anxiety, or at least inspired by such treatment protocols.

As for depression, there is a parallel literature on guided text-based self-help (bibliotherapy) and computerized CBT, both of which are important precursors of guided ICBT. As with CBT for anxiety disorder in general there are certain components that are needed for the treatment to work. For example, homework completion is probably crucial, and CBT clinicians may pause here and reflect on the importance of client activities outside of the therapy room. Another probable requirement is that the client must be provided a treatment rationale and be willing to experience aversive feelings in order to improve (e.g., in order for the exposure to work). A third consideration is the role of the therapist when treating anxiety disorders. In particular, when things do not work out as planned it may be crucial for the client to have a therapist to ask questions and to guide the client further.

We next discuss the different anxiety disorders covered in this chapter. Bearing in mind that co-morbidity is the rule rather than the exception, it is still the case that clients with diagnosed anxiety disorders have been found to respond very well to guided ICBT. For each condition a brief introduction of the condition is provided (e.g., social anxiety disorder) followed by a description of the treatment programs. Commentary on the research support for each program is given, as we are dealing with many conditions and programs. Questions regarding effects of ICBT versus face-to-face CBT are addressed, and where available the evidence regarding effectiveness will be given (i.e., if guided ICBT works in clinically representative conditions).

Panic disorder

We begin with a reminder on what panic disorder is. Panic disorder is an anxiety disorder characterized by recurrent and unexpected panic attacks. A panic attack is defined as a discrete period of intense fear or discomfort in the absence of real danger. In the *DSM-IV* a panic attack is further defined as being accompanied by at least four of 13 somatic or cognitive symptoms developed abruptly and reaching a peak within 10 minutes (APA, 2000). Symptoms can include sweating, palpitations, trembling, feeling of choking, nausea, dizziness, depersonalization, fear of losing control and fear of dying. Recurrent, unexpected panic attacks are required for a diagnosis of panic disorder (with or without agoraphobia) (APA, 2000). The attacks should be followed by at least one month of persistent concern about having another attack and/or worry about the possible implications or consequences of the attacks and/or significant behavioural change related to the attacks. The frequency and severity of panic attacks may vary among individuals suffering from panic disorder, but when a diagnosis can be confirmed it is likely that the individual suffers from a debilitating condition with marked negative consequences for quality of life (Taylor, 2006). Panic disorder is a common disorder with a lifetime prevalence of 1.5 to 3.5% (Taylor, 2000).

Research on guided ICBT for panic disorder has been conducted since the late 1990s, making panic disorder one of the conditions for which we have the longest experience. Table 8.1 presents an overview of five programs for panic disorder that have been tested in research. One of the first ICBT programs for panic disorder was developed by the late Jeff Richards and his group in Australia (Klein & Richards, 2001). The *Panic online* program has been updated and expanded from its first version. For example, in one version stress management was included (Richards et al., 2006). The program includes six modules and contains controlled breathing, progressive muscle relaxation, cognitive restructuring and interoceptive and situational exposure. It ends with relapse prevention. This program has been found to work in efficacy studies with psychologists doing the guidance and with general practitioners providing guidance in a study that could be regarded as an effectiveness study (Shandley et al., 2008). It has been found to be as effective as face-to-face CBT (Kiropoulos et al., 2008). This last study included 86 persons with panic disorder who were randomized to either ICBT ($n = 46$) or face-to-face CBT ($n = 40$). Effects were similar and both treatments lead to significant reductions in panic disorder symptoms and related problems. Interestingly, both treatments were rated as credible and satisfying but the contact with the therapist was more appreciated in the face-to-face condition. However, as expected ICBT required significantly less therapist time than the face-to-face treatment.

In Australia a second research group (Gavin Andrews and Nick Titov), has more recently developed a program for panic disorder which has been tested in one controlled trial (Wims et al., 2010) and found to be effective. There are to my knowledge no effectiveness studies or comparisons with face-to-face CBT for this program. Participants with panic disorder were however included in an effectiveness trial that focused on adherence (Hilvert-Bruce et al., 2012).

In Sweden a panic treatment was developed at about the same time as in Australia, and this program, called *panikprojektet*, was extended from an initial six weeks (Carlbring et al., 2001) to 10 weeks (Carlbring et al., 2006). The treatment has also been compared with applied relaxation (Carlbring et al., 2003), and also with individual face-to-face CBT showing equal outcomes (Carlbring et al., 2005). This latter study was small; it included 49 participants. Results showed large within-group effects (Cohen's $d = 0.80$ for the ICBT group and $d = 0.93$ for the face-to-face treatment group) and there were no significant differences between the two treatments.

Another Swedish research group developed a separate 10-week program for panic disorder that has been tested in clinical settings. First, they did a small open trial (Bergström et al., 2009), followed by a larger controlled trial in which it was found that guided Internet CBT was as effective as face-to-face group CBT (Bergström et al., 2010). Both of these studies recruited participants in a regular medical setting. Most recently, this program has been the topic of a large effectiveness trial. In a recent report from this database, all 562 patients who had received treatment for their panic disorder at the Internet Psychiatry Unit at Karolinska were included (Hedman et al., 2013). The results showed large within-group effects of $d = 1.07$ to 1.55.

Finally, the researchers behind the Interapy treatment have also developed a program for panic symptoms and panic disorder, which has been tested in one controlled trial (Ruwaard et al., 2010), and in one effectiveness study (Ruwaard et al., 2012) with good outcomes for panic symptoms. The Interapy treatment is described in Chapter 7, and differs a bit from the other panic programs in that it requires more therapist time. The Interapy panic

Table 8.1 Content of programs for panic disorder and panic symptoms

Program, country of origin, target condition	Duration and number of modules	Main contents	Mode of presentation	Reference supporting use
Panic online, Australia	12 weeks Six modules	Psychoeducation, Controlled breathing Relaxation Cognitive restructuring, Exposure Relapse prevention	Standardised text-based information and guidance. Downloadable audio material, and sequenced photographic slide shows Optional stress-management program	Klein & Richards, 2001; Richards et al., 2006
Panic program Australia	Eight weeks Six online lessons	Psychoeducation, graded exposure, cognitive restructuring, physiological de-arousal,and relapse prevention	Lessons online with illustrated case stories and printable summary Therapist support via email, and participation in online discussion forum	Wims et al., 2010
Panikprojektet Sweden	10 weeks 10 treatment modules	Psychoeducation Controlled breathing Relaxation Cognitive restructuring Exposure	Downloadable pdf files and text on screen Secure contact handling system for homework and guidance via that system Homework assignments	Carlbring et al., 2001, 2006
Internet Psychiatry Unit Sweden	10 weeks 10 treatment modules	Psychoeducation Cognitive restructuring Exposure Relapse prevention	As above, with the addition of a clinical psychiatric interview before and after treatment	Bergström et al., 2009

→

Interapy Netherlands	11 weeks	Psychoeducation, awareness training, applied relaxation, cognitive restructuring and exposure	A personal interactive workbook is used by participants and a manual with templates for therapists Communication via email (within the system) Homework assignments are included	Ruwaard et al., 2010

program is described as comprising homework assignments that are based on a web-based personal interactive workbook. The therapist uses this workbook to provide feedback and further instructions. It is stated that therapists take about 20 to 40 minutes to read a client's assignment including preparation of feedback. A full panic treatment may require between 5 and 9 hours of therapist time, which is markedly longer than the other panic programs reviewed here. Ruwaard and his colleagues did a controlled trial with 58 participants and found a between-group effect size of $d = 0.70$. Interestingly, they also reported follow-up data after three years which showed that the effects were sustained. This program has also been tested in real life with effectiveness data ($N = 135$) showing large within-group effects ($d = 1.2$) (Ruwaard et al., 2012).

To sum up, there are several empirical studies supporting ICBT for panic disorder and clear indications that ICBT can be as effective as seeing a therapist in session.

Social anxiety disorder

Social anxiety disorder (SAD), previously referred to as social phobia, is defined in the *DSM-IV* as a marked and persistent fear of one or more social performance situations in which embarrassment may occur (APA, 2000). Exposure to unfamiliar people or possible scrutiny of others typically evokes anxiety and tends to be avoided or at the most endured under great distress. SAD and symptoms of social anxiety exist on a continuum, varying in severity and number of symptoms. Literature says that SAD is associated with substantial impairment in quality of life (Hofmann et al., 2004) and is highly prevalent, with prevalence rates well above 10% (Furmark, 2002). A large epidemiological study estimated lifetime and 12-month prevalence of social phobia to be 12.1 and 7.1%, respectively (Ruscio et al., 2008). SAD may vary in severity, and most researchers distinguish between more limited specific (e.g., speaking in front of an audience) versus generalized social (Hofmann et al., 2004) phobia in which problems occur in several social situations. An overview of programs for SAD is presented in Table 8.2. There are a large number of controlled trials on guided ICBT for SAD (Andersson et al., 2014), and at least five different programs. The first ICBT program for SAD to be developed and tested was from Sweden (Andersson et al., 2006). This program was finalised in 2003 and has since then been tested in more than 10 separate trials. Originally, the treatment was a nine-module treatment delivered within nine weeks,

Table 8.2 Content of programs for social anxiety disorder

Program, country of origin, target condition	Duration and number of modules	Main contents	Mode of presentation	Reference supporting use
SOFIE program Sweden Social anxiety disorder	9 to 15 weeks Nine modules	Psychoeducation Cognitive restructuring Exposure and attention-shifting exercises Social skills relapse prevention	Downloadable pdf files and text on screen Secure contact handling system for homework and guidance via that system Also available in a shorter version as web-app for smartphones	Andersson et al., 2006
Social phobia self-help program Switzerland	Five sessions that are available for 10 weeks	Psychoeducation Cognitive restructuring Exposure and attention-shifting exercises Social skills relapse prevention	57 web sites Therapist contact and homework within the portal	Berger et al., 2011
Shyness Australia Social anxiety disorder	10 weeks Six online lessons	Psychoeducation Exposure cognitive restructuring Information on relapse prevention	Lessons online with illustrated case stories and printable summary Therapist support via email and participation in online discussion forum Different versions exist	Titov et al., 2008

but in later trials a longer 15-week version was tested. A more recent version of the program has been developed, which is a briefer adaption for presentation on smartphones (Dagöö et al., in press).

The program has also been translated and tested in Romania in a controlled trial (Tulbure et al., 2013). Following the first study, the SOFIE program has been investigated in six different published trials (see Andersson et al., 2013, for review), the most recent being a large trial with 200 participants (Andersson et al., 2012b). In that study, treatment was compared against participation in a moderated online discussion forum. The roles of therapist experience and knowledge acquisition were also investigated (Andersson et al., 2012b). Results showed a moderate between-group effect size at post-treatment (Hedges g effect size $g = 0.75$), and effects were maintained at one-year follow-up. Knowledge about SAD, and confidence in that knowledge, increased following treatment. There were no differences between experienced and novice therapists in terms of effects, but the more experienced therapists spent less time when guiding the participant.

The SOFIE program has been tested in an effectiveness trial against group CBT (Hedman et al., 2011a), and found to be equally effective and more cost-effective (Hedman et al., 2011b). Different ways of providing guidance have been studied, including telephone support (Carlbring et al., 2007) and additional live exposure sessions (Tillfors et al., 2008). The SOFIE program has been found to yield long-term effects (Carlbring et al., 2009; Hedman et al., 2011c) for as long as five years after treatment completion. The Swedish program has been translated and tested in Romania with similar promising outcomes (Tulbure et al., 2013).

Berger and co-workers have published three controlled trials on their program. This program is similar to the Swedish program but has more online interactive features. Participants are able to freely navigate through a total of 57 web sites, and the treatment is divided into five sessions that are available for 10 weeks. In the first trial they randomized 52 individuals who were diagnosed with SAD following an interview either in person or over the phone (Berger et al., 2009). Results on the main social anxiety outcome measures showed a between-group effect size of $d = 0.82$ (treatment vs. waitlist). In their second trial (Berger et al., 2011) they randomized 81 individuals diagnosed with SAD into three conditions: unguided treatment, guided treatment and flexible support which was stepped up according to need. Comments on this trial are given later, in the section on the role of guidance and support, but here it suffices to say that all three conditions lead to reductions in SAD symptoms (within group $d = 1.47$), with small differences between the groups. There is also a study in which the role of providing an interview before the treatment was tested (Boettcher et al., 2012). There are no effectiveness trials or comparisons with face-to-face treatment.

The third program, the *Shyness Program*, was developed in Australia (Titov et al., 2008). This program is presented as online lessons for a duration of eight weeks. There are six online lessons supported by a therapist, with parts of the content presented as an illustrated story about a young man with SAD. It has been tested in at least seven trials and found to be effective against waiting-list control (always with large between-group effect sizes). It has also been tested in an effectiveness trial (Aydos et al., 2009) and against face-to-face CBT (Andrews et al., 2011), showing equal outcomes.

There is one program from Spain (Botella et al., 2010), with a focus on public speaking fear. This program is not covered in detail, but both in terms of content and effects, the program appears to be similar to the three previously described programs for SAD.

As with panic disorder, there are many trials in favour of ICBT for SAD, and in fact even more and larger studies than for panic. There are yet few large studies on ICBT versus face-to-face CBT, and few effectiveness studies. Overall, however, all studies clearly show that ICBT works in short term and in the long run.

Generalized anxiety disorder

Generalized anxiety disorder (GAD) is a highly prevalent anxiety disorder characterized by excessive worry or anxiety about everyday events that may be internal, external, and originating in the past, present and/or future (APA, 2000). Since several situations and stimuli are capable of eliciting worry, GAD can become a crippling disorder, preventing the individual from taking part in and enjoying important areas of everyday life (Tyrer & Baldwin, 2006). It has been estimated that GAD has a lifetime prevalence of 1.3 to 5.9% and a 12-month prevalence of 1.2 to 1.9% (Tyrer & Baldwin, 2006). While pharmacological treatment options exist, various psychological treatments have been tested and established effects, mainly in the form of individual face-to-face CBT.

There are two ICBT programs that have been developed specifically for GAD. The first to be published was the *Worry Program* from Titov and Andrews' group in Sydney, Australia (Table 8.3). The second is from the Swedish group and was published first when three-year follow-up data had been collected.

The Worry Program has been tested in two controlled trials and in one effectiveness trial. The first controlled trial on the Australian Worry Program included 48 persons with GAD who were randomized to treatment or waiting list control. Mean between-group effect size for the GAD measures was $d = 1.1$ at post-treatment (Titov et al., 2009a). A total of 39 completed the post-treatment measures (81%), and 18 (75%) of the treatment group participants completed all six lessons within the required time frame. In a second trial the researchers investigated clinician-assisted versus technician-assisted versus delayed treatment (Robinson et al., 2010). In this interesting study with 150 participants the authors found that the treatment worked for both treatment conditions, with large effects compared to the controls and small differences between the two forms of support. This program has also been investigated in a large effectiveness study ($N = 588$), with similar large effects as in the controlled trials (Mewton et al., 2012).

The Swedish ICBT program for GAD called ORIGO has been investigated in two controlled trials. The first study, by Paxling et al. (2011), had 89 participants and included one- and

Table 8.3 Content of programs for generalized anxiety disorder

Program, country of origin, target condition	Duration and number of modules	Main contents	Mode of presentation	Reference supporting use
Worry program Australia	Nine-week and six online lessons	Psychoeducation Cognitive therapy Beliefs about worry Graded exposure Core beliefs Relapse prevention	Lessons online with illustrated case stories and printable summary Therapist support via email, and participation in online discussion forum	Titov et al., 2009
ORIGO Sweden	Eight weeks and eight modules	Psychoeducation Applied relaxation Worry time Cognitive restructuring Worry exposure Problem solving Sleep management Relapse prevention	Downloadable pdf files and text on screen Secure contact handling system for homework and guidance via that system	Paxling et al., 2011

three-year follow-ups. Duration of the treatment was eight weeks. The mean number of treatment modules completed was 4.8 out of 8 possible. The between-group effect size on the main GAD outcome measure at post-treatment was $d = 1.11$. Results at three-year follow-up showed sustained treatment effects.

The ORIGO program has also been tested against psychodynamic Internet treatment in a trial (Andersson et al., 2012c). In that study with 81 participants there were small differences between the two treatments and large within-group effect sizes. The waiting-list control group also improved immediately after the treatment period, but at three-month follow-up the effects were in favour of ICBT versus control ($d = 0.76$) and also in favour of the dynamic treatment compared to the controls ($d = 0.64$). A follow-up at 18 months post-treatment showed continued reduced symptoms of worry.

In sum, there is not much evidence on the effects of ICBT for GAD, and there are no published trials on ICBT versus face-to-face treatment. The findings to date do, however, indicate that ICBT can be effective and that it works in real life.

Posttraumatic stress disorder

Posttraumatic stress disorder (PTSD) is a diagnosis that involves disturbing recurring flashbacks, avoidance or numbing of memories of a traumatic event and hyperarousal. PTSD is common and disabling and may affect as many as 6% of the adult population in a 12-month period (APA, 2000). While evidence-based treatments exist, there are many who do not seek treatment. The effects of ICBT on trauma symptoms and PTSD have been investigated in several studies and there are also several programs (see Table 8.4).

Interapy is probably the most validated ICBT program for PTSD, as it has been tested in several trials. The five-week treatment involves much therapist contact and includes structured writing assignments that take place through an online database. Communication between therapist and patient is text based and asynchronous (see previous description for other disorders in this book). Lange et al. (2003) randomly allocated persons with a history of trauma exposure to either Interapy ($n = 122$) or to a waiting list control group ($n = 62$). Results immediately post-treatment and at six-week follow-up showed large reductions of trauma symptoms (between group Cohen's d for the intrusion symptoms $d = 1.2$, and for the avoidance symptoms $d = 1.3$ at post-treatment). Interapy has also been tested as a treatment for complicated grief (Wagner et al., 2006). It has also been translated and tested in a study conducted with participants from Iraq (Wagner et al., 2012). Data from a large sample of patients with PTSD treated in a clinic have also been reported, showing that the treatment works (Ruwaard et al., 2012). The Interapy PTSD treatment has not been directly compared with face-to-face CBT. However, it has been implemented in the Interapy clinic, with large within-group effects (d above 1.0) reported by Ruwaard et al. (2012) for a sample of 477 individuals with diagnosed PTSD.

Another program, *self-help program for traumatic event-related consequences*, was developed for trauma-related symptoms and tested in a small controlled trial (Hirai & Clum, 2005). This eight-week program has to my knowledge only been tested in one small trial with 36 individuals who were randomized to either treatment ($n = 18$) or to a waiting-list control condition ($n = 18$). Results at post treatment showed no statistical interactions on the trauma measures, which probably was due to low statistical power. However, between-group effect size for avoidance was $d = 0.85$, and $d = 0.62$ for the intrusion symptoms.

Litz and co-workers developed the *DE-STRESS* program. This program has also only been tested in one controlled trial (Litz et al., 2007) and this eight-week program contains

Table 8.4 Content of programs for posttraumatic stress disorder

Program, country of origin, target condition	Duration and number of modules	Main contents	Mode of presentation	Reference supporting use
Interapy Netherlands	Five weeks with two weekly 45-minute writing assignments (10 essays in total)	Psychoeducation, structured writing assignments, self-confrontation, cognitive reappraisal, sharing and farewell ritual	A personal interactive workbook is used by participants and a manual with templates for therapists Communication via email (within the system) Homework assignments are included	Lange et al., 2003
Self-help program for traumatic event-related consequences United States	Eight weeks	Psychoeducation Relaxation Breathing retraining Cognitive restructuring Writing exposure	Interactive cognitive-behavioural program Only technical assistance over email	Hirai & Clum, 2005
DE-STRESS United States	Eight weeks with 56 total possible log-ons (daily)	Psychoeducation Self-monitoring Stress management Exposure Writing sessions	Initial face-to-face meeting Support via email Planned phone conversation	Litz et al., 2007
PTSD program Australia	Eight weeks Seven lessons	Psychoeducation Control of physical sensations Cognitive therapy Graded exposure Cognitive restructuring Relapse prevention	Online lessons; a summary/ homework assignment for each lesson; an online discussion forum for each lesson, moderated by the therapist; regular automatic reminders and notification emails; and instant messaging to	Spence et al., 2011

			allow secure email-type messages with a clinician Access to additional written resources about assertiveness skills and anger management, panic, strategies for improving sleep, diet, exercise, reducing drug and alcohol use, further examples of exposure	
Tellus program Sweden	Eight weeks Eight modules	Psychoeducation Breathing retraining Imaginal and in vivo exposure Cognitive restructuring Relapse prevention	Downloadable pdf files and text on screen Secure contact handling system for homework and guidance via that system	Ivarsson et al., 2014

similar ingredients to the other PTSD programs. In their randomized controlled trial, the authors had an active control group, which is uncommon in this research field. The authors randomized their study participants to either self-management Internet-based CBT ($n = 24$) or to a supportive counselling Internet treatment ($n = 21$). The majority of the supportive counselling intervention dealt with self-monitoring of non-trauma-related concerns and hassles, including writing about these experiences. Dropout rate was 27%, with 33 out of 45 completing treatment. Treatment was not purely Internet based, as an initial two-hour face-to-face session was included. Participants were also in contact with the therapists via email and phone. Since two active treatments were compared in this study, between-group effect sizes are likely to be smaller than in previous trials in which the active treatment has been compared with a waiting-list condition. However, a between-group effect size of $d = 0.41$ was found in favour of the CBT treatment. The authors also reported follow-up data by considering treatment completers at six-month follow-up, with a between-group effect size of $d = 0.95$ for their overall measure of PTSD symptoms. Using intent-to-treat analyses, they reported that a significantly greater percentage of cases in the CBT group no longer met criteria for PTSD at the six-month follow-up. Data from a six-month follow-up were similar to the post treatment.

A program that was developed in Australia has also been tested in a controlled trial (Spence et al., 2011). The seven-module program includes common elements in CBT for PTSD and was found to work fairly well in the controlled trial which included 42 individuals with PTSD. Effects at post treatment were small compared to the control group ($d = 0.47$), but there were large within-group effects. No effectiveness studies or comparisons with face-to-face treatments have been published for this program.

In my group in Sweden we have also developed and tested one program for PTSD called *Tellus* in a controlled trial with promising effects (Ivarsson et al., 2014). We included 61 persons in the trial and the results showed a large between-group effect at post-treatment ($d = 1.25$). The results at one-year follow-up showed that treatment gains were maintained.

In addition to these programs that have been tested in controlled trials there are programs that have only been tested in open trials, with one not only focusing on PTSD (Ruggierio et al., 2006), and one directly aimed at PTSD developed by Klein and co-workers (2009) showing promising results.

In sum, there are many studies showing that ICBT can be a useful treatment for PTSD for a range of different target groups. Large-scale controlled trials with diagnosed PTSD are still lacking, as are direct comparative trials against face-to-face treatment.

Obsessive-compulsive disorder, health anxiety, specific phobia

The conditions reviewed above were all the subject of controlled trials. Here some additional programs for which there have been fewer studies are covered (see Table 8.5).

For obsessive-compulsive disorders there are two programs that have been evaluated in research. The Swedish program was first evaluated in a pilot study and then in a controlled trial (Andersson et al., 2012a). The trial included 101 participants who were diagnosed with OCD and randomized to either treatment or to an attention control condition, consisting of online supportive therapy. Results on the Yale–Brown Obsessive Compulsive Scale (YBOCS) administered by blinded assessors showed a between-group effect size of $d = 1.12$ at post treatment. Results were sustained at four-month follow-up.

The second OCD program is from Australia. As with the Swedish program it was first tested in a pilot trial. The controlled trial included three groups. A total of 56 individuals were diagnosed with OCD and diagnosed to either ICBT, bibliotherapy CBT or to a waiting list control group (Wootton et al., 2013). Results on the YBOCS showed that both treatments lead to improvements and the between-group effect size at post treatment was $d = 1.57$ (ICBT vs. control). Bibliotherapy and ICBT did not differ (small effect in favour of ICBT), and results for both treatments were maintained at three-month follow-up.

Severe health anxiety (earlier referred to as hypochondriasis) has been the subject of only one program, developed by Hedman et al. (2011c) following some pilot work. This program shares features of OCD treatment and was tested in a trial with 81 persons diagnosed with severe health anxiety who were randomized to ICBT or attention control (online discussion forum). Between-group effect size at post treatment on the Health Anxiety Inventory was $d = 1.62$. A follow-up at six months post treatment showed that the effects were maintained.

Very little has been done on guided ICBT for specific phobias. My group has conducted two small trials in which we compared live one-session exposure against guided ICBT (Andersson et al., 2009, 2013). The first trial was on spider phobia and included 30 participants. As expected the one-session treatment worked well, but so did the ICBT condition. The main outcome measure was the behavioural approach test (BAT), and as secondary measures the

Table 8.5 Content of programs for obsessive-compulsive disorder, severe health anxiety and specific phobia

Program, country of origin, target condition	Duration and number of modules	Main contents	Mode of presentation	Reference supporting use
ICBT for OCD Sweden	10 weeks 10 modules	Psychoeducation Cognitive restructuring Exposure and response prevention planning and later in vivo Tailored according to OCT subtypes Work with values Relapse prevention	Downloadable pdf files and text on screen Secure contact handling system for homework and guidance via that system Modules also available as audio-files	Andersson et al., 2012a
The OCD course Australia	Five online lessons	Psychoeducation Cognitive errors Exposure and response prevention Relapse prevention	Online lessons, and twice weekly telephone support	Wootton et al., 2013
Health anxiety program Sweden	12 weeks with 12 modules	Psychoeducation Mindfulness training Cognitive restructuring Exposure and response prevention Relapse prevention	Same as the Swedish OCD program	Hedman et al., 2011d
Specific phobia (spider and snake) Sweden	Five weeks With four to five modules	Psychoeducation Exposure instructions Cognitive therapy Maintenance program	Downloadable pdf files and text on screen Video in which exposure is modelled Secure contact handling system for homework and guidance via that system	Andersson et al., 2009, 2013

authors used questionnaires measuring anxiety symptoms and depression. Results showed that the groups did not differ at post treatment or follow-up, with the exception of the proportion showing clinically significant change on the BAT. At post treatment 46.2% of the Internet group and 85.7% in the live-exposure group achieved this change. In a second trial (Andersson et al., 2013) with 30 participants who had snake phobia, we found similar effects. At post treatment 61.5% of the Internet group and 84.6% in the one-session group achieved a clinically significant improvement on the BAT. Thus these small trials showed indications that face-to-face treatment was somewhat better than ICBT.

Overall, there is a need for replications of the OCD studies and the health anxiety study. The specific phobia treatment is promising and a different version aimed at children showed promising effects in a pilot trial (Vigerland et al., 2013). However, larger studies are needed.

Mixed anxiety and depression

Transdiagnostic treatment and tailored ICBT programs have been developed and tested in recent years. Examples are given in Table 8.6. Another example is provided in Chapter 7, with the Taylor and Wellness programs (Table 7.1).

There are two different approaches to transdiagnostic ICBT. One is based on the idea of having the same material for all patients (with optional tailoring in the form of extra material) and the other is based on tailoring all material with the exception of initial modules and the last module. The first can be referred to as the Australian approach and the second the Swedish approach.

Titov et al. in Australia have conducted at least three controlled trials on therapist-guided transdiagnostic ICBT (in addition to the one on depression presented in the previous chapter). The target groups have been mixed anxiety and depression. In their first trial with a slightly different program they randomized 86 participants with mixed anxiety/depression to either treatment or control. Between-group effects at post treatment were in the moderate range and clearly in favour of the treatment (Titov et al., 2010).

In another more recent trial, 77 individuals were randomized to either treatment or waitlist (Titov et al., 2011) and an updated version of the program was used. Between-group effect sizes were again in the moderate range (e.g., $d = 0.56$ for their generic anxiety measure), although within-group effects were larger. Adherence was very good with 81% of the treatment group participants completing the eight allocated lessons within the 10-week treatment period.

A third trial had a different design. Here the researchers included 131 individuals with different anxiety disorders and randomized them into three groups: clinician-supported treatment versus coach-supported treatment versus waitlist control (Johnston et al., 2011). The main difference between the two forms of providing support was that the coach was not allowed to provide clinical advice or to elaborate, expand upon or add to the existing information or skills provided in the program. In the main analyses they combined the two active groups (but there was a tendency in favour of the coach group). In this trial the between-group effects (comparing treatment against no treatment) were large. This program as in the previous study was an expanded version and included extra material (i.e. additional written resources that included guidelines about managing low mood, improving sleep, etc.). Adherence to the prescribed lessons was high with over 70% completing the eight lessons.

Table 8.6 Content of programs based on unified treatment or tailored ICBT

Program, country of origin, target condition	Duration and number of modules	Main contents	Mode of presentation	Reference supporting use
Wellbeing program *Australia*	10 weeks Eight online lessons	Transdiagnostic Psychoeducation Cognitive therapy Control of physical symptoms Behavioural activation Graded exposure More on cognitive therapy (e.g., core beliefs) Problem solving Relapse prevention Additional text modules are available	Online lessons Online discussion forum, automatic reminders, text messaging Stories from the front line Therapist guided	Titov et al., 2011
Tailored Internet intervention for anxiety (Nova) *Sweden*	Up to 10 weeks but flexible 25 modules that are prescribed according to symptom profile Four modules are fixed: psychoeducation, cognitive restructuring and relapse prevention	Modules on depression, panic, social anxiety, worry, trauma, stress management, concentration problems, problem solving, mindfulness and relaxation	Downloadable pdf files and text on screen Secure contact handling system for homework and guidance via that system	Carlbring et al., 2010

Overall, transdiagnostic ICBT is a promising treatment approach, although effects in some trials have been smaller than in diagnosis-specific studies. See Figure 8.1 for an example of how the program looks.

The second approach to handling co-morbidity and overlap between anxiety disorders and depression is to tailor the treatment according to patient profile. This idea came from the fact that the group I work with had completed several trials and developed programs for specific disorders. Hence by rewriting the treatment modules and making them more generic it became possible to prescribe tailored programs based on self-report and clinical interviews. This is probably not strange to experienced clinicians, who in their everyday clinics tend to adapt their treatments according to their patients' problems and wishes (often based on case conceptualisations). However, tailored ICBT requires some structure as the starting point, rationale, and the end of the treatment

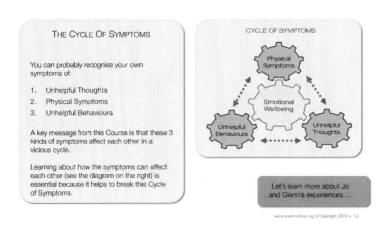

Figure 8.1 Another example from the Wellbeing program.

needs to be fixed. Between the first psychoeducation and the last (relapse prevention module), different modules are recommended. This gives the clinician an important role and tailoring can be done in collaboration with the patient, or the patient can do it himself (Andersson et al., 2011).

In the first controlled trial on tailored ICBT, 54 participants were randomized to a 10-week treatment program or to a control group. Mean between-group effect size including measures of anxiety, depression and quality of life was Cohen's $d = 0.69$ at post treatment. The study also included long-term follow-ups at one- and two-year intervals (Carlbring et al., 2010). Adherence is not as straightforward to calculate as in programs with fixed modules, but an average of about nine modules were prescribed and eight were completed. However, only about 60% completed all their prescribed modules.

A second controlled trial on tailored ICBT for anxiety disorders has been conducted by our research group. This study targeted panic symptoms and involved 57 participants randomized to an eight-week treatment program or to a control condition. Results showed large between-group effects at post treatment and the effects were maintained one year later (Silfvernagel et al., 2012). This study also investigated the importance of age (18 to 30 years vs. 31 to 45 years), but this did not appear to make a difference. There are two additional unpublished studies on tailored ICBT for anxiety disorders; one is conducted in a primary care setting and the second is a trial with older adults with anxiety disorders. Both show significant effects and moderate to large effect sizes.

A crucial question when it comes to tailoring is whether it is better to tailor than to use diagnosis-specific treatment. For depression, there was preliminary evidence that tailoring was better for the more severe patients (see Chapter 7). In the field of anxiety disorder I know of only one trial in which Berger et al. (in press) randomly allocated 132 individuals with anxiety disorders to either tailored guided ICBT, standardized disorder-specific ICBT or to a wait-list control. In this study tailoring did not appear to be either worse or better than diagnosis-specific treatment. Mean between-group effect sizes were $d = 0.80$ for the tailored treatment and $d = 0.82$ for the standardized treatment, versus wait-list controls. This is an important study as it shows that tailoring does not alter the effects of ICBT. Interestingly, there was no difference on rating of treatment satisfaction. In contrast to the findings by Johansson et al. (2012) there were no clear indications that tailored treatment was better than the standardised treatment for patients with more severe conditions.

On the other hand, a large proportion had SAD as their main diagnosis and the tailoring was not done in the same way as in the Swedish studies. However, given the large effects of diagnosis-specific treatments and that co-morbid conditions can respond to diagnosis-specific treatments (e.g., worry decreasing following treatment for panic disorder; see Titov et al., 2009b, for an example involving SAD), it may be that tailoring is more important for subclinical cases or cases with mixed problems involving not just anxiety (e.g., health problems, insomnia and major depression).

An interesting observation is that the Australian and Swedish approaches overlap to some extent. By providing access to separate texts in the Australian approach and by having fixed modules in the Swedish approach the content might differ less than it seems. On the other hand the mode or presentation is different as the Swedish tailored system is heavily text based in contrast to the online lessons in the Australian approach. Ongoing studies in my group have blurred the distinction even more by having more fixed modules and mix between delivery formats (e.g., smartphone delivery).

In sum, tailored and transdiagnostic ICBT approaches are promising and broaden the number of patients who can take advantage of ICBT. It is not yet clear how well transdiagnostic ICBT compares to diagnosis-specific ICBT, and only one study on anxiety in which tailored and standardized ICBT have been compared. The roles of patient preference and patient choice have not been studied much, with only one open study showing that patients can make decisions on the content of the treatment following description of the modules to choose from (Andersson et al., 2011).

Different target groups

In this chapter we have mainly covered ICBT for adults with anxiety disorders, but there is an emerging literature on ICBT for children and adolescents. Spence et al. (2011) did a trial on adolescents with anxiety disorders which showed that ICBT can be as effective as face-to-face therapy for this age group. The same research group has also studied the effects of ICBT for children (March et al., 2009). While the effects were perhaps not as large as seen in trials with adults, the results are promising and in the Swedish pilot study on specific phobia in children aged 8 to 12 years, large within-group effects were found (Vigerland et al., 2013). Overall, however, there has not been much done on anxiety disorders in children and adolescents using ICBT.

A second target group that has been the subject of relatively little research is ICBT for older adults. Zou et al. (2012) conducted an open pilot trial with 22 participants and found large within-group effects. Effectiveness data by Mewton et al. (2013) indicate that older adults are more likely to complete all online lessons in the treatment program when compared with their younger counterparts. However, these data are from an automated program, rendering the study less applicable to the guided ICBT format. As mentioned, we in Sweden have completed a controlled trial on tailored ICBT for older adults showing promising results, but there is clearly a need for more studies in this field.

Other target groups include persons in other countries (see Wagner et al., 2012) and clinicians who work with different therapeutic approaches than CBT. In my group we have conducted two controlled trials on anxiety using psychodynamic treatment approaches (the one on GAD was mentioned earlier). The most recent study by Johansson et al. (2013) was based on affect-focused therapy for mixed anxiety and depression. The study showed a large effect on depression symptoms but somewhat smaller effects on anxiety measures.

Discussion regarding the effects of guided ICBT for anxiety disorders

Overall, it should be clear by the overview in this chapter that there are several studies showing that guided ICBT can be effective for anxiety disorders, and there are also several reviews showing this (e.g., Cuijpers et al., 2009). While there are not many direct comparisons, we did a meta-analysis in which we found no differences between ICBT and face-to-face therapy (Andersson, Cuijpers et al., in press). As seen in this chapter there are also studies on how ICBT works in regular clinical settings (Andersson & Hedman, 2013), and also long-term follow-up studies. In addition, there are some studies on health economy and ICBT with most showing that ICBT is cost-effective (see Chapter 6).

There are also previous computerized programs that were developed before widespread use of the Internet, such as FearFighter for panic and anxiety, which is available in some parts of the United Kingdom (**http://www.fearfighter.com**). This program was originally developed for CD ROM and presented on stand-alone computers at general practice settings, but later research was done on Internet administration of the program (Schneider et al., 2005) with good results.

However, there are still several outstanding questions. We do not know much about predictors of treatment outcome and the mechanisms involved in generating good outcome. Thus, more studies on moderators and mediators are needed. Those that exist do not generate a consistent picture (e.g., Andersson et al., 2008; see also Chapter 6). As with many ICBT studies in general, the studies on anxiety disorders often include people with above-average education, and while a vast majority of people in many European countries have access to the Internet, this is not always the case and sometimes it is not even a majority.

In addition, there is knowledge to be gained by doing qualitative research on how patients experience ICBT. Some work has been done here for depression, but very little on anxiety disorder patients. Although guided ICBT and face-to-face therapies are about equally effective, it is unlikely that they work via exactly the same mechanisms. For example, exposure to feared objects can be frightening, and ICBT may be a way for clients to go through the steps at their own pace. However, it is much easier to avoid drifting from evidence-based therapy in ICBT.

What about other approaches?

Psychodynamic Internet treatment has already been covered, which in many ways is similar to guided ICBT with the exception of the theoretical rationale and contents of treatment modules. The therapist role may also differ somewhat. But there is another distinctly different way to use the Internet to treat anxiety disorders that has been much less successful: attention bias modification for social anxiety disorder. We have done a series of studies using this treatment format and there are also at least two more groups who have found the same negative results that attention bias modification, as it has been tested at least, is unlikely to work for SAD (e.g., Carlbring et al., 2012; Neubauer et al., 2013). Given the uncertainties regarding attention bias modification delivered via the Internet I will not comment more on this new form of treatment except to state that more research is needed.

Practical implications and key points

- Guided ICBT has been found to be effective for a range of anxiety disorders with sustained effects over time.

- ICBT for anxiety disorders may be as effective as face-to-face CBT, which gives weight to patient preferences.

- Most research and clinical experience are from adults, and less is known regarding ICBT for children and adolescents with anxiety disorders, and also older adults.

- Recent studies suggest that transdiagnostic and tailored ICBT can be useful in the treatment of anxiety disorders, but less is known regarding the difference between diagnosis-specific treatments and these new forms of ICBT.

- More research is needed regarding predictors and mediators of treatment outcome in ICBT for anxiety disorders.

- Attention bias modification has to date only showed marginal effects when delivered via the Internet for social anxiety disorder.

References

Andersson E, Enander J, Andrén P, Hedman E, Ljótsson B, Hursti T, Bergström J, Kaldo V, Lindefors N, Andersson G, Rück C. (2012a). Internet-based cognitive behaviour therapy for obsessive-compulsive disorder: A randomised controlled trial. *Psychological Medicine, 42,* 2193–2203.

Andersson G, Carlbring P, Furmark T. (in press). Internet-delivered treatments for social anxiety disorder In J Weeks, editor. *Handbook of Social Anxiety Disorder.* New York: Wiley-Blackwell.

Andersson G, Carlbring P, Furmark T, and on behalf of the SOFIE Research Group. (2012b). Therapist experience and knowledge acquisition in Internet-delivered CBT for social anxiety disorder: A randomized controlled trial. *PloS ONE, 7(5),* e37411.

Andersson G, Carlbring P, Furmark T. (2014). Internet-delivered treatments for social anxiety disorder In J. Weeks (ed.), *Handbook of Social Anxiety Disorder* (pp. 569–587). New York: Wiley-Blackwell.

Andersson G, Carlbring P, Grimlund A. (2008). Predicting treatment outcome in Internet versus face to face treatment of panic disorder. *Computers in Human Behavior, 24,* 1790–1801.

Andersson G, Carlbring P, Holmström A, Sparthan E, Furmark T, Nilsson-Ihrfelt E, Buhrman M, Ekselius L. (2006). Internet-based self-help with therapist feedback and in-vivo group exposure for social phobia: A randomized controlled trial. *Journal of Consulting and Clinical Psychology, 74,* 677–686.

Andersson G, Cuijpers P, Carlbring P, Riper H, Hedman E. (In press). Internet-based vs. face-to-face cognitive behaviour therapy for psychiatric and somatic disorders: A systematic review and meta-analysis. *World Psychiatry.*

Andersson G, Estling, F, Jakobsson E, Cuijpers P, Carlbring P. (2011). Can the patient decide which modules to endorse? An open trial of tailored Internet treatment of anxiety disorders. *Cognitive Behaviour Therapy, 40,* 57–64.

Andersson G, Hedman E. (2013). Effectiveness of guided Internet-delivered cognitive behaviour therapy in regular clinical settings. *Verhaltenstherapie, 23*, 140–148.

Andersson G, Paxling B, Roch-Norlund P, Östman G, Norgren A, Almlöv J, Georén L, Breitholtz E, Dahlin M, Cuijpers P, Carlbring P, Silverberg F. (2012c). Internet-based psychodynamic vs. cognitive behavioural guided self-help for generalized anxiety disorder: A randomised controlled trial. *Psychotherapy and Psychosomatics, 81*, 344–355.

Andersson G, Waara J, Jonsson U, Malmaeus F, Carlbring P, Öst L-G. (2009). Internet-based self-help vs. one-session exposure in the treatment of spider phobia: A randomized controlled trial. *Cognitive Behaviour Therapy, 38*, 114–120.

Andersson G, Waara J, Jonsson U, Malmeus F, Carlbring P, Öst L-G. (2013). Internet-based vs. one-session exposure treatment of snake phobia: A randomized controlled trial. *Cognitive Behaviour Therapy, 42*, 284–291.

Andrews G, Davies,M, Titov N. (2011). Effectiveness randomized controlled trial of face to face versus Internet cognitive behaviour therapy for social phobia. *Australian and New Zealand Journal of Psychiatry, 45*, 337–340.

Aydos L, Titov N, Andrews G. (2009). Shyness 5: The clinical effectiveness of Internet-based clinician-assisted treatment of social phobia. *Australasian Psychiatry, 17*, 488–492.

Berger T, Boettcher J, Caspar F. (In press). Internet-based guided self-help for several anxiety disorders: A randomized controlled trial comparing a tailored with a standardized disorder-specific approach. *Psychotherapy*.

Berger T, Caspar F, Richardson R, Kneubühler B, Sutter D, Andersson G. (2011). Internet-based treatment of social phobia: A randomized controlled trial comparing unguided with two types of guided self-help. *Behaviour Research and Therapy, 48*, 158–169.

Berger T, Hohl E, Caspar F. (2009). Internet-based treatment for social phobia: A randomized controlled trial. *Journal of Clinical Psychology, 65*, 1021–1035.

Bergström J, Andersson G, Karlsson A, Andreewitch S, Rück C, Carlbring P, Lindefors N. (2009). An open study of the effectiveness of Internet treatment for panic disorder delivered in a psychiatric setting. *Nordic Journal of Psychiatry, 63*, 44–50.

Bergström J, Andersson G, Ljótsson B, Rück C, Andréewitch S, Karlsson A, Carlbring P, Andersson E, Lindefors N. (2010). Internet- versus group-administered cognitive behaviour therapy for panic disorder in a psychiatric setting: A randomised trial. *BMC Psychiatry, 10*, 54.

Boettcher J, Berger T, Renneberg B. (2012). Does a pre-treatment diagnostic interview affect the outcome of Internet-based self-help for social anxiety disorder? A randomized controlled trial. *Behavioural and Cognitive Psychotherapy, 40*, 513–528.

Botella C, Gallego MJ, Garcia-Palacios A, Guillen V, Banos RM, Quero S, Alcaniz M. (2010). An Internet-based self-help treatment for fear of public speaking: A controlled trial. *Cyberpsychology, Behavior and Social Networking, 13*, 407–421.

Carlbring P, Apelstrand M, Sehlin H, Amir N, Rousseau A, Hofmann S, Andersson G. (2012). Internet-delivered attention training in individuals with social anxiety disorder – a double blind randomized controlled trial. *BMC Psychiatry, 12, 66*.

Carlbring P, Bergman Nordgren L, Furmark T, Andersson G. (2009). Long term outcome of Internet delivered cognitive-behavioural therapy for social anxiety disorder: A 30-month follow-up. *Behaviour Research and Therapy, 47*, 848–850.

Carlbring P, Bohman S, Brunt S, Buhrman M, Westling BE, Ekselius L, Andersson G. (2006). Remote treatment of panic disorder: A randomized trial of Internet-based cognitive behavioral therapy supplemented with telephone calls. *American Journal of Psychiatry, 163*, 2119–2125.

Carlbring P, Ekselius L, Andersson G. (2003). Treatment of panic disorder via the Internet: A randomized trial of CBT vs. applied relaxation. *Journal of Behavior Therapy and Experimental Psychiatry, 34*, 129–140.

Carlbring P, Gunnarsdóttir M, Hedensjö L, Andersson G, Ekselius L, Furmark T. (2007). Treatment of social phobia: Randomized trial of Internet delivered cognitive behaviour therapy and telephone support. *British Journal of Psychiatry, 190*, 123–128.

Carlbring P, Maurin L, Törngren C, Linna E, Eriksson T, Sparthan E, Strååt M, Marquez von Hage C, Bergman-Nordgren L, Andersson G. (2011). Individually-tailored, internet-based treatment for anxiety disorders: A randomized controlled trial. *Behaviour Research and Therapy, 49*, 18–24.

Carlbring P, Nilsson-Ihrfelt E, Waara J, Kollenstam C, Buhrman M, Kaldo V, Söderberg M, Ekselius L, Andersson G. (2005). Treatment of panic disorder: Live therapy vs. self-help via Internet. *Behaviour Research and Therapy, 43*, 1321–1333.

Carlbring P, Westling BE, Ljungstrand P, Ekselius L, Andersson G. (2001). Treatment of panic disorder via the Internet – a randomized trial of a self-help program. *Behavior Therapy, 32*, 751–764.

Cuijpers P, Marks I, van Straten A-M, Cavanagh K, Gega L, Andersson G. (2009). Computer-aided psychotherapy for anxiety disorders: A meta-analytic review. *Cognitive Behaviour Therapy, 38*, 66–82.

Dagöö J, Persson Asplund R, Andersson Bsenko H, Hjerling S, Holmberg A, Westh S, Öberg L, Ljótsson B, Carlbring P, Furmark T, Andersson G. (In press). Cognitive behavior therapy versus interpersonal psychotherapy for social anxiety disorder delivered via smartphone and computer: A randomized controlled trial. *Journal of Anxiety Disorders*.

Furmark T. (2002). Social phobia: Overview of community surveys. *Acta Psychiatrica Scandinavica, 105*, 84–93.

Hedman E, Andersson E, Ljótsson B, Andersson G, Rück C, Lindefors N. (2011b). Cost-effectiveness of Internet-based cognitive behavior therapy vs. cognitive behavioral group therapy for social anxiety disorder: Results from a randomized controlled trial. *Behaviour Research and Therapy, 49*, 729–736.

Hedman E, Andersson G, Ljótsson B, Andersson E, Rück C, Asmundson GJG, Lindefors N. (2011d). Internet-based cognitive-behavioural therapy for severe health anxiety: Randomised controlled trial. *British Journal of Psychiatry, 198*, 230–236.

Hedman E, Andersson G, Ljótsson B, Andersson E, Rück C, Mörtberg E, Lindefors N. (2011a). Internet-based cognitive behavior therapy vs. cognitive behavioral group therapy for social anxiety disorder: A randomized controlled non-inferiority trial. *PloS ONE, 6(3)*, e18001.

Hedman E, Furmark T, Carlbring P, Ljótsson B, Rück C, Lindefors N, Andersson G. (2011c). Five-year follow-up of Internet-based cognitive behaviour therapy for social anxiety disorder. *Journal of Medical Internet Research, 13(2)*, e39.

Hedman E, Ljótsson B, Rück C, Bergström J, Andersson G, Kaldo V, Jansson L, Andersson E, Blom K, El Alaoui S, Falk L, Ivarsson J, Nasri B, Rydh S, Lindefors N. (2013). Effectiveness of Internet-based cognitive behaviour therapy for panic disorder in routine psychiatric care. *Acta Psychiatrica Scandinavica, 128*, 457–467.

Hilvert-Bruce Z, Rossouw PJ, Wong N, Sunderland M, Andrews G. (2012). Adherence as a determinant of effectiveness of Internet cognitive behavioural therapy for anxiety and depressive disorders. *Behaviour Research and Therapy, 50*, 463–468.

Hirai M, Clum GA. (2005). An Internet-based self-change program for traumatic event related fear, distress, and maladaptive coping. *Journal of Traumatic Stress, 18*, 631–636.

Hofmann SG, Heinrichs N, Moscovitch DA. (2004). The nature and expression of social phobia: toward a new classification. *Clinical Psychology Review, 24*, 769–797.

Ivarsson D, Blom M, Hesser H, Carlbring P, Enderby P, Nordberg R, Andersson G. (2013). Guided Internet-delivered cognitive behaviour therapy for post-traumatic stress disorder: A randomized controlled trial. *Submitted manuscript.*

Ivarsson D, Blom M, Hesser H, Carlbring P, Enderby P, Nordberg R, Andersson G. (2014). Guided Internet-delivered cognitive behaviour therapy for post-traumatic stress disorder: A randomized controlled trial. *Internet Interventions, 1*, 33–40.

Johansson R, Björklund M, Hornborg C, Karlsson S, Hesser H, Ljótsson B, Rousseau A, Frederick RJ, Andersson G. (2013). Affect-focused psychodynamic psychotherapy for depression and anxiety through the Internet: A randomized controlled trial. *PeerJ, 1*, e102.

Johansson R, Sjöberg E, Sjögren M, Johnsson E, Carlbring P, Andersson T, Rousseau A, Andersson G. (2012). Tailored vs. standardized Internet-based cognitive behavior therapy for depression and comorbid symptoms: A randomized controlled trial. *PLoS ONE, 7*(5), e36905.

Johnston L, Titov N, Andrews G, Spence J, Dear BF. (2011). A RCT of a transdiagnostic Internet-delivered treatment for three anxiety disorders: Examination of support roles and disorder-specific outcomes. *PLoS ONE, 6*, e28079.

Kiropoulos LA, Klein B, Austin DW, Gilson K, Pier C, Mitchell J, Ciechomski L. (2008). Is Internet-based CBT for panic disorder and agoraphobia as effective as face-to-face CBT? *Journal of Anxiety Disorders, 22*, 1273–1284.

Klein B, Mitchell J, Gilson K, Shandley K, Austin D, Kiropoulos L, Abbott J, Cannard G. (2009). A therapist-assisted Internet-based CBT intervention for posttraumatic stress disorder: Preliminary results. *Cognitive Behaviour Therapy, 38*, 121–131.

Klein B, Richards JC. (2001). A brief Internet-based treatment for panic disorder. *Behavioural and Cognitive Psychotherapy, 29*, 113–117.

Lange A, Rietdijk D, Hudcovicova M, van den Ven J-P, Schrieken B, Emmelkamp PMG. (2003). Interapy: A controlled randomized trial of the standardized treatment of posttraumatic stress through the Internet. *Journal of Consulting and Clinical Psychology, 71*, 901–909.

Litz BT, Engel CC, Bryant RA, Papa A. (2007). A randomized, controlled proof-of-concept trial of an Internet-based, therapist-assisted self-management treatment for posttraumatic stress disorder. *American Journal of Psychiatry, 164*(11), 1676–1683.

March S, Spence SH, Donovan CL. (2009). The efficacy of an Internet-based cognitive-behavioral therapy intervention for child anxiety disorders. *Journal of Pediatric Psychology, 34*, 474–487.

Mewton L, Sachdev PS, Andrews G. (2013). A naturalistic study of the acceptability and effectiveness of Internet-delivered cognitive behavioural therapy for psychiatric disorders in older Australians. *PLoS ONE, 8*, e71825.

Mewton L, Wong N, Andrews G. (2012). The effectiveness of Internet cognitive behavioural therapy for generalized anxiety disorder in clinical practice. *Depression and Anxiety, 29*, 843–849.

Neubauer K, von Auer M, Murray E, Petermann F, Helbig-Lang S, Gerlach AL. (2013). Internet-delivered attention modification training as a treatment for social phobia: A randomized controlled trial. *Behaviour Research and Therapy, 51*, 87–97.

Paxling B, Almlöv J, Dahlin M, Carlbring P, Breitholtz E, Eriksson T, Andersson G. (2011). Guided Internet-delivered cognitive behavior therapy for generalized anxiety disorder: A randomized controlled trial. *Cognitive Behaviour Therapy, 40*, 159–173.

Richards JC, Klein B, Austin DW. (2006). Internet CBT for panic disorder: Does the inclusion of stress management improve end-state functioning? *Clinical Psychologist, 10*, 2–15.

Robinson E, Titov N, Andrews G, McIntyre K, Schwencke G, Solley K. (2010). Internet treatment for generalized anxiety disorder: A randomized controlled trial comparing clinician vs. technician assistance. *PloS ONE, 5*, e10942.

Ruggiero KJ, Resnick HS, Acierno R, Coffey SF, Carpenter MJ, Ruscio AM, Stephens RS, Kilpatrick DG, Stasiewicz PR, Roffman RA, Bucuvalas M, Galea S. (2006). Internet-based intervention for mental health and substance use problems in disaster-affected populations: A pilot feasibility study. *Behavior Therapy, 37*, 190–205.

Ruscio AM, Brown TA, Chiu WT, Sareen J, Stein MB, Kessler RC. (2008). Social fears and social phobia in the USA: Results from the National Comorbidity Survey Replication. *Psychological Medicine, 38*, 15–28.

Ruwaard J, Broeksteeg, J, Schrieken B, Emmelkamp, P, Lange, A. (2010). Web-based therapist-assisted cognitive behavioral treatment of panic symptoms: A randomized controlled trial with a three-year follow-up. *Journal of Anxiety Disorders, 24*, 387–396.

Ruwaard J, Lange, A, Schrieken B, Dolan CV, Emmelkamp P. (2012). The effectiveness of online cognitive behavioral treatment in routine clinical practice. *PLoS ONE, 7(7)*, e40089.

Schneider AJ, Mataix-Cols D, Marks IM, Bachofen M. (2005). Internet-guided self-help with or without exposure therapy for phobic and panic disorders. *Psychotherapy and Psychosomatics, 74*, 154–164.

Shandley K, Austin DW, Klein B, Pier C, Schattner P, Pierce D, Wade V. (2008). Therapist-assisted, Internet-based treatment for panic disorder: Can general practitioners achieve comparable patient outcomes to psychologists? *Journal of Medical Internet Research, 10(2)*, e14.

Silfvernagel K, Carlbring P, Kabo, J, Edström, S, Eriksson J, Månson L, Andersson G. (2012). Individually tailored Internet-based treatment of young adults and adults with panic symptoms: A randomized controlled trial. *Journal of Medical Internet Research, 14(3)*, e65.

Spence J, Titov N, Dear BF, Johnston L, Solley K, Lorian C, Wootton B, Zou J, Schwenke G. (2011). Randomized controlled trial of Internet-delivered cognitive behavioral therapy for posttraumatic stress disorder. *Depression and Anxiety, 28*, 541–550.

Spence SH, Donovan CL, March S, Gamble A, Anderson RE, Prosser S, Kenardy J. (2011). A randomized controlled trial of online versus clinic-based CBT for adolescent anxiety. *Journal of Consulting Clinical Psychology, 79*, 629–642.

Taylor CB. (2006). Panic disorder. *British Medical Journal, 332*, 951–955.

Taylor S. (2000). *Understanding and treating panic disorder. Cognitive-behavioral approaches*. Chichester: Wiley.

Tillfors M, Carlbring P, Furmark T, Lewenhaupt S, Spak M, Eriksson A, Ekselius L, Westling B, Andersson G. (2008). Treating university students with social phobia and public speaking fears: Internet delivered self-help with or without live group exposure sessions. *Depression and Anxiety, 25*, 708–717.

Titov N, Andrews G, Johnston L, Robinson E, Spence J. (2010). Transdiagnostic Internet treatment for anxiety disorders: A randomized controlled trial. *Behaviour Research and Therapy, 48*, 890–899.

Titov N, Andrews G, Robinson E, Schwencke G, Johnston L, Solley K, Choi I. (2009a). Clinician-assisted Internet-based treatment is effective for generalized anxiety disorder: Randomized controlled trial. *Australian and New Zealand Journal of Psychiatry, 43*, 905–912.

Titov N, Andrews G, Schwencke G, Drobny J, Einstein D. (2008). Shyness 1: Distance treatment of social phobia over the Internet. *The Australian and New Zealand Journal of Psychiatry, 42*, 585–594.

Titov N, Dear BF, Schwencke G, Andrews G, Johnston L, Craske MG, McEvoy P. (2011). Transdiagnostic Internet treatment for anxiety and depression: A randomised controlled trial. *Behaviour Research and Therapy, 49*, 441–452.

Titov N, Gibson M, Andrews G, McEvoy P. (2009b). Internet treatment for social phobia reduces comorbidity. *The Australian and New Zealand Journal of Psychiatry, 43*, 754–759.

Tulbure BT, Szentagotai A, David O, Stefan S, Månsson KNT, David D, Andersson G. (2013). Internet-delivered cognitive-behavioral therapy for social anxiety disorder in Romania: A randomized controlled trial. Under review.

Tyrer P, Baldwin D. (2006). Generalised anxiety disorder. *Lancet, 368*, 2156–2166.

Vigerland S, Thulin U, Svirsky L, Öst L-G, Ljótsson B, Lindefors N, Andersson G, Serlachius E. (2013). Internet-delivered CBT for children with specific phobia: A pilot study. *Cognitive Behaviour Therapy, 42*, 303–314.

Wagner B, Knaevelsrud C, Maercker A. (2006). Internet-based cognitive-behavioral therapy for complicated grief: A randomized controlled trial. *Death Studies, 30*, 429–453.

Wagner B, Schulz W, Knaevelsrud C. (2012). Efficacy of an Internet-based intervention for posttraumatic stress disorder in Iraq: A pilot study. *Psychiatry Research, 195*, 85–88.

Wims E, Titov N, Andrews G, Choi I. (2010). Clinician-assisted Internet-based treatment is effective for panic: A randomized controlled trial. *Australian and New Zealand Journal of Psychiatry, 44*(7), 599–607.

Wootton BM, Dear BF, Johnston L, Terides MD, Titov N. (2013). Remote treatment of obsessive-compulsive disorder: A randomized controlled trial. *Journal of Obsessive-Compulsive and Related Disorders, 2*, 375–384.

Zou JB, Dear BF, Titov N, Lorian CN, Johnston L, Spence J, Knight RG, Anderson T, Sachdev P. (2012). Brief Internet-delivered cognitive behavioral therapy for anxiety in older adults: A feasibility trial. *Journal of Anxiety Disorders, 26*, 650–655.

📖 Further reading

Andersson G, Carlbring P, Ljótsson B, Hedman E. (2013). Guided Internet-based CBT for common mental disorders. *Journal of Contemporary Psychotherapy, 43*, 223–233.

Hedman E, Ljótsson B, Lindefors N. (2012). Cognitive behavior therapy via the Internet: A systematic review of applications, clinical efficacy and cost-effectiveness. *Expert Review of Pharmacoeconomics and Outcomes Research, 12*, 745–764.

Marks IM, Cavanagh K, Gega L. (2007). *Hands-on help. Maudsley monograph no. 49.* Hove: Psychology Press.

Chapter 9

Guided ICBT: somatic conditions

What you will learn

In this chapter you will learn about:

- How somatic disorders involving psychological components can be effectively treated with guided ICBT.
- Contents of a selection of programs for somatic disorders.
- Effects in research and in clinical settings.
- Other approaches and future challenges.

Case

Maria worked as a secretary for her whole working life and was happily married with two children who no longer lived at home. She and her husband spent some time at the local pub and two years ago they went and listened to a local rock band there. Maria sat a bit too close to the loudspeakers and after that event she developed constant ringing in her ears (tinnitus). At first she was in shock, but after a while she got more used to it. Now after two years it was still a problem and had even gotten a bit worse. She felt tired and could not work as efficiently as she used to. At the hospital she had been offered some advice and hearing tests, but not much more than that as her hearing was pretty intact. In addition, she was noise sensitive and so never went to the pub when she knew it would be loud. Almost by coincidence she met an old friend on the street one day who talked about his tinnitus and told her that he had now started a treatment on the Internet that was a research project in the local university hospital. Maria contacted the researchers and was called in for an interview. Eventually she received ICBT, which helped her get more used to her tinnitus, although the loudness of the tinnitus remained more or less the same. During the treatment she learned about relaxation and coping, and was able to apply these methods in her daily life.

Guided ICBT for somatic conditions

My first study on ICBT was on headache (Ström et al., 2000), and since that time in the late 1990s we have continued to do research on somatic disorders. There are also other research groups in the world who focus on somatic disorders when doing studies on guided ICBT.

In fact, various forms of ICBT have been developed and tested for somatic problems (see Hedman et al., 2012), but far from all are based on CBT and there are also many in which support and guidance is not included; for example the program for insomnia, Shut-i, mentioned in Chapter 5.

In this chapter we describe a selection of programs and approaches that fall under the heading of *guided ICBT*. Overall, not much is different from the approaches and studies reviewed in the last two chapters on depression and anxiety. There is an overlap in how CBT is conducted for psychiatric and somatic conditions, and there are also some adaptations that need to be made in order for an ICBT program to be suitable for a specific somatic problem such as irritable bowel syndrome (IBS).

Psychological treatments for somatic problems in general require a multidisciplinary setting and proper assessment and diagnosis of the medical condition at hand. For this reason, medical specialists should be involved in the process. Although many somatic problems may be medically unexplained, a bio-psycho-social perspective is needed, as there may be treatable causes and complicating factors involved. For IBS, for example, it is important to identify cases where there is a risk of a malign underlying condition. The same goes for tinnitus, chronic pain, insomnia, and others. Typically, however, the patient will have already been examined from a medical point of view. For conditions like cancer, ICBT is called for after medical treatment has been implemented.

Some programs for somatic conditions are reviewed here. Some may be missed, as the field is growing rapidly. The information here is based on our experiences, as we were among the first to do guided ICBT for somatic problems and also likely among the first to implement ICBT as a regular treatment in a medical setting (i.e. treatment for tinnitus).

Headache

The first program developed by my group was for chronic headache. This was a rather primitive IT-solution in which we emailed text files and communicated via the media (Ström et al., 2000). The contents of the program were relaxation, time management and problem solving. The program lasted for six weeks. Forms and registrations were collected via the Internet and this was something we immediately recognised as an advantage over traditional forms of data collection. This first trial involved 102 participants who were randomized to treatment or control. Unfortunately the dropout rate was substantial in this trial (52% in the treatment group), but as seen in this book we later found ways to prevent this, and overall guidance and a clear deadline tend to lead to much less dropout from ICBT trials in studies on somatic problems. Effects in the first headache trial were moderate, but as this was a very promising new way to deliver treatment we pursued the research.

A second headache trial with more or less the same program was conducted in which we tried to boost the effects and adherence by adding scheduled telephone calls (Andersson et al., 2003). This was a smaller trial, with 44 participants, and there was no waitlist control group. We did manage to reduce the dropout rate to 29% in the telephone support group and 35% in the control group. Results showed significant reductions in headache-related disability, but my impression is that we recruited a more severe and chronic group in this trial and the effects were not impressive on a measure called headache index (which showed effects in the first trial). Since then we have not done any more studies on headache, and the treatment was implemented by a private company called Livanda.

Another research group from the United States was inspired by our work and conducted a separate trial (Devineni & Blanchard, 2005). Their program included progressive relaxation, limited biofeedback with autogenic training and stress management. The study involved 139 participants who were allocated to treatment or waitlist control. The dropout rate was 38%, which is more or less in line with the preceding Swedish headache trials (i.e. higher than seen in current trials). Results showed a large effect on the headache index ($d = 0.88$), with 38.5% showing a clinically significant change (defined as a 50% reduction in headache index).

A third research group has developed and tested ICBT for headache, but for children and adolescents (Trautmann & Kröner-Herwig, 2010). Their study involved 68 participants, and results were in favour of the treatment. They had much less dropout (only five from the ICBT condition).

To my knowledge there are two additional programs for headache, with a focus on migraine (Bromberg et al., 2012; Hedborg & Muhr, 2011). Both showed promising results. Overall, it is clear that more research is needed on ICBT for headache, which is a costly and common problem in society that often goes untreated apart from medication (Andrasik, 2007).

Chronic pain

Chronic pain has been the topic of ICBT research, and one of the first studies was performed by my research group (e.g., Buhrman et al., 2004). Several programs and versions of programs exist, which is reflected in the observation that there are now enough studies to perform a meta-analysis (Macea et al., 2010). The contents of the pain programs often reflect the multidisciplinary character of pain management treatments. Thus relaxation training, cognitive therapy and physiotherapy exercises are often included.

We have done a series of trials on chronic pain in my group. In the first trial ($N = 56$) with a six-week treatment and a waitlist control group, we found reductions of pain catastrophizing (Buhrman et al., 2004), and the dropout rate was only 9% ($n = 5$), which we believed was caused by having regular phone calls with the participants. In our second pain trial we thus removed the phone calls but added a live interview to secure diagnoses (Buhrman et al., 2011). Results in this trial ($N = 54$) were somewhat weaker but still significant for the pain catastrophizing outcome. The treatment was longer and more comprehensive than in the first study, but again the dropout rate was low ($n = 5$).

While treatment effects can be found following rehabilitation of chronic pain, a well-known problem is the relapse rates (Williams et al., 2012). We addressed this issue in one study by recruiting patients from a pain clinic who had received rehabilitation earlier but who had residual pain problems (Buhrman et al., 2013a). We included 72 persons who were randomized to either treatment for eight weeks or to a control group who were invited to participate in a moderated online discussion forum. The treatment program was adapted to be in line with the rehabilitation program they had received earlier at the clinic. Results showed effects on the pain catastrophizing measure again, and a six-month follow-up exhibited maintenance of improvements. This study is unique in that continued treatment may be called for in chronic conditions like pain, but resources are limited, rendering ICBT a possible cost-effective option.

Given the relatively weak results in our pain trials (and CBT for chronic pain in general) we decided to try another approach and developed a program based on acceptance and commitment therapy (Buhrman et al., 2013b). The program is presented in Table 9.1.

We included 76 patients with chronic pain who were randomized to either treatment for seven weeks or to a control group that participated in a moderated online discussion forum. Results showed significant increases regarding activity engagement and pain willingness, and reductions were found on measures of pain-related distress, anxiety and depressive symptoms. A six-month follow-up showed maintenance of improvements. However, when compared to the results we usually see in the treatment of anxiety and depression, effects were more modest and in the moderate range (e.g., the effect sizes). Another Swedish pain management program has been evaluated with promising results (Brattberg, 2006), and overall the research in this field is very active.

In light of the somewhat disappointing results of ICBT for chronic pain (when compared to other conditions), a study by the Australian group led by Blake Dear and Nick Titov is interesting in that it found large treatment effects. The program (*Pain Course*) is presented in Table 9.1, and an example is provided in Figure 9.1. In their trial they included 63 participants with pain and randomized them into immediate treatment or waitlist control. A three-month follow-up was also included. Standard measures of psychological well-being were included as well as measures of pain-related distress. Effects were in the moderate to large range, with strong effects on pain catastrophizing, kinesiophobia and disability. To date, this is probably the study with most promising results with guided ICBT for chronic pain.

There are other studies on pain and pain-related conditions, for example a controlled study on multiple sclerosis fatigue showing good results (Moss-Morris et al., 2012), a study on a CBT-based family intervention for children and their parents (Palermo et al., 2009) and a study on children and adolescents with pain (Hicks et al., 2006). Overall, ICBT for chronic pain conditions is a promising research field.

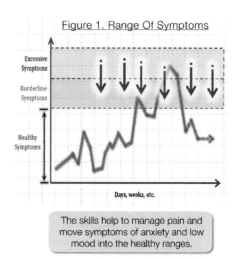

Figure 9.1 From the Pain Course by Dear and Titov.

Irritable bowel syndrome (IBS)

IBS is a common functional gastrointestinal disorder that affects 5 to 11% of the adult population in most countries. IBS symptoms include abdominal pain or discomfort combined with diarrhoea and/or constipation (Blanchard, 2001). ICBT for IBS has been developed by

Table 9.1 Content of selection programs for somatic disorders

Program, country of origin, target condition	Duration and number of modules	Main contents	Mode of presentation	Reference supporting use
ACT for chronic pain *Sweden*	Seven weeks Eight modules	Psychoeducation, mindfulness, defusion, goal setting, values, willingness, maintenance, all being derived from ACT Homework included	Downloadable pdf files and text on screen Audio files with instructions Secure contact handling system for homework and guidance via that system	Buhrman et al., 2013b
The Pain Course *Australia*	Five online lessons over eight weeks	Lessons covered psychoeducation, cognitive therapy, controlled breathing, activity scheduling, pacing and relapse prevention Homework assignments, and nine written resources that provided information about sleep hygiene, treatments for chronic pain, problem solving, assertiveness, managing attention and core beliefs	Online didactic lessons, automatic emails, weekly telephone calls, secure email contact	Dear et al., 2013
IBS treatment *Sweden*	10-week modules divided into five sequential steps	Modules on psychoeducation, mindfulness, exposure exercises Homework	Downloadable pdf files and text on screen Secure contact handling system for homework and guidance via that system	Ljótsson, Falk et al., 2011b

→

ICBT for tinnitus Sweden	Six to nine weeks of treatment with 11 modules and five optional modules	Applied relaxation in six steps, positive imagery, focus exercises Exposure to tinnitus, sound enrichment, cognitive restructuring in two steps, sleep management, concentration management, hypersensitivity to sound, hearing tactics Relapse	Similar to above	Kaldo et al., 2008

two separate research groups. The first study was by Hunt et al. (2009), who did a small controlled trial on a five-week program. A total of 31 participants were randomized to either treatment or waitlist control. The treatment included modules on psychoeducation, cognitive therapy, catastrophic thinking, exposure therapy and behavioural experiments. Treatment effects were large, but there was a substantial dropout rate (38% in the treatment group). To my knowledge there are no more recent trials on this program.

About the same time as the U.S. program was developed, we in Sweden developed a program which was first tested in an open face-to-face trial (Ljótsson et al., 2010a) and later transferred to the Internet format. In a subsequent controlled trial (Ljótsson, Falk et al., 2011b), we investigated the effects of the ICBT program (see Table 9.1). The trial included 86 participants who were randomized to treatment or a control condition (an online discussion forum). Dropout was low (5%). Between-group effects were moderate to large for IBS-symptom and secondary outcomes. For the primary outcome (Gastrointestinal Symptom Rating Scale modified for IBS [GSRS-IBS]), the between-group effect was large (Cohen's $d = 1.21$). Effects were maintained at three-month follow-up and in a subsequent one-year follow-up.

The Swedish IBS program has been tested in further trials. In one effectiveness trial we recruited participants from a gastroenterological clinic (Ljótsson et al., 2011a). Sixty-one patients were randomized to 10 weeks of ICBT or a waiting list control. Health economic data were also collected. The between-group effect size on GSRS-IBS was Cohen's $d = 0.77$. Improvements in the ICBT group were maintained at 12-month follow-up and ICBT was more cost-effective than the waiting list, with an 87% chance of leading to reduced societal costs combined with clinical effectiveness.

In the largest published study to date, Ljótsson et al. (2011b) tested the ICBT program against a credible Internet-based stress management condition. This study is one of the few in which ICBT has been tested against a credible control (and this was attested by similar credibility ratings in this study). The trial included 195 participants who were randomized to either the ICBT treatment which focused on exposure (Table 9.1) or to the stress management treatment which emphasized symptom control through relaxation techniques, dietary adjustments and problem-solving skills. Results showed significant advantage of the ICBT group, and on the GSRS-IBS the between-group effect was $d = 0.38$ at post-treatment and

$d = 0.44$ at six-month follow-up. This study clearly showed the specificity of the program as both treatments lead to improvements but still differed in favour of the ICBT condition. ICBT for IBS is thus well validated, but independent replications and further research on mechanisms of change are needed (Ljótsson et al., 2013).

Tinnitus

Tinnitus is defined as ringing or other sounds in the ears with no external origin (Baguley et al., 2013). For most cases with tinnitus there is no cure and hence CBT has been developed and investigated showing moderate to large effects on measures of tinnitus-related distress. Tinnitus is my main research field and the area in which I have practiced as a clinician for 20 years. Thus, tinnitus became the second topic for ICBT research we developed, directly after the first trial on headache back in the late 1990s.

Tinnitus is interesting as ICBT was disseminated almost directly and has been delivered as a regular clinical treatment since the late 1990s in the Audiology Department at Uppsala Academic Hospital, Sweden. The first trial was conducted around that time, with participants recruited via advertisements (Andersson et al., 2002). This was the first version of our program and it was tested in a sample of 117 individuals who were randomized to the treatment or waitlist control. There was a large dropout in the treatment group (51%), but some returned to the study at a one-year follow-up. The six-week program included 10 treatment components including applied relaxation (in five steps), sound enrichment, insomnia management, cognitive therapy, advice on concentration and physical activity and finally relapse prevention.

Effects at post treatment were small. An effectiveness study of the same program showed somewhat greater results ($N = 77$), but there was no control group (Kaldo-Sandström et al., 2004). The program was then updated and increased in length. This newer version is presented in Table 9.1, and a screenshot example is provided in Figure 9.2. It was tested in a small controlled trial against live group treatment (Kaldo et al., 2008). In the trial 51 participants with tinnitus were randomly allocated to either guided ICBT or to face-to-face group treatment. There was no significant difference between the two treatments and within-group effect size for the Internet treatment was $d = 0.73$ and for the group treatment $d = 0.64$. The Internet treatment consumed less therapist time and was hence 1.7 times as cost-effective as the group treatment.

The ICBT tinnitus treatment was shortened slightly and translated into English and tested in a trial in Australia against an information control condition (Abbott et al., 2009). The treatment was no better than the control condition and the dropout rate was high.

In the most recent controlled trial we developed a new Internet treatment for tinnitus based on acceptance and commitment therapy (ACT) (Hesser et al., 2012). This program was compared against the previous ICBT program and a control condition in the trial which included 99 participants. Results showed moderate to large effects for both treatments against the control group, and results were maintained at one-year follow-up. Thus ACT via the Internet worked just as well. The ICBT program has also been translated into German and found to work in two controlled trials. An effectiveness study on the ICBT program ($N = 293$) showed moderate effects ($d = 0.58$) (Kaldo et al., 2013).

Finally, a separate program for recent onset tinnitus has been developed and tested by a German research group that showed promising results in a large trial with 304 participants (Nyenhuis et al., 2013). In sum, there are now trials showing good outcomes for tinnitus distress both in controlled trials and in clinical settings, but also trials with more modest outcomes. As is often concluded, larger trials are needed in this field.

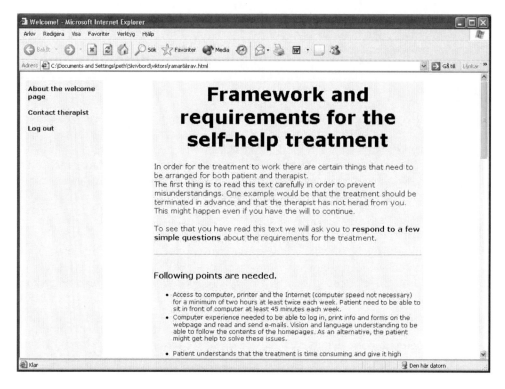

Figure 9.2 Example from the tinnitus program from Uppsala, Sweden.

Insomnia

Insomnia is a common condition that is linked with psychopathology and impaired quality of life (Espie, 2002). In addition to the studies conducted on automated ICBT (e.g., Ritterband et al., 2009), there are studies on guided ICBT. Insomnia is interesting as it may be that automated programs are more suitable for this condition than for psychiatric conditions like moderate depression (where research indicates that unguided programs are inferior to guided).

The first controlled trial on ICBT for insomnia was the one we did here in Sweden (Ström et al., 2004). We included 109 participants with insomnia in the study and randomized them to either treatment or waiting-list control. The treatment lasted for five weeks and consisted of sleep restriction, stimulus control and cognitive restructuring. The dropout rate was 24% and results showed statistically significant improvements in the treatment group on many outcome measures, including total sleep time, total wake time in bed and sleep efficiency. There were however some improvements in the control group as well.

Vincent and Lewycky (2009) did a controlled trial which involved minimal therapist contact. They included 118 participants and had a 33% attrition rate. Results were however in favour of the treatment (with 35% of the treated participants rating themselves as much improved).

In a trial by Lancee et al. (2013) the role of support was investigated. With 129 participants randomized to ICBT for insomnia with minimal support and 133 to the same treatment without support, the authors found a clear advantage for the supported group on most sleep measures and secondary measures ($d = 0.3$ to 0.5).

van Straten and coworkers (2014) conducted a randomized controlled trial on guided ICBT for insomnia and included 118 patients from the general population. Participants were randomly assigned to either immediate treatment or to a waitlist control group. A majority of the treated participants completed the intervention (72.9%), and results showed moderate to large between-group effect sizes.

In conclusion, there are an emerging number of controlled trials on guided ICBT for insomnia and other trials on unguided ICBT. While the literature on insomnia may reflect the general finding that guided interventions are superior to unguided, there is a great potential for unguided interventions as well given the high prevalence of insomnia and the low access to evidence-based psychological treatments.

Cancer

Cancer comes in various forms, and psychological interventions have a clear role as persons who survive cancer may suffer from psychological distress (Moorey & Greer, 2002). To the best of my knowledge there are yet few programs and trials on guided ICBT for cancer-related distress, although there are several trials on online support groups and a few on unguided programs (e.g., Owen et al., 2005; Ritterband et al., 2012).

David et al. (2013) conducted a controlled trial on guided ICBT for hematologic cancer patients. They randomized 186 patients to either four weeks of treatment or waiting list. While the study suffered from a fairly high dropout rate (44% in the treatment group), results showed significant improvements in cancer-related distress.

In Sweden we have conducted a controlled trial on guided ICBT for women with breast cancer and residual psychological distress. Instead of a waiting-list group the control group participated in an online moderated discussion group. The study included 70 patients, and results at post treatment showed an average between-group effect size of $d = 0.50$.

Other health conditions

There are several other health conditions for which ICBT has been developed and tested. One is erectile dysfunction, for which there are at least two independent programs and controlled studies. The first program was developed and tested in Australia (McCabe & Price, 2008), showing promising outcomes. Another one is from our group in Sweden, which was tested in a study involving 78 participants. No between-group effects were found initially ($d = 0.1$), but the effects increased at the six-month follow-up ($d = 0.88$) (Andersson et al., 2011). A Dutch group conducted a controlled trial on their program and found that Internet-based sex therapy was efficacious for male erectile disorder but not for premature ejaculation (van Lankveld et al., 2009). There are more studies in this field including studies on female sexual dysfunction (Hucker & McCabe, in press; Jones & McCabe, 2011).

Another example for which there is somewhat less research is diabetes. In one controlled trial van Bastelaar et al. (2011) evaluated guided ICBT for persons with type 1 or type 2 diabetes and co-morbid depressive symptoms. They included 255 participants in the trial which involved two conditions: treatment or waiting list. ICBT was found to be effective with a small effect size ($d = 0.29$) if all participants were included, but when analyzing completers only the effect was larger ($d = 0.70$). Attrition from the study was 32% for the post-assessment, and was higher in the treatment group. Overall, the findings are important given the scope of the problem with diabetes and co-morbid depressive symptoms, but perhaps less promising than for other conditions. There are other Internet treatment studies in this field but not necessarily based on CBT (see Beatty & Lambert, 2013, for review).

A third example could be heart disease, and there are indeed studies on this using the Internet, but to the best of my knowledge there are no controlled trials on guided ICBT (Munro et al., 2013). In the review by Beatty and Lambert (2013) other problems were covered such as epilepsy and fatigue. It is likely that more health conditions are covered in research currently, as this field has developed at a very fast rate.

Stress

Guided ICBT would be suitable for stress-related problems but there have been relatively few trials since the first trial conducted by my group in 2003 (Zetterqvist et al., 2003). In that study we included 85 participants who were randomized either to treatment or to a waiting-list control group. Treatment included applied relaxation, problem solving, time management and cognitive restructuring. Improvements were seen in both groups, but with greater improvements in the ICBT group.

A more recent controlled study by Morledge et al. (2013) investigated Internet-based mindfulness training and found promising results but a relatively high dropout rate. It is likely that more studies will appear in this field, including studies on different target groups, for example young persons (Vliet & Andrews, 2009) and persons with work-related stress (Ruwaard et al., 2007).

Addictions

There are also several studies on the treatment of addictions, including alcohol use (Riper et al., 2011), smoking (Civljak et al., 2013) and cannabis use (Tait et al., 2013). Most studies have not been on guided ICBT and tend to have small to moderate effect sizes overall. Another problem area that has been investigated in controlled trials is pathological gambling (Carlbring & Smit, 2008), showing positive outcomes.

Eating disorders and obesity

Eating disorders, and in particular binge eating and bulimia nervosa, have been found to be suitable for guided self-help (Fairburn, 2013), and guided self-help has also been tested via the Internet by several independent research groups.

Sanchez-Ortiz et al. (2011) in the United Kingdom tested the effects of a program called "Overcoming Bulimia Online" in a controlled trial including 76 participants with bulimia nervosa or eating disorder not otherwise specified. Support was provided via email and the treatment period lasted for three months. Effects were compared against a waiting-list control group and results were in favour of the treatment. In another earlier trial a Swedish research group found positive effects as well (Ljótsson et al., 2007), with the therapist interaction being via the Internet but the self-help treatment being the book by Fairburn, *Overcoming Binge Eating*. A third example is a trial by the Dutch group behind Interapy, who also have developed a program for bulimic symptoms and tested the effects in a controlled trial involving 105 participants who were randomly allocated to online CBT, bibliotherapy or a waiting-list group (Ruwaard et al., 2013). Online CBT was found to be superior to the other groups in this trial, and improvements were sustained at follow-up one year later. In another trial with 155 participants guided ICBT was directly compared against guided bibliotherapy. There were no differences between the formats in the study (Wagner et al., 2013).

There are several other trials on eating disorders and for persons with a risk of developing eating disorders (Zabinski et al., 2003), but not all are based on CBT. Aardoom et al. (2013)

conducted a systematic review on Internet treatments for eating disorders. They located and included 21 studies and concluded that Internet-based treatments were superior to waiting lists in reducing eating disorder psychopathology and frequency of binge eating and purging, and in improving quality of life. As repeatedly stated in this book it has also been found that inclusion of face-to-face assessments and therapist support enhanced study compliance.

In another recent review a smaller number of studies were included (Dolemeyer et al., 2013), but they also concluded that there is evidence in favour of ICBT for eating disorder pathology. To the best of my knowledge there are no studies on anorexia nervosa using ICBT. Overall, ICBT for eating disorder is a growing research field and will probably be disseminated into regular clinics, given the need for evidence-based treatment.

Several studies on Internet-delivered treatments for obesity exist, some of which have been based on CBT protocols. In a review by Tate et al. (2011) it was concluded that interventions have produced weight losses of 4 to 7 kg over six months to one year when support via email, automated messages or chat rooms is provided. There are other research groups who have studied ICBT for obesity (e.g., Morgan et al., 2009, see Arem & Irwin, 2011, for review). Overall, this is a difficult area for research when it comes to compliance and long-term effects, but given the health implications of obesity further research should be conducted.

Discussion on the effects of ICBT for health problems

As we have seen in this chapter, there are numerous examples of how ICBT has been used for various health and lifestyle problems. We did a review some years ago (Cuijpers et al., 2008), and since that time the field has rapidly expanded. The more recent review by Beatty and Lambert (2013) included many more studies, and there are many more that are not yet published.

In spite of this fervent research activity there is little consistency in the field. For example, the role of guidance is not always addressed, and there are few studies in which co-morbidity across problems has been focused. A preliminary conclusion, based on a recent meta-analysis of face-to-face versus ICBT studies (Andersson et al., in press) suggests that ICBT can be as effective as face-to-face delivery of CBT for health problems. However, when it comes to direct comparisons there are still very few studies. In addition, progress in some areas is slow, as the first trials on ICBT for health problems are more than 15 years old.

There is a need for each of the conditions covered here to do further research on moderators and mediators of outcome. We need to know more about for whom ICBT is suitable, and more research on the mechanisms of change would also be welcomed. There are studies on long-term effects of ICBT for health problems, but mostly only one year after treatment. Thus the long-term effects are not well known. In terms of research activities the somatic field lags behind as well when it comes to effectiveness studies (Andersson & Hedman, 2013), and there are few permanent clinical implementations for which data have been published.

As with ICBT for psychiatric conditions, implementation of ICBT for somatic problems involves some challenges and requirements. One concern is the need for proper medical diagnosis, as self-reported problems without face-to-face interaction can lead to misdiagnosis. For example, albeit rare, unilateral tinnitus can be a sign of a benign tumour, vestibular schwannoma (also known as acoustic neuroma), which may require immediate surgery and definitely needs to be detected. Headache can be a sign of a more serious neurological condition, and pain in the stomach can be a sign of a serious disease. This can at least partly be solved by requiring that patients be seen by at least their general practitioner before engaging in ICBT, but another option is to implement ICBT in settings where patients are seen and diagnosed anyway.

A second concern relates to attitudes and how ICBT is aligned with other services. This has been mentioned earlier, but in somatic health care it may be that the psychological treatments in general are not standard and hence ICBT needs to be described carefully as being one format of CBT and not something totally different.

A third aspect to consider before implementation is the role of the clinicians providing the services. Special training in ICBT is needed, but if other professionals handle the contact with the patient it may be important to develop strategies for supervision.

A fourth aspect of ICBT is the technical solutions. In Sweden patients often have access to health care contacts via the Internet and this can be a way into the ICBT portal, but this is not the case in many other countries. Patient security is always crucial, but in particular when treatments are implemented into regular care.

Practical implications and key points

- ICBT has been developed and tested for a range of health problems and lifestyle problems.

- For many conditions ICBT appears to work as well as face-to-face CBT; for example in the treatment of tinnitus-related distress.

- In addition to health problems such as headache, ICBT has been developed for eating disorders and obesity, addictions and stress.

- There are issues to consider when implementing ICBT in regular health care, and appropriate diagnostic procedures are needed before recommending ICBT.

References

Aardoom JJ, Dingemans AE, Spinhoven P, Van Furth EF. (2013). Treating eating disorders over the Internet: A systematic review and future research directions. *International Journal of Eating Disorders, 46*, 539–552.

Abbott JM, Kaldo V, Klein B, Austin D, Hamilton C, Piterman L, Andersson G. (2009). A cluster randomised controlled trial of an Internet-based intervention program for tinnitus distress in an industrial setting. *Cognitive Behaviour Therapy, 38*, 162–173.

Andersson E, Walén C, Hallberg J, Paxling B, Dahlin, M, Almlöv J, Källström R, Wijma K, Carlbring P, Andersson G. (2011). A randomized controlled trial of guided Internet-delivered cognitive behavioral therapy for erectile dysfunction. *Journal of Sexual Medicine, 8*, 2800–2809.

Andersson G, Cuijpers P, Carlbring P, Riper H, Hedman E. (In press). Internet-based vs. face-to-face cognitive behaviour therapy for psychiatric and somatic disorders: A systematic review and meta-analysis. *World Psychiatry*.

Andersson G, Hedman E. (2013). Effectiveness of guided Internet-delivered cognitive behaviour therapy in regular clinical settings. *Verhaltenstherapie, 23*, 140–148.

Andersson G, Lundström P, Ström L. (2003). Internet-based treatment of headache. Does telephone contact add anything? *Headache, 43*, 353–361.

Andersson G, Strömgren T, Ström L, Lyttkens L. (2002). Randomised controlled trial of Internet based cognitive behavior therapy for distress associated with tinnitus. *Psychosomatic Medicine, 64*, 810–816.

Andrasik F. (2007). What does the evidence show? Efficacy of behavioural treatments for recurrent headaches in adults. *Neurogical Sciences, 28*(Suppl 2), S70–S77.

Arem H, Irwin M. (2011). A review of web-based weight loss interventions in adults. *Obesity Review, 12*, e236–e243.

Baguley DM, Andersson G, McKenna L, McFerran DJ. (2013). *Tinnitus: A multidisciplinary approach* (2nd ed.). Chichester: Wiley.

Beatty L, Lambert S. (2013). A systematic review of Internet-based self-help therapeutic interventions to improve distress and disease-control among adults with chronic health conditions. *Clinical Psychology Review, 33*, 609–622.

Blanchard EB. (2001). *Irritable bowel syndrome. Psychosocial assessment and treatment.* Washington, DC: American Psychological Association.

Brattberg G. (2006). Internet-based rehabilitation for individuals with chronic pain and burnout: A randomized trial. *International Journal of Rehabilitation Research, 29*, 221–227.

Bromberg J, Wood ME, Black RA, Surette DA, Zacharoff KL, Chiauzzi EJ. (2012). A randomized trial of a web-based intervention to improve migraine self-management and coping. *Headache, 52*, 244–261.

Buhrman M, Fältenhag S, Ström L, Andersson G. (2004). Controlled trial of Internet-based treatment with telephone support for chronic back pain. *Pain, 111*, 368–377.

Buhrman M, Fredriksson A, Edström G, Shafiei D, Tärnqvist C, Ljótsson B, Hursti T, Gordh T, Andersson G. (2013a). Guided Internet-delivered cognitive-behavioral therapy for chronic pain patients who have residual symptoms after rehabilitation treatment: Randomized controlled trial. *European Journal of Pain, 17*, 753–765.

Buhrman M, Nilsson-Ihrfelt E, Jannert M, Ström L, Andersson G. (2011). Guided Internet-delivered cognitive-behavioral treatment for chronic back pain reduces pain catastrophizing: A randomized controlled trial. *Journal of Rehabilitation Medicine, 43*, 500–505.

Buhrman M, Skoglund A, Husell, J, Bergström, K, Gordh T, Hursti T, Bendelin N, Furmark T, Andersson G. (2013b). Guided Internet-delivered acceptance and commitment therapy for chronic pain patients: A randomized controlled trial. *Behaviour Research and Therapy, 51*, 307–315.

Carlbring P, Smit F. (2008). Randomized trial of Internet-delivered self-help with telephone support for pathological gamblers. *Journal of Consulting and Clinical Psychology, 76*, 1090–1094.

Civljak M, Stead LF, Hartmann-Boyce J, Sheikh A, Car J. (2013). Internet-based interventions for smoking cessation. *Cochrane Database of Systematic Reviews, 7*, CD007078.

Cuijpers P, van Straten A-M, Andersson G. (2008). Internet-administered cognitive behavior therapy for health problems: A systematic review. *Journal of Behavioral Medicine, 31*, 169–177.

David N, Schlenker P, Prudlo U, Larbig W. (2013). Internet-based program for coping with cancer: A randomized controlled trial with hematologic cancer patients. *Psychooncology, 22*, 1064–1072.

Dear BF, Titov N, Perry KN, Johnston L, Wootton BM, Terides MD, Rapee RM, Hudson JL. (2013). The Pain Course: a randomised controlled trial of a clinician-guided Internet-delivered cognitive behaviour therapy program for managing chronic pain and emotional well-being. *Pain, 154*, 942–950.

Devineni T, Blanchard EB. (2005). A randomized controlled trial of an Internet-based treatment for chronic headache. *Behaviour Research and Therapy, 43*, 277–292.

Dolemeyer R, Tietjen A, Kersting A, Wagner B. (2013). Internet-based interventions for eating disorders in adults: A systematic review. *BMC Psychiatry, 13*, 207.

Espie CA. (2002). Insomnia: conceptual issues in the development, persistence, and treatment of sleep disorders in adults. *Annual Review of Psychology, 53*, 215–243.

Fairburn CG. (2013). *Overcoming binge eating* (2nd ed.). New York: Guilford Press.

Hedborg K, Muhr C. (2011). Multimodal behavioral treatment of migraine: an Internet-administered, randomized, controlled trial. *Upsala Journal of Medical Sciences, 116*, 169–186.

Hedman E, Ljótsson B, Lindefors N. (2012). Cognitive behavior therapy via the Internet: A systematic review of applications, clinical efficacy and cost-effectiveness. *Expert Review of Pharmacoeconomics and Outcomes Research, 12*, 745–764.

Hesser H, Gustafsson T, Lundén C, Henriksson O, Fattahi KEJ, Zetterqvist Westin V, Carlbring P, Mäki-Torkko E, Kaldo V, Andersson G. (2012). A randomized controlled trial of Internet-delivered cognitive behavior therapy and acceptance and commitment therapy in the treatment of tinnitus. *Journal of Consulting and Clinical Psychology, 80*, 649–661.

Hicks CL, von Baeyer CL, McGrath PJ. (2006). Online psychological treatment for pediatric recurrent pain: A randomized evaluation. *Journal of Pediatric Psychology, 31*, 724–736.

Hucker A, McCabe MP. (In press). An online, mindfulness-based, cognitive-behavioral therapy for female sexual difficulties: Impact on relationship functioning. *Journal of Sex and Marital Therapy*.

Hunt MG, Moshier S, Milonova M. (2009). Brief cognitive-behavioral Internet therapy for irritable bowel syndrome. *Behaviour Research and Therapy, 47*, 797–802.

Jones LM, McCabe MP. (2011). The effectiveness of an Internet-based psychological treatment program for female sexual dysfunction. *Journal of Sexual Medicine, 8*, 2781–2792.

Kaldo V, Haak T, Buhrman M, Alfonsson S, Larsen, HC, Andersson G. (2013). Internet-based cognitive behaviour therapy for tinnitus patients delivered in a regular clinical setting – outcome and analysis of treatment drop-out. *Cognitive Behaviour Therapy, 42*, 146–158.

Kaldo V, Levin S, Widarsson J, Buhrman M, Larsen HC, Andersson G. (2008). Internet versus group cognitive-behavioral treatment of distress associated with tinnitus. A randomised controlled trial. *Behavior Therapy, 39*, 348–359.

Kaldo-Sandström V, Larsen HC, Andersson G. (2004). Internet-based cognitive-behavioral self-help treatment of tinnitus: Clinical effectiveness and predictors of outcome. *American Journal of Audiology, 13*, 185–192.

Lancee J, van den Bout J, Sorbi MJ, van Straten A. (2013). Motivational support provided via email improves the effectiveness of Internet-delivered self-help treatment for insomnia: a randomized trial. *Behaviour Research and Therapy, 51*, 797–805.

Ljótsson B, Andersson G, Andersson E, Hedman E, Lindfors P, Andréewitch S, Rück C, Lindefors N. (2011a). Acceptability, effectiveness, and cost-effectiveness of Internet-based exposure treatment for irritable bowel syndrome in a clinical sample: a randomized controlled trial. *BMC Gastroenterology, 11*, 110.

Ljótsson B, Andréewitch S, Hedman E, Rück C, Andersson G, Lindefors N. (2010a). Exposure and mindfulness based therapy in the treatment of irritable bowel syndrome – an open pilot study. *Journal of Behavior Therapy and Experimental Psychiatry, 41*, 185–190.

Ljótsson B, Falk L, Wibron Vesterlund A, Hedman E, Lindfors P-J, Rück C, Hurst T, Andréewitcha, S, Jansson L, Lindefors N, Andersson G. (2010b). Internet-delivered exposure and mindfulness based therapy for irritable bowel syndrome – a randomized controlled trial. *Behaviour Research and Therapy, 48*, 531–539.

Ljótsson B, Hedman E, Andersson E, Hesser H, Lindfors P, Hursti T, Rydh S, Rück C, Lindefors N, Andersson G. (2011b). Internet-delivered exposure based treatment vs. stress management for irritable bowel syndrome: A randomized trial. *American Journal of Gastroenterology, 106*, 1481–1491.

Ljótsson B, Hesser H, Andersson E, Lindfors P-J, Hursti T, Rück C, Lindefors N, Andersson G, Hedman E. (2013). Mechanisms of change in exposure-based Internet-treatment for irritable bowel syndrome. *Journal of Consulting and Clinical Psychology, 81*, 1113–1126.

Ljótsson B, Lundin C, Mitsell K, Carlbring P, Ramklint M, Ghaderi A. (2007). Remote treatment of bulimia nervosa and binge eating disorder: A randomized trial of Internet-assisted cognitive behavioural therapy. *Behaviour Research and Therapy, 45*, 649–661.

Macea DD, Gajos K, Daglia Calil YA, Fregni F. (2010). The efficacy of Web-based cognitive behavioral interventions for chronic pain: A systematic review and meta-analysis. *Journal of Pain, 11*, 917–929.

McCabe M, Price E. (2008). Internet-based psychological and oral medical treatment compared to psychological treatment alone for ED. *Journal of Sexual Medicine, 5*, 2338–2346.

Moorey S, Greer S. (2002). *Cognitive behaviour therapy for people with cancer*. Oxford: Oxford University Press.

Morgan PJ, Lubans DR, Collins CE, Warren JM, Callister R. (2009). The SHED-IT randomized controlled trial: evaluation of an Internet-based weight-loss program for men. *Obesity, 17*, 2025–2032.

Morledge TJ, Allexandre D, Fox E, Fu AZ, Higashi MK, Kruzikas DT, Pham SV, Reese PR. (2013). Feasibility of an online mindfulness program for stress management – a randomized, controlled trial. *Annals of Behavioral Medicine, 46*, 137–148.

Moss-Morris R, McCrone P, Yardley L, van Kessel K, Wills G, Dennison L. (2012). A pilot randomised controlled trial of an Internet-based cognitive behavioural therapy self-management programme (MS Invigor8) for multiple sclerosis fatigue. *Behaviour Research and Therapy, 50*, 415–421.

Munro J, Angus N, Leslie SJ. (2013). Patient focused Internet-based approaches to cardiovascular rehabilitation – a systematic review. *Journal of Telemedicine and Telecare, 19*, 347–353.

Nyenhuis N, Zastrutzki S, Weise C, Jager B, Kroner-Herwig B. (2013). The efficacy of minimal contact interventions for acute tinnitus: A randomised controlled study. *Cognitive Behaviour Therapy, 42*, 127–138.

Owen JE, Klapow JC, Roth DL, Shuster JL Jr, Bellis J, Meredith R, Tucker DC. (2005). Randomized pilot of a self-guided Internet coping group for women with early-stage breast cancer. *Annals of Behavioral Medicine, 30*, 54–64.

Palermo TM, Wilson AC, Peters M, Lewandowski A, Somhegyi H. (2009). Randomized controlled trial of an Internet-delivered family cognitive-behavioral therapy intervention for children and adolescents with chronic pain. *Pain, 146*, 205–213.

Riper H, Spek V, Boon B, Conijn B, Kramer J, Martin-Abello K, Smit F. (2011). Effectiveness of E-self-help interventions for curbing adult problem drinking: a meta-analysis. *Journal of Medical Internet Research, 13*, e42.

Ritterband LM, Bailey ET, Thorndike FP, Lord HR, Farrell-Carnahan L, Baum LD. (2012). Initial evaluation of an Internet intervention to improve the sleep of cancer survivors with insomnia. *Psychooncology, 21*, 695–705.

Ritterband LM, Thorndike FP, Gonder-Frederick LA, Magee JC, Bailey ET, Saylor DK, Morin CM. (2009). Efficacy of an Internet-based behavioral intervention for adults with insomnia. *Archives of General Psychiatry, 66*, 692–698.

Ruwaard J, Lange A, Bouwman M, Broeksteeg J, Schrieken B. (2007). E-mailed standardized cognitive behavioural treatment of work-related stress: a randomized controlled trial. *Cognitive Behaviour Therapy, 36*, 179–192.

Ruwaard J, Lange A, Broeksteeg J, Renteria-Agirre A, Schrieken B, Dolan CV, Emmelkamp P. (2013). Online cognitive-behavioural treatment of bulimic symptoms: A randomized controlled trial. *Clinical Psychology and Psychotherapy, 20*, 308–318.

Sanchez-Ortiz VC, Munro C, Stahl D, House J, Startup H, Treasure J, Williams C, Schmidt U. (2011). A randomized controlled trial of Internet-based cognitive-behavioural therapy for bulimia nervosa or related disorders in a student population. *Psychological Medicine, 41*, 407–417.

Ström L, Pettersson R, Andersson G. (2000). A controlled trial of self-help treatment of recurrent headache conducted via the Internet. *Journal of Consulting and Clinical Psychology, 68*, 722–727.

Ström L, Pettersson R, Andersson G. (2004). Internet-based treatment for insomnia: A controlled evaluation. *Journal of Consulting and Clinical Psychology, 72*, 113–120.

Tait RJ, Spijkerman R, Riper H. (2013). Internet and computer based interventions for cannabis use: a meta-analysis. *Drug and Alcohol Dependence, 133*, 295–304.

Tate DF. (2011). A series of studies examining Internet treatment of obesity to inform Internet interventions for substance use and misuse. *Substance Use and Misuse, 46*, 57–65.

Trautmann E, Kröner-Herwig B. (2010). A randomized controlled trial of Internet-based self-help training for recurrent headache in childhood and adolescence. *Behaviour Research and Therapy, 48*, 28–37.

van Bastelaar KM, Pouwer F, Cuijpers P, Riper H, Snoek FJ. (2011). Web-based depression treatment for type 1 and type 2 diabetic patients: A randomized, controlled trial. *Diabetes Care, 34*, 320–325.

van Lankveld JJ, Leusin P, van Diest S, Gijs L, Slob AK. (2009). Internet-based brief sex therapy for heterosexual men with sexual dysfunctions: A randomized controlled pilot trial. *Journal of Sexual Medicine, 6*, 2224–2236.

van Straten A, Emmelkamp J, de Wit J, Lancee J, Andersson G, van Someren EJW, Cuijpers P. (2014). Guided Internet-delivered cognitive behavioral treatment for insomnia: A randomized trial. *Psychological Medicine, 44*, 1521–1532.

Vincent N, Lewycky S. (2009). Logging on for better sleep: RCT of the effectiveness of online treatment for insomnia. *Sleep, 32*, 807–815.

Vliet HV, Andrews G. (2009). Internet-based course for the management of stress for junior high schools. *Australian and New Zealand Journal of Psychiatry, 43*, 305–309.

Wagner G, Penelo E, Wanner C, Gwinner P, Trofaier ML, Imgart H, Waldherr K, Wober-Bingol C, Karwautz AF. (2013). Internet-delivered cognitive-behavioural therapy v. conventional guided self-help for bulimia nervosa: Long-term evaluation of a randomised controlled trial. *British Journal of Psychiatry, 202*, 135–141.

Williams AC, Eccleston C, Morley S. (2012). Psychological therapies for the management of chronic pain (excluding headache) in adults. *Cochrane Database of Systematic Reviews, 11*, CD007407.

Zabinksi MF, Celio AA, Wilfley DE, Barr Taylor CB. (2003). Prevention of eating disorders and obesity via the Internet. *Cognitive Behaviour Therapy, 32*, 137–150.

Zetterqvist K, Maanmies J, Ström L, Andersson G. (2003). Randomized controlled trial of Internet-based stress management. *Cognitive Behaviour Therapy, 3*, 151–160.

 Further reading

Beatty L, Lambert S. (2013). A systematic review of Internet-based self-help therapeutic interventions to improve distress and disease-control among adults with chronic health conditions. *Clinical Psychology Review, 33*, 609–622.

Chapter 10

Other applications of the Internet

What you will learn

In this chapter you will learn about:

- Real-time ICBT.

- The use of modern mobile phones in ICBT.

- Use of web-based support systems.

- Training and supervision.

- Advice on how to set up a service and integrate with existing services.

Case

Rachel had been in therapy for her depression and personality disorder for about a month. Therapy was conducted with face-to-face sessions via web-camera, as Rachel lived far from the specialist centre. She and the therapist also worked via a web portal where homework and psychoeducation were provided, and in addition a contact messenger system was included. This was useful as the therapist and Rachel worked according to the dialectical behaviour therapy protocol (Linehan, 1993), because there was some self-harm involved (albeit not suicidal intent). Rachel used her smartphone in the treatment as well, in the form of an application used for behavioural activation. Her therapist had several similar patients and received supervision weekly via the Internet, and had completed two extra courses on CBT via the Internet. Thus the treatment for Rachel was not the ordinary face-to-face, but the blended form of treatment suited her well and the therapy progressed.

Real-time Internet-delivered CBT and email therapy

The main focus of this book has been guided self-help, for which there is an abundance of empirical support. Less research has been done on the feasibility of delivering CBT directly in real time via web-camera (e.g., Skype or similar programs). Real-time ICBT does not save much therapist time but it has many of the advantages of guided self-help ICBT; for example there is no need to travel to the therapist's office, material may be used. It also has unique advantages such as the therapist being able to interact with the patient and pick up signs of distress or problems in the therapy. The disadvantages mirror those in regular CBT. As in regular face-to-face CBT, sessions need to be scheduled, the therapist cannot as easily consult a colleague if difficult questions arise, and as in face-to-face therapy the real-time ICBT treatment is not based on text and film clips (blending is of course possible).

Not all CBT clinicians or researchers are aware of the literature on telephone-based CBT, for which several controlled trials have been conducted showing good outcomes (Leach & Christensen, 2006). Telephone-based CBT is similar to real-time online CBT in many ways. Research on real-time online CBT is, however, still limited. An excellent exception was a large-scale depression study by Kessler et al. (2009), which was published in the *Lancet*. In their trial they included 297 persons with depression who were randomly assigned to either real-time ICBT and treatment as usual or to treatment as usual only from the general practitioner. Results were in favour of the ICBT condition with a between-group effect size of $d = 0.61$ at four-month follow-up and also significant at eight months. There are few similar trials on this treatment format, in particular if studies on videoconferencing are not included (Richards & Viganó, 2013). A systematic review identified only six controlled trials (Dowling & Rickwood, 2013), and of these studies not many were based on CBT. Most likely clinicians use the Internet to provide CBT in real time, for example by using Skype, but the research to date is not sufficient. One exception was a small controlled study on web-camera delivered CBT for youth with obsessive-compulsive disorder (Storch et al., 2011), in which the authors found a large between-group effect of $d = 1.36$.

In previous chapters I have referred to email-based CBT, and while the Interapy program involves much therapist-patient interaction (Lange et al., 2003), it is not conducted in real time and includes other material in addition to the correspondence. Overall, there are few studies on email-based CBT, but the limited evidence to date suggests that this treatment format might work well but that it is more time consuming than guided self-help. In our only trial on this format the email therapy worked well as a treatment for depression (Vernmark et al., 2010), but given the substantially longer therapist time we did not continue with this approach. The email therapy was manualized, and the manual was based on CBT principles for treating depression. Hence there was a focus on a case conceptualization and subsequent applications of components commonly used in CBT for depression, including behavioural activation and cognitive restructuring. Each treatment was tailored for each patient in the email therapy. The between-group effect size against waiting-list control was $d = 0.96$. To my knowledge there are few if any other direct comparisons between email therapy and guided self-help in the Internet format. It should be noted, however, that email therapy is widely practiced across the world and hence this treatment format would benefit from more scientific studies.

Mobile-phone-based CBT

As I write this book many studies are being conducted using modern mobile phone technology (smartphones) for the delivery of psychological treatments, and these are often based on CBT (Donker et al., 2013). One feature of mobile technology is that the therapist may reach the client outside of the therapy room, and the client does not need to sit in front of a computer (Boschen & Casey, 2008). Other possibilities include gathering real-time data via ecological momentary assessment (EMA), and physiological data and activity monitoring (Warmerdam et al., 2012). While this is a new field, initial findings suggest that smartphone and computer delivery do not differ in terms of effect (Watts et al., 2013). However, the smartphone format may require shortening of text material and other presentation forms such as videos given the smaller format of the screen.

Two smartphone applications are presented in Figure 10.1. The program to the right is called Viary and has been developed in association with our research in Sweden (Ly et al., 2012, 2014). Following the initial development we tested the behavioural activation app called "Viary" against the commercially available Mindfulness app. We randomized 81 participants to either Viary (behavioural activation) or to the Mindfulness app. Both interventions were guided by therapists. The results showed large within-group effect sizes for both groups but no significant interaction effects of group and time. Subgroup analyses showed that the behavioural activation app was more effective than the Mindfulness app among participants with higher initial severity of depression. In contrast, the Mindfulness app worked better than the behavioural activation app among participants with lower initial severity.

Another study on smartphone treatment was conducted by a group in Australia. The program, called *myCompass*, was tested in a trial with 720 participants (Proudfoot et al., 2013). In this case it was an automated program. In line with previous ICBT studies, the effects were somewhat smaller than in guided treatments, but a strength of the study was the use of an attention control group.

Several studies on smartphones are in progress, including blended treatments in which smartphone apps and regular ICBT or face-to-face therapies are blended. However, overall relatively few CBT studies have been conducted using mobile phone applications (Mohr et al., 2013). There are studies using text messaging as an adjunct to treatment, but the more current applications use the advantages of smartphones.

Figure 10.1 Screenshots from two smartphone apps: Mindfulness and behavioural activation.

Developing Internet-based "support systems" for regular face-to-face CBT

Many CBT clinicians will probably continue seeing their clients face-to-face but may benefit from using modern information technology as an adjunct in their treatments. In a large-scale study, Roy-Byrne and colleagues (2010) evaluated a system called CALM, which includes a computer-assisted program aimed to optimize the delivery of CBT by non-expert care managers. This is a form of support system for the therapist, and it has recently been adapted for Internet delivery.

We in Sweden have developed another Internet-based support system for CBT (see Figure 10.2). This support system includes basic CBT components such as goal setting and upcoming homework assignments, and a library of interventions gathered from existing ICBT treatments. In a pilot trial we included 15 patients with mild to moderate anxiety or depression (or both), and eight therapists who conducted the treatments (Månsson et al., 2013). Initial evaluation of the results pre-post show large within-group effect sizes (d = 1.62 to 2.43). There are no controlled studies investigating if CBT with a support system is better than standard CBT, but at least the clients in the Månsson et al. study were satisfied with the system.

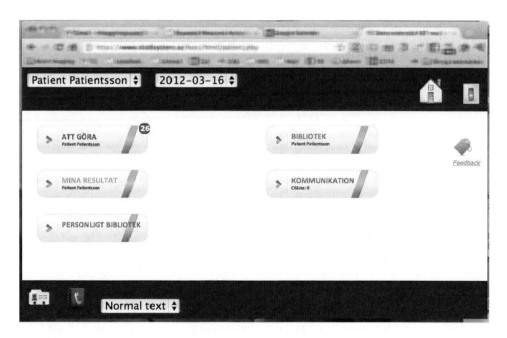

Figure 10.2 Screenshot for a support system for CBT.

Training and supervision

The Internet has not only changed the world when it comes to the delivery of psychological treatments, it has also on a much larger scale changed the educational system. Online education is increasingly used in the training and supervision of CBT clinicians, and a literature on this topic has emerged, although there are few controlled studies (as is the case for training CBT in general).

In one early study in this field, Sholomskas et al. (2005) randomized 78 clinicians to three forms of training in CBT. The first condition was a review of a CBT manual only, the second condition a review of the manual plus access to a CBT training web site and the third condition a review of the manual plus a didactic seminar followed by supervised casework. Results showed that the CBT training web site condition was effective; for example adherence scores increased following training ($d = 0.88$ when compared against the manual only).

In a controlled study by Weingardt and colleagues (2009), 147 substance abuse counsellors completed eight self-paced online CBT training modules in addition to attending four weekly group supervision sessions using web conferencing software. The randomized part of this study was that participants received one of two versions of the training program (varying the degree of adherence promotion). Counsellors in both conditions demonstrated similar improvements in CBT knowledge and self-efficacy.

In a third controlled study Dimeff et al. (2009) evaluated the efficacy of three methods of training 150 community mental health providers in Dialectical Behavior Therapy skills. The first method was a written treatment manual, the second an interactive multimedia online training and the third a two-day instructor-led training workshop. Results indicated that learner satisfaction with the training was highest in the online training and the instructor-led workshop condition, but interestingly the online training led to increased knowledge of the treatment than the live instruction.

Westbrook et al. (2012) reported data from an open evaluation of online CBT training called OCTC Online. This program included video presentations by trainers, accompanying PowerPoint slides and video demonstrations of key clinical techniques. In the study 94 participants completed ratings before and after training, and results showed effects on satisfaction ratings and self-confidence.

In another open study, Kobak et al. (2013) developed an Internet-based therapist CBT training program for anxiety disorders and tested the effects in a small pilot study. The program included an interactive multimedia online tutorial for didactic training on CBT concepts, and videoconference involving feedback. Results showed a significant increase in knowledge of CBT concepts and a significant increase in clinical skills.

Finally, Rakovshik et al. (2013) conducted a controlled study on the effects of Internet-based training (IBT) in CBT theory, assessment and formulation for participants in Russia with limited previous knowledge or training in CBT. This is an interesting study as it illustrates the potential of Internet-delivered education across country borders. The study included 63 participants who received immediate online CBT training or waited. Results showed differences in favour of the training group on measures of CBT assessment and formulation skills (between-group effects sizes ranging between $d = 0.77$ and 1.10).

In regard to online supervision I am not aware of any systematic research studies but it is likely that many CBT clinicians are supervised over Skype and similar systems. I see no major concerns when doing this as long as confidentiality is secured, for example when showing film clips of sessions. It has been argued that some in-person supervision sessions are needed when training clinicians in CBT (Bennett-Levy & Perry, 2009), but in any case supervision from a distance using modern information technology is likely here to stay.

There is a great need to develop Internet-based training methods in CBT in order to make the training cost-effective and scalable (Fairburn & Cooper, 2011), as well as to provide training to less advanced regions in the world where training resources are scarce. More research is needed in this field.

How to set up a service

There is an emerging database showing that ICBT can be transferred and delivered in routine clinical practice, and a few examples of this have been cited in the book. We recently reviewed the available evidence on how well therapist-guided ICBT works in routine clinical settings (Andersson & Hedman, 2013). Following literature searches, we identified four controlled trials and eight open studies, involving a total of 3,888 patients. Included were studies on panic disorder, social anxiety disorder, generalized anxiety disorder, posttraumatic stress disorder, depression, tinnitus and irritable bowel syndrome (many of these studies have already been mentioned in this book). All indicated that it is possible to transfer ICBT to clinical practice with sustained effects and moderate to large effect sizes. However, what model to use for service delivery was not clear. Implementing ICBT is context dependent, and not much has been written on the topic (Andersson et al., 2010).

A distinction can be made between clinical implementations where ICBT becomes part of the regular services and separate "virtual clinics" in which all services are provided via the Internet, or the previously mentioned open web sites with no therapist interaction at all (e.g., MoodGYM). In our work in Sweden we have mainly focused on the first, namely integrating ICBT as a regular clinical service. The first service to be implemented as a permanent treatment option was the tinnitus clinic in Uppsala, Sweden, which started in 1999. This may be one of the first in the world as part of a regular specialist service in a hospital (many other ICBT treatments also ran at that time but not as part of hospital services; e.g., Interapy in the Netherlands). In Sweden we also launched a specialist service for the treatment of psychiatric disorders (the Internet Psychiatry Unit at Karolinska Hospital, Stockholm), which was officially launched in 2007, but began earlier. There are probably many more examples in the world, but few published papers and to my knowledge no manual on how to set up the service. There are many challenges when starting ICBT as a regular service. We identified four aspects that we regarded as important for dissemination of ICBT (Andersson et al., 2010):

1) Patients need to be informed about ICBT, as do clinicians. A clear presence on the Internet as well as ongoing research may facilitate this. Incorporation of ICBT in treatment guidelines may also facilitate dissemination (which has been the case in Sweden).

2) When setting up a service for ICBT it is important to consider how co-workers and fellow therapists view it. Attitudes probably differ and it may be wise to present ICBT as an option rather than a replacement for regular services. It may be a good idea to provide training in ICBT (Hadjistavropoulos et al., 2011, 2012).

3) The organisational structure is crucial when implementing ICBT in specialist health care settings. Depending on the setting it may be preferable to host the program within the specialist setting instead of adopting and using a program beyond control of the staff who deliver the program. Patient security and responsibility must be cleared before treatment is provided.

4) Reimbursement of services is crucial for implementation. It is possible to arrange solutions for ICBT, but my experience is that it is easier if the patients are seen at least once in person. Another aspect is how the clinician who provides the support is funded (e.g., if a patient treated via the Internet counts the same way as a regular patient).

In addition to the above, clinical routines and patient management models should be prepared. At the Internet Psychiatry Unit in Stockholm this involves careful psychiatric diagnostic procedures, and continues outcome monitoring including "red flags" in case of deterioration (e.g., Hedman et al., 2014).

There are other aspects of implementing guided ICBT in regular clinical practice. In the United Kingdom and Sweden we have tax-funded health care, and citizens are covered by national health insurance. This is not the case in many countries in which insurance companies may be responsible. Another crucial aspect is whether health service infrastructure and IT policies will allow ICBT (e.g., Andrewes et al., 2013).

Practical implications and key points

- There are studies on real-time ICBT showing positive outcomes. This could be considered as a treatment option, but takes more clinician time than guided self-help.

- Modern mobile phones and in particular smartphones are currently being investigated as tools to be used in CBT. Studies show promising outcomes but there are yet few controlled studies. It is likely that smartphone applications will be blended with face-to-face services or with guided self-help via the Internet in the near future.

- A new way to integrate modern information technology with face-to-face CBT has emerged by means of Internet-based support systems. This is likely to be helpful in training new therapists and also to secure adherence to treatment manuals and facilitate interactions between therapists and clients.

- Access to therapist training in CBT is limited, and one way to increase reach is to provide training and supervision via the Internet. There are studies showing that web-based training in CBT is feasible but there are yet little data to support supervision over the Internet.

- Setting up a service with guided ICBT is much dependent on the context and will be influenced by attitudes and how well ICBT can be aligned with existing services. There are separate specialist services that are online only, but also examples of implementations in regular health care. Data from effectiveness studies show that ICBT works in the clinic just as well as in research studies.

References

Andersson G, Carlbring P, Kaldo V, Cuijpers P. (2010). Challenges and potential solutions in integrating Internet-based CBT into specialist services. In J Bennett-Levy, H Christensen, P Farrand, K Griffiths, D Kavanagh, B Klein, M Lau, J Proudfoot, D Richards, J White, C Williams, editors. *Oxford guide to low intensity CBT interventions* (pp. 495–501). Oxford: Oxford University Press.

Andersson G, Hedman E. (2013). Effectiveness of guided Internet-delivered cognitive behaviour therapy in regular clinical settings. *Verhaltenstherapie, 23*, 140–148.

Andrewes H, Kenicer D, McClay CA, Williams C. (2013). A national survey of the infrastructure and IT policies required to deliver computerised cognitive behavioural therapy in the English NHS. *BMJ Open, 3*, e002277.

Bennett-Levy J, Perry H. (2009). The promise of online cognitive behavioural therapy training for rural and remote mental health professionals. *Australasian Psychiatry, 17*(Suppl 1), S121–S124.

Boschen MJ, Casey LM. (2008). The use of mobile telephones as adjuncts to cognitive behavioral psychotherapy. *Professional Psychology: Research and Practice, 39*, 546–552.

Dimeff LA, Koerner K, Woodcock EA, Beadnell B, Brown MZ, Skutch JM, Paves AP, Bazinet A, Harned MS. (2009). Which training method works best? A randomized controlled trial comparing three methods of training clinicians in dialectical behavior therapy skills. *Behaviour Research and Therapy, 47*, 921–930.

Donker T, Petrie K, Proudfoot J, Clarke J, Birch MR, Christensen H. (2013). Smartphones for smarter delivery of mental health programs: A systematic review. *Journal of Medical Internet Research, 15*(11), e247.

Dowling M, Rickwood D. (2013). Online counseling and therapy for mental health problems: A systematic review of individual synchronous interventions using chat. *Journal of Technology in the Human Services, 31*, 1–21.

Fairburn CG, Cooper Z. (2011). Therapist competence, therapy quality, and therapist training. *Behaviour Research and Therapy, 49*, 373–378.

Hadjistavropoulos HD, Thompson M, Ivanov M, Drost C, Butz CJ, Klein B, Austin DW. (2011). Considerations in the development of therapist-assisted Internet cognitive behavior therapy service. *Professional Psychology: Research and Practice, 42*, 463–471.

Hadjistavropoulos HD, Thompson M, Klein B, Austin DW. (2012). Dissemination of therapist-assisted Internet cognitive behaviour therapy: development and open pilot study of a workshop. *Cognitive Behaviour Therapy, 41*, 230–240.

Hedman E, Ljótsson B, Kaldo V, Hesser H, El Alaoui S, Kraepelin M, Andersson E, Rück C, Svanborg C, Andersson G, Lindefors N. (2014). Effectiveness of Internet-based cognitive behaviour therapy for depression in routine psychiatric care. *Journal of Affective Disorders, 155*, 49 58.

Kessler D, Lewis G, Kaur S, Wiles N, King M, Weich S, Sharp DJ, Araya R, Hollinghurst S, Peters TJ. (2009). Therapist-delivered Internet psychotherapy for depression in primary care: A randomised controlled trial. *Lancet, 374*, 628–634.

Kobak KA, Craske MG, Rose RD, Wolitsky-Taylor K. (2013). Web-based therapist training on cognitive behavior therapy for anxiety disorders: A pilot study. *Psychotherapy, 50*, 235–247.

Lange A, van de Ve, J-P, Schrieke, B. (2003). Interapy: Treatment of post-traumatic stress through the Internet. *Cognitive Behaviour Therapy, 32*, 110–124.

Leach LS, Christensen H. (2006). A systematic review of telephone-based interventions for mental disorders. *Journal for Telemedicine and Telecare, 12*, 122–129.

Linehan MM. (1993). *Cognitive-behavioral treatment of borderline personality disorder*. New York: Guilford Press.

Ly KH, Dahl J, Carlbring P, Andersson G. (2012). Development and initial evaluation of a smartphone application based on acceptance and commitment therapy. *SpringerPlus, 1*, 11.

Ly KH, Trüschel A, Jarl L, Magnusson S, Windahl T, Johansson R, Carlbring P, Andersson G. (2014). Behavioral activation vs. Mindfulness-based guided self-help treatment administered through a smartphone application: A randomized controlled trial. *BMJ Open, 4*, e003440.

Månsson KNT, Ruiz E, Gervind E, Dahlin M, Andersson G. (2013). Development and initial evaluation of an Internet-based support system for face to face cognitive behavior therapy: A proof of concept study. *Journal of Medical Internet Research, 15*, e280.

Mohr DC, Burns MN, Schueller SM, Clarke G, Klinkman M. (2013). Behavioral Intervention Technologies: Evidence review and recommendations for future research in mental health. *General Hospital Psychiatry, 35,* 332–338.

Proudfoot J, Clarke J, Birch M-R, Whitton A, Parker G, Manicavasagar V, Harrison V, Christensen H, Hadzi-Pavlovic D. (2013). Impact of a mobile phone and web program on symptom and functional outcomes for people with mild-to-moderate depression, anxiety and stress: A randomised controlled trial. *BMC Psychiatry, 13,* 312.

Rakovshik SG, McManus F, Westbrook D, Kholmogorova AB, Garanian NG, Zvereva NV, Ougrin D. (2013). Randomized trial comparing Internet-based training in cognitive behavioural therapy theory, assessment and formulation to delayed-training control. *Behaviour Research and Therapy, 51,* 231–239.

Richards D, Vigano N. (2013). Online counseling: A narrative and critical review of the literature. *Journal of Clinical Psychology, 69,* 994–1011.

Roy-Byrne P, Craske MG, Sullivan G, Rose RD, Edlund MJ, Lang AJ, Bystritsky A, Welch SS, Chavira DA, Golinelli D, Campbell-Sills L, Sherbourne CD, Stein MB. (2010). Delivery of evidence-based treatment for multiple anxiety disorders in primary care: A randomized controlled trial. *Journal of the American Medical Association, 303,* 1921–1928.

Sholomskas DE, Syracuse-Siewert G, Rounsaville BJ, Ball SA, Nuro KF, Carroll KM. (2005). We don't train in vain: a dissemination trial of three strategies of training clinicians in cognitive-behavioral therapy. *Journal of Consulting and Clinical Psychology, 73,* 106–115.

Storch EA, Caporin, NE, Morgan JR, Lewin AB, Rojas A, Brauer L, Larson MJ, Murphy TK. (2011). Preliminary investigation of web-camera delivered cognitive-behavioral therapy for youth with obsessive-compulsive disorder. *Psychiatry Research, 189,* 407–412.

Vernmark K, Lenndin J, Bjärehed J, Carlsson M, Karlsson J, Öberg J, Carlbring P, Eriksson T, Andersson G. (2010). Internet administered guided self-help versus individualized email therapy: A randomized trial of two versions of CBT for major depression. *Behaviour Research and Therapy, 48,* 368–376.

Warmerdam L, Riper H, Klein M, van den Ven P, Rocha A, Ricardo Henriques M, Tousset E, Silva H, Andersson G, Cuijpers P. (2012). Innovative ICT solutions to improve treatment outcomes for depression: The ICT4 Depression project. *Studies in Health Technology and Informatics, 181,* 339–343.

Watts S, Mackenzie A, Thomas C, Griskaitis A, Mewto, L, Williams A, Andrews G. (2013). CBT for depression: A pilot RCT comparing mobile phone vs. computer. *BMC Psychiatry, 13,* 49.

Weingardt KR, Cucciare MA, Bellotti C, Lai WP. (2009). A randomized trial comparing two models of web-based training in cognitive-behavioral therapy for substance abuse counselors. *Journal of Substance Abuse and Treatment, 37,* 219–227.

Westbrook D, McManus F, Clark G, Bennett-Levy J. (2012). Preliminary evaluation of an online training package in cognitive behaviour therapy: Satisfaction ratings and impact on knowledge and confidence. *Behavioural and Cognitive Psychotherapy, 40,* 481–490.

📖 Further reading

Mohr DC, Burns MN, Schueller SM, Clarke G, Klinkman M. (2013). Behavioral Intervention Technologies: Evidence review and recommendations for future research in mental health. *General Hospital Psychiatry, 35,* 332–338.

Chapter 11

Conclusions and future directions

In this book we have covered a major part of what is relevant for a CBT clinician and researcher to consider when it comes to the Internet. Some aspects may be familiar already, as the Internet without any doubt has changed our society in the last 15 to 20 years. When seeing clients in 2014, a CBT clinician can almost take for granted that the client or the significant others have searched the Internet for information. Perhaps they even searched Google for information about the therapist. This was covered in Chapter 2. Of course not all patients use the Internet, but a majority most likely do.

There are also resources for patients on the Internet, as covered in Chapters 2 and 3. Much more could be said about this, and the reader may come up with examples of uses (and misuses) of the Internet that I have failed to mention. Assessment procedures are likely to be delivered via the Internet in the very near future.

Outcome monitoring is becoming unavoidable in modern health care services, and Chapter 4 covered what we know about psychometrics and how suitable web administration of questionnaires can be – with one caveat. Diagnosis of a condition is hard to make without any direct interaction with the patient. It is possible that at least some patients can be seen using a web camera, but in somatic health care settings there will always be a need to see the patient in person (even if we manage to measure things like heart rate from a distance).

For many clinical implementations in general, including my own experiences of implementing tinnitus treatment and treatments for depression and anxiety, live meetings can usefully precede Internet-delivered CBT (ICBT).

The need to see the patient and guide him through the treatment requires resources, and unguided open access treatment should be seen as a complement to more intensive ICBT with therapist support. While it is pretty clear by now that unguided treatments usually lead to more dropout and perhaps lower effects than guided treatments, they have their place, given their almost limitless reach. Some of these programs were covered in Chapter 5, and it can be said again that these unguided programs may work very well together with face-to-face CBT, even if we know relatively little about the effects of such combined treatments.

I have devoted most of this book to guided ICBT for several conditions (Chapters 6 through 9). This is a treatment format that shares features with bibliotherapy, as most of the treatment is delivered via text, and the guidance is minimal. I am still somewhat surprised at how well this form of treatment works, and in spite of many references in this book, all of the studies supporting guided ICBT have not been mentioned.

For many years I hesitated to say that guided ICBT was as effective as seeing a therapist. Now I think we can say that there will be patients who will not benefit from ICBT and who will be better served by regular face-to-face CBT, but given the fact that at least 13 direct comparative studies between ICBT and face-to-face CBT now show equivalent outcomes between the two formats (and there are a few more), I feel more confident in saying that ICBT may be as effective as face-to-face CBT, and perhaps in some cases even more effective.

This last statement may be puzzling or even irritating to regular CBT clinicians who like myself have spent years with clients and pursued training and license to practice CBT. It remains to be investigated why it is so, but I feel that ICBT can help some patients to better remember their therapy, and that the self-paced format can be beneficial as well.

This leads me to another conclusion – I suspect that modern information technology and face-to-face CBT will blend. We recently did a trial in my research group where we found that 10 sessions of behavioural activation for depression were no more effective than just four sessions with the added feature of a smartphone application devoted to behavioural activation. In other words, the use of modern information technology could in this case allow for six fewer sessions without any loss of effect. In another project mentioned in Chapter 10, we have developed a web-based support system for CBT. This together with online CBT education and supervision is likely to change the future of CBT, perhaps even more than guided ICBT, which may be slower to be disseminated.

As we reach the end of this book, I bring up some areas for further development. It is clear that ICBT is much less developed for children, adolescents and older persons. The research on these target groups is much less well developed, with only a handful of trials.

As noted in this book, I focused on rather traditional targets for treatment such as mood and anxiety disorders. But there is an interesting new trend to instead do transdiagnostic treatment and also develop treatments for problems in life that are not necessarily part of a diagnostic system such as the *DSM-5* (*Diagnostic and Statistical Manual of Mental Disorders,* 5th ed.). There have been studies on perfectionism, concerns about infertility and procrastination, to give a few examples, and my hope is that we will be able to develop treatments for other problems as well.

In my own research I have just started running trials on the treatment of problems in association with interpersonal violence; another project dealt with couples' therapy over the Internet. This research is not out yet, but is very exciting as it opens up new opportunities for research and clinical treatments.

Another potential advantage with ICBT is that treatments can fairly easily be adapted to specific target groups and languages. I mentioned earlier our experiences of translation of our programs to Romanian and German, and there are other examples.

Cultural sensitivity is another issue; for example, for religious persons a program can be tailored specifically for their belief systems. There are many opportunities here and in reaching less well-served parts of the world, but there will likely be some hurdles as well, as admittedly ICBT is something that has been developed by researchers in our part of the world and may not apply to other cultures.

Readers may have noted that I deliberately avoided focusing on the technology side of ICBT. I have not mentioned virtual reality applications, which are likely to be both cheaper and accessible via modern information technology, and I did not cover "serious gaming" applications. These will perhaps be useful as new and attractive ways to deliver CBT in the future, but one of the tricks behind the success of guided ICBT is that it is just another way to present the methods and techniques usually presented in CBT. Thus, exposure to feared situations in face-to-face CBT (in the form of instructions to do homework exposures) is no different from what is conveyed in ICBT. Exposure to real situations is the shared feature. Thus exposure to pictures and films on the computer (and not in real life) is something different, and indeed bias modification training as well which is probably one of the less successful applications of ICBT to date (even if this may change with better programs).

I end this book by hoping that in the future we will see more and better uses of the Internet as a way to deliver CBT. Internet applications will increase access to evidence-based treatments, and for many people suffering from psychological distress this may turn out to be the only possible way to get treatment. Having said that, face-to-face CBT will continue to exist and the future probably lies in blended solutions where ICBT and more traditional CBT exist together.

Index